User's Guide
to the
VAX/VMS
Operating System

User's Guide
to the
VAX/VMS
Operating System

Corey Sandler

Scott, Foresman and Company
Glenview, Illinois   London

DEC, MicroVAX, VAX and VMS are trademarks of Digital Equipment Corp of Maynard, Mass.

Any use of these trademarks or others in this book are for the editorial purposes of this book and are not intended in any way to infringe on the rights of the trademark holders.

The following drawings are reprinted from Digital Equipment Corporation copyrighted publication, with permission. Figure 1-2, ZT220 terminal; Figure1-3, LK201 keyboard; Figure 1-4, WTS-Plus keyboard; and, Figure 1-7, ZT320 set-up directory screen.

Library of Congress Cataloging-in-Publication Data

Sandler, Corey
   User's guide to the VAX/VMS operating system.
   Includes index.
   1. VAX/VMS (Computer operating system) I. Title.
QA76.76.063S35   1988   005.4′44   88-11500
ISBN 0-673-38173-0

1 2 3 4 5 6 7 RRC 93 92 91 90 89 88

Copyright © 1989 Corey Sandler.
All Rights Reserved.
Printed in the United States of America.

ISBN 0-673-38173-0

Notice of Liability

The information in this book is distributed on an "As Is" basis, without warranty. Neither the author nor Scott, Foresman and Company shall have any liability to customer or any other person or entity with respect to any liability, loss, or damage caused or alleged to be caused directly or indirectly by the programs contained herein. This includes, but is not limited to, interruption of service, loss of data, loss of business or anticipatory profits, or consequential damages from the use of the programs.

Scott, Foresman professional books are available for bulk sales at quantity discounts. For information, please contact Marketing Manager, Professional Books Group, Scott, Foresman and Company, 1900 East Lake Avenue, Glenview, IL 60025.

Contents

Introduction: Learning to Drive a VMS Vehicle   1

    What Do VAX and VMS Mean?   **3**
    Some Important Concepts of VAX and VMS   **6**
    Applications on a VAX   **8**
    How This Book Is Structured   **8**

1   **The Terminal Solution**   9

    Terminal-to-Host Communications   **9**
    The VT Family of Terminals   **11**
    A Tour of the VT220   **16**
    A Tour of the VT320   **21**
    The Standard Digital Keyboard   **22**
    Using Set-Up to Customize Your Terminal   **36**

2   **A Few Small Steps for VMS Users**   55

    Logging In   **55**
    Passwords   **58**

3   **The Digital Command Language**   60

    Levels of Computer Language   **60**
    Some Facts about DCL   **61**
    DCL Commands   **62**
    Help Is Always at Hand   **70**

4 Files 74

File Specifications 74
Global Characters 77
File Manipulation 81
Directories and Subdirectories 86

5 Symbolic Logic 88

Real Symbolic Examples 89
Creating Your Own Symbols 91
Local and Global Symbols 94
Lexical Functions 95

6 Logical Names 96

Creation of Logical Names 96
Keeping Track of What Goes Where 99
Logical Name Tables 101
Search Lists 104

7 DCL Expressions 106

Character String Expressions 106
Integer String Expressions 107
Operations 107
String Operations 109
String to Integer Conversion 110
Evaluation of an Expression 114

8 Your Electronic Postman 115

Reading Your Mail 116
Sending a Message 121
Using the Keypad for Commands in Mail 126
Reading a Map of Mail 130
Everything You Need to Know about Your Mail Account 130

CONTENTS □ vii

     Help Is in the Mail **131**
     A Mail Dictionary **132**

9 **The Million-Dollar Phone Call 149**

     Phone Commands **150**
     Dialing a Call **151**
     Conference Calls **152**
     Directory Assistance **152**
     Answering the Call **153**
     Hanging Up **154**
     Sending a File **154**
     How To Phone for Help **155**
     Placing a Call on Hold **155**
     The Computer as an Answering Machine **156**
     Rejecting an Incoming Phone Call **156**
     Effects of Keyboard Characters **157**

10 **A Dictionary of Selected DCL Commands and Statements 158**

11 **Error Messages 289**

     Types of Error Messages **289**
     Recovering from an Error **291**
     VMS Error Message Directory **292**

    Glossary 339

    Index 365

For Janice, Willie & Tessa, always.

User's Guide
to the
VAX/VMS
Operating System

Introduction: Learning to Drive a VMS Vehicle

In order to operate an automobile, you don't have to know how to design and build an engine. You do, though, have to learn to drive the car.

Think of this book as a driver's manual for VAX computers from Digital Equipment Corp.* It will not attempt to teach you how to construct a computer; there are no lessons on assembly language programming, and you won't find a single hint that requires a screwdriver to implement.

Who should buy this book? Let's start with system managers. Understand that this is not a technical reference book and is not intended to provide the information needed to operate a VAX computer system. But a system manager wears many hats—with one of those roles often being that of a teacher.

This book can serve as an introduction to VAX/VMS for the innocent user: the sort of person whose job it is to use a computer as a tool or for whom a computer is a means to an end and not an end in itself.

The user of this book should be an accountant, a secretary, a lawyer, a writer, a clerk, or any other nontechnical person who is given a job to be completed with the assistance of a VAX mini- or microcomputer.

---

* DEC, VAX, VMS, and VT are trademarks of Digital Equipment Corp. These terms, and any other trademarks mentioned in this book, are used for editorial purposes and are not intended to infringe on the rights of the trademark holder.

Which computers and terminals are germane to this book? Well, for most users, the answer is any VAX computer and any VT or VT-compatible terminal. Here is a partial list:

Computers:

MicroVAX I
MicroVAX II
MicroVAX 2000
MicroVAX 3000 family
VAXmate personal computer (in VMS mode)
VAXstation family
VAX 11/700 family
VAX 6200 family
VAX 8000 family

Terminals:

Digital VT52
Digital VT100
Digital VT220
Digital VT240
Digital VT241
Digital VT320
Digital VT330
Digital VT340

Compatible VT terminals from makers including CIE, Falco, GraphOn, Human Designed Systems, Hewlett-Packard, IBM, Lanpar, Liberty, Microterm, Televideo, Texas Instruments, Wyse, and others. Look for VT compatibility in the product description or specifications.

You'll also want to use this book as a reference to the VMS operating system if you are signing onto a VAX system from a PC or other computer using "terminal emulator" software, which allows one type of hardware to emulate another. An example of this is software for IBM PCs, Apple Macintoshes, or similar devices that allows this class of microcomputer to perform VMS functions. You'll need to keep the terminal emulator manual alongside this book to help you in necessary conversions from the PC keyboard to a VAX-like keyboard.

If you were to follow the cable from your desktop to your company's computer room, you would almost certainly find a bookshelf filled with orange binders—depending on the complexity of your system, you may find books lined up for as much as 10 feet. These are the system manager's and the programmer's guides to VAX/VMS hardware and software.

The goal of this book is to be a distillation and a simplification of those dozens of complex manuals.

- You'll learn about the structure of VAX hardware and the VMS operating system to help you understand the requirements of the job you are performing.
- You'll find a short course in DCL (Digital Command Language) to help you customize your computer account and perform necessary housekeeping with your files and mail.
- You'll read about the capabilities of the "phone" and mail services that are built into VMS.
- You'll learn how to use the extensive help system that is built into VMS.
- You'll learn about the range of error codes and messages that are part of VMS to help you diagnose problems by yourself.
- And you'll find a glossary of computer and VAX-specific terms that will help you understand this book, as well as manuals for many application programs you may use.

WHAT DO VAX AND VMS MEAN?

VAX is the trademark, from Digital Equipment Corp., for an extensive line of computers based on an architecture, or design, called Virtual Address Extended. The VAX line includes multi-million dollar, mainframe-like "clusters" of large computers in the VAX 8700 class, as well as the extremely popular MicroVAX II and MicroVAX 3000 family of minicomputers and the even smaller and more affordable MicroVAX 2000 workstations and the VAXmate microcomputer.

The unifying link between these dozens of machines is the VMS (Virtual Memory System) operating system, the control program that instructs the computer on how to deal with users, files, peripherals, networks, and its internal memory and processor. VMS is compatible across all members of the VAX series, and a program that is written for one VAX machine should run on any other VAX machine.

From the standpoint of the user, the only difference between the low end of the VAX line and the high end is speed—the amount of time it takes to run a program and the response time of the computer to the number of users signed on at a particular moment.

The operating system is the tie that binds. VMS includes elements named *system services* (housekeeping facilities, memory management, and control over the input and output functions), *device drivers* (special coding to operate particular terminals, printers, and other devices), *schedulers* (to control the priorities of various jobs underway), and *system executive* (supervisory functions at the system level).

All computers must have an operating system of some sort. On IBM PCs and compatibles, the operating system is called PC-DOS or MS-DOS; Apple uses its own (incompatible) operating systems on its Apple II and Macintosh line of computers. IBM has a whole set of incompatible or partially compatible operating systems across its line of minicomputers and mainframes.

The concept of an operating system is to serve as a sort of interpreter between the human user and the inarticulate machine. If you were to tell your friend, "Drive on down to the supermarket and pick up a loaf of bread, please," the communication would succeed because your friend (we hope)

- speaks the same language you do, and therefore can understand the meaning of each of the words you used;
- understands the contextual concept of the verb *drive*: to enter into an automobile and control its actions;
- can determine that *the supermarket* is a logical equivalent to *Joe's Grocery Store at the corner of Highland Avenue and Meadow Lane;*
- retains a mental map that includes the location of appropriate roads to the supermarket;
- knows what bread is, and understands the concept of a *loaf* as a particular measure of bread.

As you can see, communication is extremely complex even in such a simple sentence. In fact, we need to understand that there are many other levels of even more complex communication that are inherent in such a conversation.

For example, when your friend is asked to *drive*, what you are suggesting includes the following: Locate the proper car. Locate the proper key. Locate the door. Locate the keyhole in the door. Insert the key and open the lock. Open the door. Sit in the driver's seat. Insert the key in the ignition. Examine the various controls and gauges—transmission, fuel level, oil level, and so on—for proper settings. Turn on the engine. Place the car in gear. Drive away. And all this represents only the very first step in driving to the grocery store.

All the while, there is another, lower level of communication that is going on inside your friend's brain. If *locate the car* is the instruction, your friend must consult a database of information to determine the proper color, shape, and location of the automobile, for example.

And then there is the lowest and most direct level of communication. Let us say that your friend has placed himself in the driver's seat and is about to turn the ignition key. On an unconscious level, but still a very important element of his actions, are instructions that tell the body to contract one set of muscles and extend the other to move the arm and hand.

Now, back to a computer operating system such as VMS. If we have a file named "TEST" and we want to print it, we may need to issue a command as simple as

PRINT TEST   <Return>

to accomplish the task. This is a very high level of communication between the user and the computer, made possible by the operating system.

To begin with, a critical element of VMS's abilities is the acceptance and interpretation of input from various sources, including in this case a computer keyboard.

Next, the interpreter function of VMS translates the verb PRINT into the detailed set of instructions that the VAX computer requires, including the name of the printer, its location, and its particular needs. It then takes the file name, TEST, and applies to it the necessary information of the user's name and the location of the file, any special attributes assigned to the file, and so on.

Under VMS, commands are issued using the Digital Command Language (DCL). You'll learn most of the common DCL commands in this book.

This book is current through the release of VMS version 4.7. In computer terminology, the higher the release number the later the version: Version 4.7 is a later version than 4.6, for example. Numbers to the left of the decimal point change infrequently, representing major revisions to the product. Numbers to the right of the decimal point are changed for minor improvements or correction of small problems, called "bugs," in earlier versions. Very minor changes, often implemented to make allowance for slight differences required for new hardware, are often signified by changes two places to the right of the decimal, as in a version called 4.25.

A major revision of VMS, called version 5.0, was released by Digital Equipment Corp. in mid-1988. That product is "downwardly compatible" with earlier versions, meaning that commands and abilities of older versions are retained and expanded upon in the new software.

The MicroVAX models generally use an operating system called MicroVMS, which is a subset of the full VMS system, but the differences are very small, and should not be apparent to the user.

SOME IMPORTANT CONCEPTS OF VAX AND VMS

At the heart of VAX/VMS is the concept of virtual memory. A standard computer has a finite memory limit. If it is a 256K-byte computer, the system cannot accommodate an operating system and program larger than that size (256 kilobytes is equal to 256 * 1024, or 262,144 bytes.) In such a conventional system, the only way to deal with larger programs or larger files is to add memory. Memory, although declining in price, still represents a substantial investment for most systems. And, in any case, many operating systems have finite limits on the amount of memory they (or the central processing unit [CPU] they manage) can oversee.

Such an operating system is not feasible in a large system with multiple users, or in a large system running very large programs.

Virtual memory, used in VAX/VMS systems, is the ability of the computer to address and use more memory than its CPU physically contains. A 1-megabyte VAX processor can address not just the one million (actually 1024 × 1024, or 1,048,576) physical addresses in its memory, but because of its 32-bit address length, more than 4 billion storage locations (1111 1111 1111 1111 1111 1111 1111 1111 in binary representation.)

The simple trick behind VAX/VMS's impressive abilities is its recognition of the fact that no matter how large the job is, the computer works on only one bit at a time. Like a human being reading a huge book, the computer "reads" only one page at a time, shuttling it in and out of memory as needed.

You can think of the printed page as permanent storage, like the files stored on disk drives or other systems by the computer. The brain of the computer (like a human being) is considerably more volatile, essentially capable of dealing only with the here and now.

Another important concept is multiprocessing. This is the ability of a VAX/VMS system to run more than one program at a time, usually because it has to deal with more than one user at a time. It is not precise to think in terms of running more than one program at the same instant—only one task is actually taking place—but the extremely fast computer can move around quickly from one job to another.

There are two common ways to accomplish multiprocessing. The older scheme is called "timesharing," in which the processing time of a computer is divided into equal "slices," or clock segments, and then allocated on a rotating basis to each user. The more modern and more efficient system, employed by VAXs under VMS, allocates time on the basis of need and priority.

Another element of the VAX/VMS package worth understanding is interactivity. This is the ability of the machine to give an immediate response to commands and programs, essentially making users feel as if they had an entire computer dedicated to them. This scheme is different from a batch environment, where responses come only when a job is completed or at an appointed time when the computer is available to respond.

APPLICATIONS ON A VAX

There are literally thousands of application programs, each of which can be customized in one way or another to the particular system and particular users of that system.

I'd suggest you read this book first for an introduction to the basic concepts of VAX computing, and then keep it alongside as you read the instruction manuals for the various applications you will employ.

Some of the more common types of applications you will encounter include:

Text Editors or Word Processors: Digital's own include EDT, TPU and DSR, which are powerful but demanding products, and WPS-Plus, a full-featured, user-oriented text package. Competitive products include IT*OS, Lex, Mass-11, Saturn-WP, Word-11, WordMarc, and WordPerfect.

Spreadsheets: SaturnCalc, 20/20

Databases: Ingres, Oracle, Sybase.

HOW THIS BOOK IS STRUCTURED

This book will start with an exploration of the only hardware many users will ever have direct contact with—the desktop terminal. From there, we will move on to an introduction to the operating system and its DCL (Digital Command Language) interface.

Later on, we'll learn about the Mail and Phone capabilities of VMS, at the heart of the network solution that has brought Digital Equipment Corp. into the corporate and educational world.

Finally, we'll go through a dictionary of DCL commands and VMS error messages, aimed at helping the innocent user take charge of the computer.

1 The Terminal Solution

Let's start with what a terminal is *not*. It is not the computer itself,* and it is not the software or the operating system or the data or task that is the reason for bringing all together. Think of it this way: The terminal is your window into the computer.

The key to proper use of a terminal is understanding how much the user can adapt the device to particular needs.

TERMINAL-TO-HOST COMMUNICATIONS

The host computer and the terminal are separated, obviously, by a length of cable that can be a few feet or many hundreds or even thousands of miles if a modem or special network is employed. A critical need, then, is for the computer to be able to match its transmission of information to the ability of the terminal to accept that data. At the same time, the terminal has to be able to have the same assurance when it is sending data to the host.

One of the first steps employed to accomplish this transmission is agreement between both ends of the line as to the speed

---

*Increasingly, desktop computers—IBM PCs and compatibles and Apple Macintoshes in particular—are being connected to VAXs. Digital also sells its own PC, the VAXmate, for multiple purpose applications. In such uses, the PC emulates a VT terminal using software or firmware. Consult the instruction manuals for any adaptations the user must be aware of for use of the keyboard and peripherals.

of characters moving over the line (often referred to as the *baud rate*) and the convention that will be used to describe individual characters (typically, a 7- or 8-bit ASCII code).

The speed of transmission of communications data is called the baud rate, which is defined as the number of discrete signal changes per time unit. The term *baud* is derived from the name of Emile Baudot, early pioneer in telecommunications. It was originally a measure of dots and dashes on telegraph lines.

The computer's internal coding—the so-called *machine language*—can be based on any set of vocabulary and rules of grammar the designers choose, for this code is resident within the machine for its own purposes only and goes nowhere else. However, if we need the computer to communicate instructions or results or data to another device, there must be a shared language. It doesn't matter whether the coding says that a value of 65 is an *A* or a *J*, or whether 128 equals an instruction to lift up a steel beam or drop it down—all that matters is that the coding is a reliable and reproducible standard between man and computer, computer and computer, or computer and machine.

One of the most commonly used codes in computers is the ASCII (American Standard Code for Information Interchange) code, which uses 7-bit binary representation for characters. In this set of 128 codes are numerical values for all 52 lowercase and uppercase letters, numbers from 0 to 9, a set of punctuation and mathematical symbols, and 32 special computer control commands for such things as escape shifts, carriage returns, and line feeds.

Remember that the ASCII code set represents characters only, and therefore is not limited to English words. The same codes can be used for any other language that shares the same characters.

The next level of cooperation between host and terminal is called *data flow control*. They do this through the use of a character input buffer and an XON/XOFF "handshaking" communication scheme.

You can think of the character input buffer as a data bucket, with a pipe bringing information in at the top and a spigot dispensing the bits of data at the bottom. In the computer model, the pipe at the top is automatically shut off when the bucket is near to overflowing. The spigot at the bottom dispenses the information that has been in the bucket for the longest time first.

(In manufacturing terms, this is called a FIFO, or *first-in, first-out*, inventory scheme.)

In the VT200 and VT300 series of terminals, the terminal has a buffer with a capacity of 256 or 254 characters, respectively. When the buffer fills to the 64- or 128-character level (as selected in the Set-Up series of menus), the terminal sends an XOFF character back along the line to the host computer. This signals the host to stop sending more characters. (A second XOFF is sent at 220 characters if the host computer continues to transmit, and a third warning is sent if the buffer becomes completely full.)

When the buffer falls below 32 characters, an XON signal is sent to the host computer to tell it to resume transmitting.

The user can choose to turn off the XON/XOFF handshaking protocol by making such a selection from within the Set-Up series of menus. If this option is chosen, there is no way to ensure that data will not be lost in transmission.

The host computer can also send an XOFF command to the terminal to tell it to stop sending data. The keyboard has a data buffer of its own. If that buffer overflows, the keyboard will *lock* and not accept further keystrokes until it receives an XON message from the host. When the LK201 keyboard is locked, the Wait indicator will illuminate.

THE VT FAMILY OF TERMINALS

There are three major families of terminals in use with VAXs: the VT100 series, the VT200 series, and the VT300 series. Each of the three was originally designed by Digital Equipment Corp. (DEC) and is still supported by the company. When we talk about the VT series, we are talking both about a specific line of Digital terminals as well as a whole marketplace of VT-compatible terminals from third-party manufacturers. The third parties typically compete with DEC on the basis of one or another of two points: price and features. Of the three DEC series, though, the VT200 series has been mimicked and enhanced by dozens of third-party vendors.

The VT200 series is also the most widely used, supplanting the VT100 devices in almost every instance. According to

Digital, it had sold more than a million devices by mid-1987, when the company's VT300 series was introduced. The initial release of the VT300 family comprised three models—a monochrome alphanumeric text terminal (VT320), a monochrome graphics model (VT330), and a color graphics terminal (VT340). Within the next few years, VT300 devices will likely make a major impact.

The VT200 family added its advanced features to those of the VT100 series; similarly, the VT300s include a superset of the features and commands of the VT200 machines. Digital went in several new directions with its VT300 family. The VT320 text terminal broke a price barrier at its launch as well as enhancing the resolution of the screen. The VT330 and VT340 models include better screens as well, while also adding a new capability of maintaining connections to two separate hosts, or two separate sessions on a single host, over a single standard cable connection.

Here is a listing of some of the features of the models from DEC in the VT200 and VT300 lines. You can expect competitive models from third-party manufacturers to equal or surpass the specifications for each device.

- VT220: 12 inch curved nonglare monochrome screen. Resolution is 800 pixels across by 240 lines in depth. In 80-column mode, characters are displayed in a 7×9-dot matrix. In 132-column mode, characters are displayed in a 7×12-dot matrix. Includes ASCII, Digital Special Graphics, and Digital Supplemental Graphics character sets. Communicates at speeds from 75 to 19.2K bits per second. Includes 25-pin EIA RS-232C, 20 mA loop host port connector, 9-pin printer port connector, and composite video output.
- VT240: 12 inch nonglare monochrome screen, available in white, green, or amber phosphors. Resolution is 800 pixels across by 240 lines in depth. In 80-column mode, characters are displayed in an 8×10-dot matrix. In 132-column mode, characters are displayed in a 5×10-dot matrix. Supports ReGIS, Tektronix 4010 and 4014 graphics protocols. Includes ASCII, UK National, Digital Special Graphics, Digital Supplemental Graphics character sets. Communicates at speeds from 75 to 19.2K bits per second. Includes EIA RS-232C, RS-423 and 20 mA interfaces.

- VT241: 13 inch nonglare color screen, with four colors displayable from a palette of 64. Resolution is 800 pixels across by 240 lines in depth. In 80-column mode, characters are displayed in an 8×10-dot matrix. In 132-column mode, characters are displayed in a 5×10-dot matrix. Supports ReGIS, Tektronix 4010 and 4014 graphics protocols. Includes ASCII, UK National, Digital Special Graphics, Digital Supplemental Graphics character sets. Communicates at speeds from 75 to 19.2K bits per second. Includes EIA RS-232C, RS-423 and 20 mA interfaces.
- VT320: 14 inch flat-surfaced antiglare monochrome screen, available in "paper" white, green, or amber phosphors. Resolution is 1200 pixels across by 300 lines in depth. In 80-column mode, characters are displayed in a 7×12-dot matrix. In 132-column mode, characters are displayed in a 7×7-dot matrix. Includes ASCII (7-bit National Replacement Character Set), 8-bit ISO Latin 1 international character sets (on international models), and DEC Special Graphic (VT100 line drawing) set. Communicates at speeds from 75 to 19.2K bits per second. Includes 6-pin RS-423 host port and 6-pin RS-423 printer port. International model adds 25-pin EIA RS-232C host port.
- VT330: 14 inch flat-surfaced antiglare monochrome screen, available in "paper" white, green, or amber phosphors, with the ability to display graphics in four shades of gray. Resolution is 800 pixels across by 500 lines in depth. In 80-column mode, characters are displayed in an 8×11- or 9×11-dot matrix. In 132-column mode, characters are displayed in a 4×9- or 5×9-dot matrix. Includes up to six pages of local memory. Supports ReGIS, Sixels, Tektronix 4010 and 4014 graphics protocols. Includes ASCII (7-bit National Replacement Character Set), 8-bit ISO Latin 1 international character sets, and DEC Technical. Communicates at speeds from 75 to 19.2K bits per second. Includes EIA RS-232C, three RS-423s, and Micro-DIN connector for mouse, tablet, or other device.
- VT340: 13 inch convex antiglare color screen, with 16 colors displayable from a palette of 4096 colors. Resolution is 800 pixels across by 500 lines in depth. In 80-column mode, characters are displayed in an 8×11- or 9×11-dot

matrix. In 132-column mode, characters are displayed in a 4×9- or 5×9-dot matrix. Includes up to six pages of local memory. Supports ReGIS, Sixels, Tektronix 4010 and 4014 graphics protocols. Includes ASCII (7-bit National Replacement Character Set), 8-bit ISO Latin 1 international character sets, and DEC Technical. Communicates at speeds from 75 to 19.2K bits per second. Includes EIA RS-232C, three RS-423s, and MicroDIN connector for mouse, tablet, or other device.

Figure 1-1 lists the various character attribute capabilities of the three principal alphanumeric terminals. The pattern is generally followed by third-party clones, although some manufacturers have enhanced the capabilities of their competitive devices.

Capabilities of Three VAX Terminals			
	VT320	**VT220**	**VT102**
Character attributes			
Blinking	Yes	Yes	Yes
Bold	Yes	Yes	Yes
Double-height	Yes	Yes	Yes
Double-width	Yes	Yes	Yes
Reverse video	Yes	Yes	Yes
Underline	Yes	Yes	Yes
Character sets			
ASCII	Yes	Yes	No[a]
DEC Special Graphics	Yes	Yes	Yes
DEC Supplemental Graphics	Yes	Yes	No
Downline-loadable	Yes	Yes	No
ISO Latin1	Yes	No	No
National replacement (NRC)	Yes	Yes	No[b]
Communication			
Baud rate to 19.2K	Yes	Yes	Yes
Composite video output	No	Yes	Yes

Figure 1-1

Capabilities of Three VAX Terminals

	VT320	VT220	VT102
Communication (*cont.*)			
Communication ports:			
DEC-423 serial	Yes	No	No
RS-232 serial	Yes	Yes	Yes
20 milliamp	No	Yes	Yes
Optional internal modem	No	Yes	No
Printer port			
Connector	6-pin DEC-423	9-pin RS-232	25-pin RS-232
Bidirectional	Yes	Yes	Yes
Compatibility			
VT52	Yes	Yes	Yes
VT100	Yes	Yes	Yes
VT102	Yes	Yes	Yes
VT220	Yes	Yes	No
Conformance level	3 (VT300 mode)	2 (VT200 mode)	1 (VT100 mode)
Display features			
Character cell			
80 columns	10×20	10×10	7×10
132 columns	×20	×10	6×10
Display size (diagonal)	14 in.	12 in.	12 in.
Display type	Flat	Convex	Convex
Nonglare screen	Etched	Coated	Coated
Pixel aspect ratio	Square	Rectangular	Rectangular
External features			
Rear panel cable cover	Yes	No	No
Tile-swivel base	Optional	No	No
25th Status line	Yes	No	No

[a]VT102 terminal's United States character set differs slightly from the ASCII set.

[b]VT102 terminal's United Kingdom character set differs slightly from the United Kingdom NRC set.

Figure 1-1 (*continued*)

A TOUR OF THE VT220

Digital's VT220 is a mature machine, well set in its forgiving ways. Weighing in at 26 pounds, plus 4.5 pounds for the keyboard, the terminal is capable of operating in a broad range of environments.

For standard domestic installations, the VT220 will operate off "110 volt" current within the range of 90 to 128 volts, 47 Hz to 63 Hz. Flipping a switch and changing a fuse on the rear of the unit allows it to plug into a "220 volt" line that provides between 180 and 268 volts, within the 47 Hz to 63 Hz frequency spread. The higher-power capability is part of a European option kit.

Looking Backward

We start our tour by looking at the rear of the terminal (see Figure 1-2). Starting at the top right of the terminal and working clockwise, we have the on/off power switch. In an adaptation of the computer programmer's binary logic, the 0 position means *off*, while the "1" position indicates the power is *on*.

Directly below the power switch is a guarded voltage selection switch. For domestic models of the VT220, the terminal comes from the factory preset for 110 volt lines; it is nevertheless a wise idea to doublecheck the setting before installing a new or transferred terminal. The switch and the nearby fuse holder should both indicate 110 volts. Follow the instructions in the pictograms of the VT220 Installation Guide to move the switch and change the fuse and holder if necessary.

At the bottom right of the terminal is a small opening for the plug from the keyboard, a connector that looks like the miniplug used to connect modern telephones to the wall. The connector can be attached only in one way.

Moving to the center, bottom, we find the PR port, for attachment of a local printer. The VT220 has a built-in serial interface for use with a number of Digital Equipment Corp. printers including the LA34/38, LA35/36, LA12, LA100, LA120, LA50, and LQP02. Numerous other printers from third-party manufacturers can also be plugged into this port. The connector employed in Figure 1-2 is a 9-pin Subminiature D Type.

A TOUR OF THE VT220 □ 17

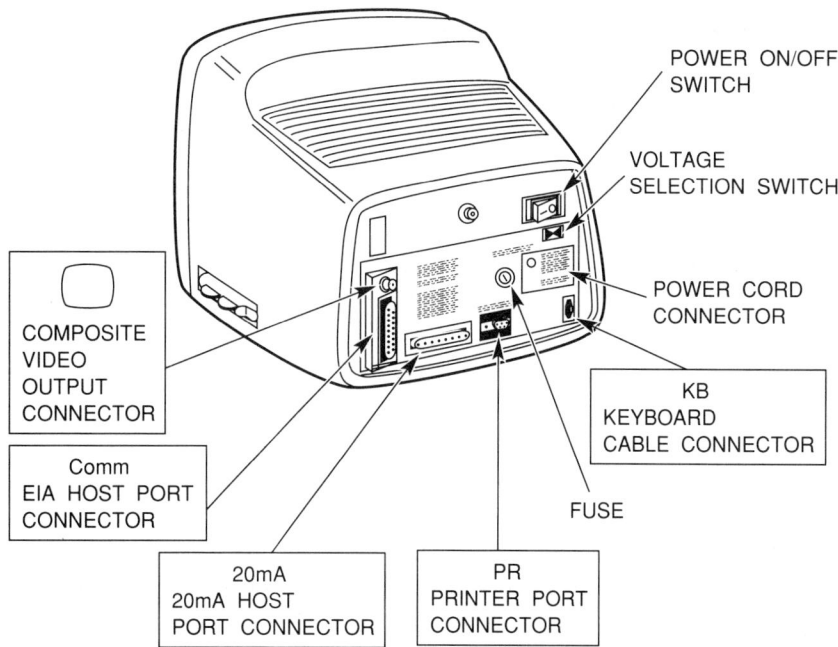

Figure 1-2 VT220 (Courtesy Digital Equipment Corp.)

The printer interface has four operating modes, selectable from within the Printer Set-Up menu of the Set-Up series:

- Normal Mode: This is the standard setting for all keyboard printing functions, such as Print Screen.
- Auto Print Mode: This mode calls upon a printer to print the previously displayed line on the terminal when the cursor moves to the next line. (The cursor moves to the next line when the terminal receives a linefeed, form feed, or vertical tab code, or when the cursor automatically wraps to the next line.) All keyboard-invoked printer functions, such as Print Screen, are also allowed in Auto Print Mode. To issue this command, the user types the Ctrl-Print Screen command and types it again to exit this mode.
- Printer Controller Mode: In this mode, the host computer assumes direct control of the printer. Characters received from the host computer go directly to the printer and are not displayed on the terminal's screen. Under Printer Controller Mode, the keyboard can not invoke printing

functions. The Set-Up key is used for access to the printer menu to turn the mode off. This mode might be used where it is of value to maintain a running printout of the computer's response to queries from the terminal.
- Local Controller Mode: This mode is used to allow keyboard output to go directly to a printer, in effect making the terminal into a typewriter. It is invoked in two steps: first by selecting Local in the general Set-Up directory and then going to the Printer Set-Up menu and invoking Printer Controller Mode.

Left of center on the bottom row is a 20 mA (20 milliamp) Host Port Connector. This is one available entrance point for the cable to link your VT220 terminal to its host computer.

At bottom left is a connector marked Comm, an EIA Host Port Connector, used for connection to a host computer or connection to a modem for telecommunications. The connector itself is a 25-pin Subminiature D Type connector. The VT220 can communicate with Bell 103, 113, and 212 type modems or devices compatible with these standards, as well as Digital's own DF02 and DF03 modems.

At top left is a circular connector for video output to a composite video monitor, used as a slave. This might be used in a classroom situation, or where the terminal is being used to drive an informational display. Note that a composite video image may be less sharp than the video circuitry employed by the VT220 for its internal monitor. The composite video output is also employed by a class of "video printers" that produce hard-copy images based on the video display.

Brightness and Contrast

Turning around to face the terminal, you will find two rotary dials on the right-hand side to adjust the intensity and contrast of the screen. The dial closest to you is the Contrast control, marked by a half-black circle; the brightness dial is marked with a pictogram of the sun. Both dials are at maximum setting when they are fully rotated toward you; the minimum setting is fully rotated away, toward the back.

Start by turning both dials to the full maximum setting. Decrease the brightness dial until the white diagonal lines on the screen just disappear. Next, decrease the contrast setting until the screen display is most readable for you. You will likely discover that the contrast setting will need adjustment over the course of the day as sunlight and interior lighting change.

If you find that you cannot obtain a satisfactory setting for your work, you should investigate a Polaroid or other antiglare screen that can be installed over the exterior face of the video tube. The screens are available from computer and business supply outlets. These antiglare screens increase the contrast between the text and background. It is also a good practice to clean the face of the monitor regularly. There are special cleaning solutions available, or you can use standard window cleaner, weakened slightly with water. Be sure to turn the terminal off before approaching it with liquid.

Operational States

The VT220 has three operational states, each selectable by the user:

- *On-Line*. This is the standard setting for the terminal, used when the device is in communication with a host computer. In the on-line state, whatever is typed on the keyboard is transmitted to the host computer for action. At the same time, data sent by the host computer is displayed on the terminal's screen.
- *Local*. This setting allows the terminal to operate as a discrete device, disconnected from the host computer. Keystrokes entered while the terminal is in local state are displayed on the terminal but not transmitted to the host computer; data sent by the host terminal is stored and then redirected to the terminal once it is returned to the on-line state.
- *Set-Up*. This setting temporarily disconnects the terminal from the host or other connected device and allows the user to change or examine the selected configuration for the terminal.

20 □ THE TERMINAL SOLUTION

Operating Modes   The VT220 has four operating modes for communications, selectable by the user:

- *VT200 Mode, 7-bit Controls.* This is the standard setting for operation of a VT220 terminal. It produces standard ANSI functions and the full range of VT220 capabilities, communicating with a host computer and its application programs using control characters made up of seven bits of code.
- *VT200 Mode, 8-bit Controls.* Same as the previous setting, with the addition of an eighth bit in control characters. Use this setting only when an application program or a modification to your host computer's operating system requires it.
- *VT100 Mode.* This setting selects a subset of the VT220's capabilities to emulate the standard ANSI functions and the character set and control characters of the earlier VT100 line of terminals. Use this setting only when an application program or operating system requires use of the less-capable VT100 terminal or its functional equivalents.
- *VT52 Mode.* This setting is a text-only mode that emulates Digital's VT52 terminal and its proprietary functions. Use this setting only when an application program or operating system requires use of the less-capable VT52 terminal or its functional equivalents.

A standard feature of the VT200 series is the automatic screen blanker, also called a CRT saver. This facility will automatically clear the image from the CRT if there has been no data received or sent in the specified period—you can adjust the time period by changing the time value listed in the Set-Up menu for the terminal.

The screen blanker serves several purposes. First of all, it prevents damage to the phosphors of the screen from the effects of having a single stationary image displayed for a great length of time. It also saves a small amount of electrical power. Finally, the screen blanker can be an element of your data security scheme, keeping information on the screen from casual viewers. (It is not a good idea, however, to leave a signed-on terminal unattended.

This is equivalent to leaving your front door wide open, with the porch light on, while you are away from home.)

The terminal display will return as soon as the terminal receives new data—a mail message or the reactivation of a suspended process, for example—or when a character key is pressed on the keyboard. A good habit to get into is the use of the Ctrl key rather than the Return or an alphanumeric character—this should restore the display without sending a command to an application program or disrupting the screen image.

A TOUR OF THE VT320

Digital's VT320 is best described as a refinement of the hugely successful VT220 line of terminals. There is nothing radically different about the new alphanumeric terminal—someone used to the VT220 will feel right at home—but there are some pleasant surprises.

Among improvements are a larger screen (14 inches diagonally, up from 12 inches), increased resolution, a sharper character set, an improved nonglare screen, and a choice of "paper" white, green, or amber phosphors. The new terminals are also priced lower. Missing from the VT320 are the rarely used composite video output jack and the 20 mA loop host connector.

The new terminal is Digital's smallest such device, weighing just 14.5 pounds, down from the 26 pounds of the VT220. It also has a very small desktop footprint.

The VT320 uses an almost-unchanged LK201 keyboard. The most significant difference is that the LED lights on the keyboard to warn of Hold, Key Lock, and other modes have been changed from red to green in color. The keyboard itself plugs into the right side of the terminal.

The power switch is located on the left side of the terminal, toward the front. The 1 position means *on*, 0 means *off*. Note that Digital has decided to offer separate American and International versions of the terminal. American units will come expecting standard 110 volt power lines, and will include an attached power cord. International units are switchable to work with 240 volt or 110 volt power, and will include detachable power cords with appropriate plugs for foreign systems.

Brightness and contrast controls are located along the right side of the terminal, at the bottom. The rotary dial closest to the user is the contrast control; the second rotary dial is the brightness control. Maximum contrast and brightness are obtained when the dials are rotated toward the front.

The VT320 includes a built-in tilt mechanism; a tilt and swivel base is available as an option.

The back of the VT320 terminal presents a much simpler face than its predecessors. Gone are the rows of (to some) unfriendly pin connectors. Instead, Digital has chosen to use modular connectors that are very similar to the small plugs now used by most telephones. Looking at the rear of the terminal, the leftmost modular port is a DEC-423 printer port. To the right of that port is a 6-pin DEC-423 (RS-423) communication port, which is used for connection to the host computer.

If the cabling in your office terminates in the previously standard 25-pin connector, you must use the 25-pin to 6-pin adapter supplied by Digital.

Note that the international version of the VT320 includes a third port, a 25-pin RS-232-C communication port, located almost exactly in the center of the rear panel. The RS-232 port is the default connector to the host system on international models, although the DEC-423 communication can be used in its stead; both ports cannot be active at the same time.

The VT320 includes the same operating states and modes as the VT200, with the addition of a standard VT320 mode.

THE STANDARD DIGITAL KEYBOARD

The basic keyboard for VT200 and VT300 terminals is called the LK201. There have been minor adjustments by Digital and some minor and not-so-minor changes by third-party manufacturers, but the general layout has remained the same. (See Figure 1-3.)

Some application programs, such as word processors, may assign nonstandard functions to some keys. In some instances, the software may come with replacement key caps to indicate the new definitions. Obviously you do not want to replace your

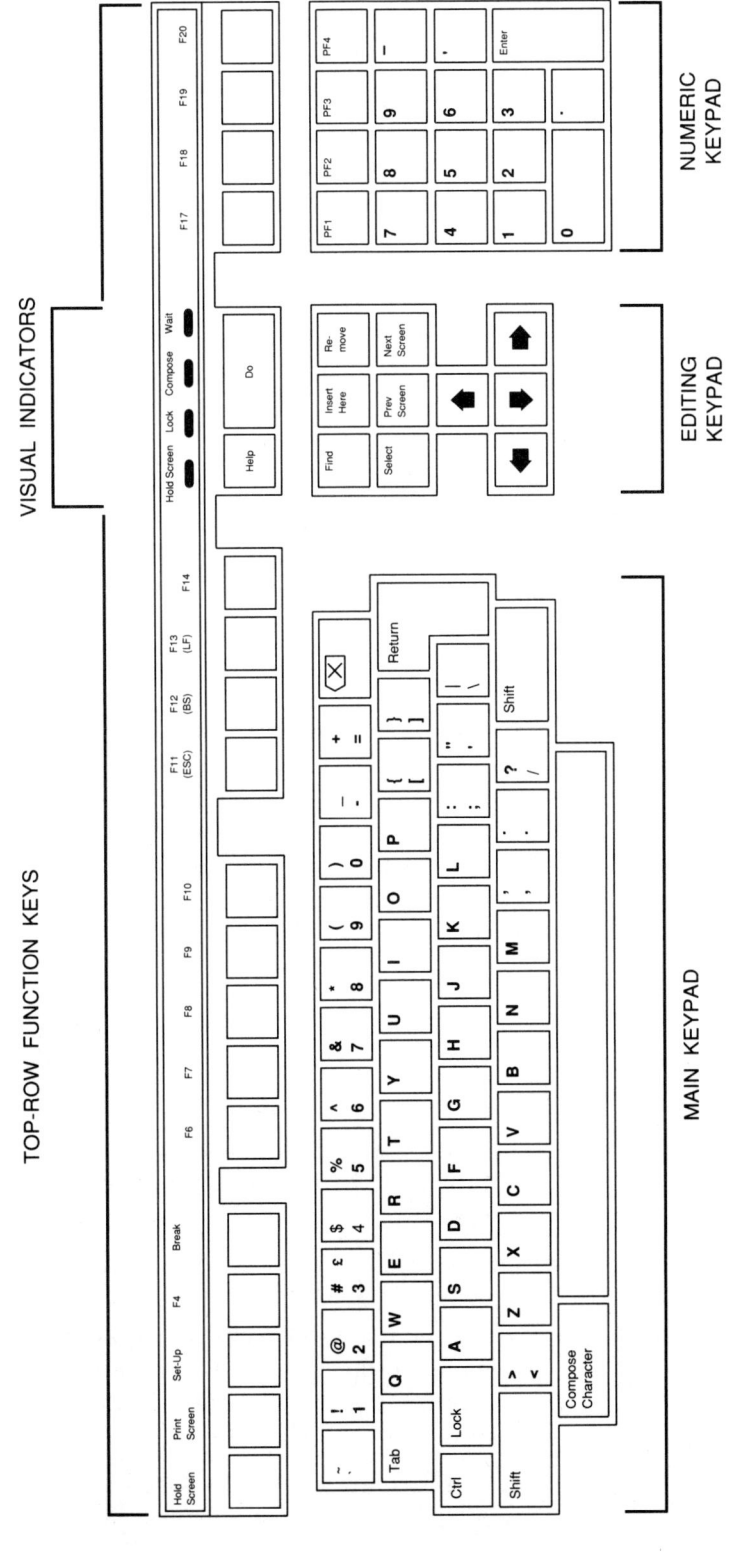

Figure 1-3

VT220 key caps unless you will be using that application quite heavily. If you make this change, you would be well advised to save the keycaps in case you change programs or move the terminal. Digital and some of the third-party companies also sell versions of their keyboards with special notations on the front face of the keycaps for such command-driven programs as WPS-Plus (Digital's most common word processor).

The LK201 keyboard has four areas: the main keyboard, the editing keypad, the auxiliary keypad, and the top-row function keys.

Main Keyboard

Very much like a standard typewriter keyboard, this section includes the A–Z alphabet characters, numerals 0 through 9, punctuation marks, and several function keys.

- Tab key: A horizontal tab command, which moves the cursor to the next tab stop.
- Ctrl key: The control key is another "shift" key on the typewriter. Just as a "Shift A" sends the capital A character to the screen and on to the host computer, the "Ctrl-A" key combination sends a different character. The user invokes a control character by holding down the Ctrl key and then typing a second character.

Note: Throughout this book, control characters will be indicated through the use of the following convention:

Ctrl-A for the character yielded by holding down the Ctrl key and typing the letter A.

Ctrl-Shift-A for a character yielded by holding down the Ctrl key and Shift key and then typing the letter A.

- Shift key: Holding down the Shift key and typing another key yields the "shifted" character for the second key. This can be a capital letter for alphabetic keys or a special character indicated in the top position on a two-character key. Some control keys act differently in the shifted and unshifted mode.

Note: Throughout this book, shifted characters will be indicated through the use of the following convention:

Shift-A for the character yielded by holding down either of the Shift keys and typing the letter A.
- Lock key: This locks the alphabetic keys into their shifted equivalents. Unaffected are the numeric keys, function keys, and other special keys.
- Return key: This key has different meanings, depending upon the context or user-selectable assignment given it. Pressing Return generates either a carriage return or a carriage return and linefeed, as determined by the selection in the Set-Up mode. It can also signify an Enter command in communication with the operating system or an application program.
- Delete key: This key sends a delete character (⌫) to the computer. In most applications, this command will erase one character to the left of the cursor. A Shift-Del key combination produces a CAN (cancel) character. The effect of the CAN character is determined by the application program.
- Compose character: This key allows the user to send special commands or characters not standard on the keyboard.

Editing Keypad

This section of the keyboard is used to send commands to the computer to move the on-screen cursor and manipulate text or other data.

- The four cursor keys will move the cursor in the direction of the arrow shown on them. Note that the left and right cursors will "wrap around" the end of a line, moving down from the right side of one line to the left side of the line below with the right arrow; or from the left side of one line up to the right side of the line above with the left arrow.
- Editing command keys ask the application program or the operating system to perform certain tasks including Prev Screen for the display of the previous 24 or 25 lines of text and Next Screen for the display of the next 24 or 25 lines of text. These keys can be used as quick substitutes for the cursor keys in many, but not all, application programs. The "Find," "Remove," "Select," and "Insert Here" keys can be used to generate certain editing functions by certain application programs.

Auxiliary Keypad

This section of the keyboard is intended for use in entering numeric data in a calculator-like layout. There are also four function keys—marked PF1, PF2, PF3, and PF4—which can be assigned special functions by the application program. Further, some programs, word processors chief among them, will take this area of the keyboard for special editing commands. (See Figure 1-4.)

The Enter key on the auxiliary keypad can be used as a transmit key for commands or data, as a return key, or for special purposes including selection of a Set-Up screen choice.

Top-Row Function Keys

Across the top of the VT220 keyboard are 20 special purpose keys that command the operating system or certain application programs. Here are some of the preassigned functions:

- Hold Screen: This key "freezes" the onscreen display, particularly useful when viewing a long directory, "typing" a lengthy file, or otherwise looking at information that is larger than the normal 25 lines of display and would otherwise scroll off the screen before the user could read it. The key acts as a toggle—striking it once holds the screen, striking it again releases the screen.
- Print Screen: If enabled by the operating system or an application program, the Print Screen key will send the text on the screen to the printer. This is a quick means to obtain a copy of downloaded data or a portion of a data file. Typing Ctrl-Print Screen sets or resets the Auto Print Mode.
- Set-Up: This key temporarily disconnects the terminal from the host and brings forth the Set-Up screen set. More details can be found later in this chapter.
- Data/Talk: An infrequently used key, this key can be used in conjunction with a modem connected to the EIA modem port on the terminal. (It has been eliminated in the VT300 series.)
- Break: A multiple function key: *Break* sends a break command if such authorization is given in the Set-Up configu-

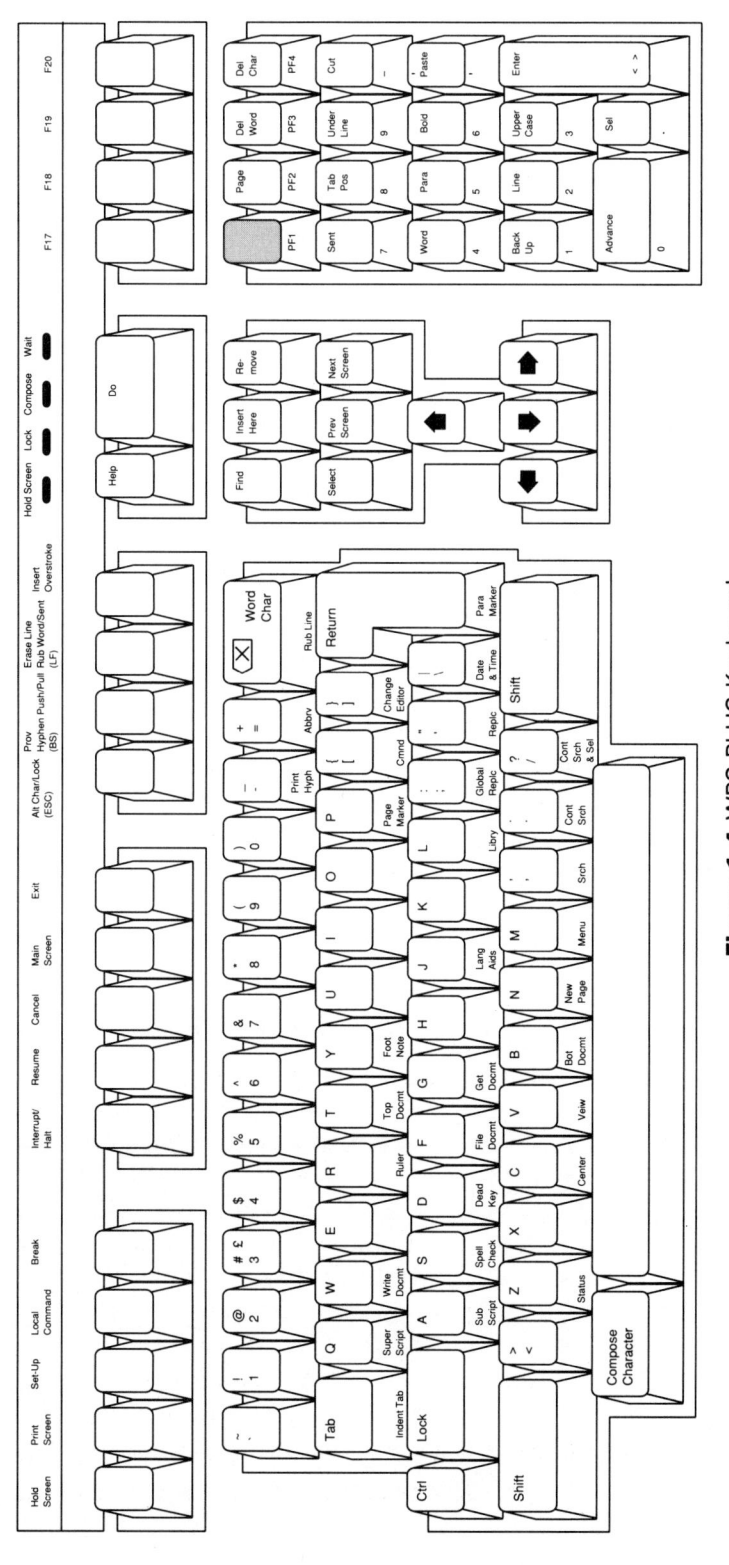

Figure 1-4 WPS-PLUS Keyboard

ration; *Shift-Break* initiates a disconnect; and *Ctrl-Break* sends the "answerback" message selected in the Set-Up configuration to the host computer.
- PF1–PF4, F14, F17–F20: These function keys are given special assignments by many applications programs.
- F11 (ESC): A function key given special assignments by many applications programs. In VT100 and VT52 modes, the F11 key generates and sends an ESC (escape) character to the host computer.
- F12 (BS): A function key given special assignments by many applications programs. In VT100 and VT52 modes, the F12 key generates and sends a BS (backspace) character to the host computer.
- F13 (LF): A function key given special assignments by many applications programs. In VT100 and VT52 modes, the F13 key generates and sends a LF (linefeed) character to the host computer.
- Help: Calls for context-sensitive help from within many application programs.
- Do: A special function key under some application programs.

Visual Indicators

The keyboard includes four status lights that help the user know about previously issued commands:

- Hold screen indicator: Glows when the hold screen command has been issued and the screen is frozen.
- Lock indicator: Glows when the shift lock key has been struck, showing that uppercase letters will be generated from the alphabetic section of the keyboard.
- Compose indicator: Glows when the user is in the midst of issuing a multikey compose command.
- Wait indicator: A signal that the host computer is unable to accept new information from the terminal for some reason. If the keyboard remains unlocked, the user can issue a **Clear Communications** command from within the Set-Up series of menus.

Audible Indicators

Two user-controlled audible indicators are also included.

- Keyclick: This option is available to give an audible assurance that a typed key has been properly delivered from the keyboard. Essentially, it is an audible aid for the very light typist. If you are the sort who punches the keys so hard they bottom out and click by themselves, this feature is of no value. (And some users would rather have near-silence as they type.) The keyclick feature can be turned off with a selection in the Set-Up menus. Note that the Shift and Ctrl keys never generate a keyclick since they are intended to be used only in combination with other keys.
- Bell: The bell sounds as part of the automatic self-test at power-up and when the computer receives a BEL (bell) character from the host computer. Depending upon selections made in the Set-Up menu, the bell can also sound when a compose error is made or when the cursor approaches the right margin.

Control Character Commands

The Ctrl key serves as another shift key on the LK201 keyboard. In various application programs, the keyboard can issue any number of special commands in combination with the Ctrl or Ctrl-Shift or Ctrl-Alt commands.

As delivered, the LK201 keyboard will issue the following commands from the DCL prompt:

Command	Description
Crtl-A or F14[a]	Sets DCL into an insert mode, rather than overstrike. Useful in editing a DCL line already on the screen. The default for this mode is selected with the **SET TERMINAL/LINE EDIT** command, and is reset at the beginning of each line.

Figure 1-5

Command	Description
Ctrl-B or Up arrow (↑)	Recalls and displays previously entered DCL commands, starting with the most recent entry and working backward through the last 20 commands in the recall buffer. Displayed commands can be edited by using the keyboard's arrow keys to move the cursor to the point to be edited. Characters typed will overwrite existing letters unless the Ctrl-A command is issued to set DCL into insert mode. Typing the Enter key sends the command to the computer for execution.
Ctrl-C or F6[a]	Interrupts a command or program. Use care in using this command and the Ctrl-Y command while in a program with an open file. In certain circumstances the use of an interrupt command could lose a working file. Displays a "cancel" statement on screen.
Ctrl-D or Left arrow (←)	In line editing, moves the cursor one character to the left.
Ctrl-E	In line editing, moves the cursor the end of the line.
Ctrl-F or Right arrow (→)	In line editing, moves the cursor one character to the right.
Ctrl-H or F12[a] or Backspace	In line editing, moves the cursor to the beginning of the line.
Ctrl-I	Preset at eight spaces, this tab key can also be set at different spacing in various editing programs.
Ctrl-J or Linefeed or F13[a]	Deletes the word to the left of the cursor.
Ctrl-K	Advances the current line to the next vertical tab position.
Ctrl-L	Commands the terminal to go to the beginning of the next page. This key is ignored when line editing is enabled.

Figure 1-5 (*continued*)

Command	Description
Ctrl-O	To suppress the display of computer output on a terminal. The command does not interrupt or stop execution, but merely turns off the display. Typing the command again resumes display. Displayed on the screen as "Output off" and "Output on" with each successive entry of the command.
Ctrl-Q	Restarts terminal output that has been suspended by the Ctrl-S command.
Ctrl-R	Retypes the current input line and leaves the cursor at the end of the line.
Ctrl-S	Suspends terminal output. To restart, use Ctrl-Q.
Ctrl-T	Temporarily suspends terminal output to display information about the current process running in your account on the VAX. Information includes your user name, the time, the sort of process you are running, and the total amount of CPU time you have used since you logged in. Invoking the process display does not affect execution of your previously called command or program, and the system will resume terminal output after the line has been displayed. Ctrl-T will work only if the system-wide login command file includes the specification **SET CONTROL = T** or if the user adds the line to his own LOGIN.COM file or enters it as an interactive command.
Ctrl-U	Clears the current command line without executing it. In line editing mode, Ctrl-U deletes characters from the beginning of the line to the cursor position.
Ctrl-V	In line editing mode, allows the user to enter one of the line editing function keys but suppresses the line editing function.

Figure 1-5 (continued)

Command	Description
Ctrl-W	Redraws, or refreshes, the current screen. This can be used to eliminate error messages, system notices, or mail notices that may have appeared on the screen.
Ctrl-X	Discards the current line by clearing out the type-ahead buffer, also causing the computer to disregard commands not yet executed.
Ctrl-Y	Interrupts a command or program and returns the user to the DCL prompt.[b]
Ctrl-Z or F10	Notifies the computer that the end of data has been reached. Used to end a file under the CREATE command or the Mail, Phone, and other modes. "Exit" appears on the screen with this command.
DELETE	Removes the last character entered at the cursor position on the terminal. Labeled as RUBOUT on some keyboards, and as on LK201 keyboards. ⌫
TAB	Moves the cursor or printhead to the next preset tab stop.
Down arrow (↓)	Displays the next line in the command recall buffer. See Ctrl-B or Up arrow.

[a] Keys available on the LK201 keyboard, used with VT200 and VT300 terminals.

[b] The user can choose whether to enable or disable the Ctrl-Y or Ctrl-T key combinations. Some applications will automatically shut off this capability as part of their protection schemes. In order to disable Ctrl-T or Ctrl-Y, enter the following from the DCL prompt:

$ SET NO_CONTROL = T (Return)

or

$ SET NO_CONTROL = Y (Return)

To restore to the default condition, enter

$ SET CONTROL = T (Return)

or

$ SET CONTROL = Y (Return)

Figure 1-5 (*continued*)

Composing Characters

VT200 and VT300 terminals are not limited just to the characters that appear on the LK201 keyboard. You can select *Compose sequences* by using the Compose character followed by two other keyboard characters.

Characters can be selected from the character set selected from the Set-Up menu. The default character set is the DEC Multinational set. Make sure that Compose is enabled (the ordinary setting) within the Keyboard Set-Up screen.

Two types of compose sequences are available: three-stroke and two-stroke. You can generate three-stroke sequences on all keyboards by first pressing the Compose character key and then striking two other keys that are among the recognized sequences. Two-stroke sequences can be generated on all keyboards except North American keyboards, and are initiated by starting the sequence with what Digital calls a "non-spacing diacritical mark"—one of the non–English-language accents (grave accent, acute accent, circumflex accent, tilde mark, diaeresis mark (umlaut) and ring mark.) These diacritical marks are not present on most North American keyboards. In this book, we will look only at the three-character compose sequences. To compose a character, find the character you want in Column 1 of Figure 1-6. Press the Compose Character key on the keyboard. The Compose indicator light will illuminate, indicating that the terminal is in the middle of a compose operation. Then type the two characters in Column 2 for the character you are composing.

When the sequence is completed, the composed character appears on the screen and the Compose indicator light goes off.

If you attempt to use an invalid sequence, the terminal will end the compose sequence and sound a warning bell. If you make a mistake and wish to end the sequence or start over, use any of the following characters:

Tab
Return
Enter
Any of the function keys in the top row
The period key on the numeric keypad
Any Ctrl-combination

34 □ THE TERMINAL SOLUTION

If you strike the Compose Character key while in the middle of composing a character, a new compose sequence will begin at that point and the original sequence will be canceled.

Note that some of the characters in Figure 1-6 duplicate characters found on the American VT keyboard.

Compose Sequences for Multinational Characters

(1)		(2)	(3)[b]	(1)		(2)	(3)[b]
"	quotation mark	¨(sp)[a]	¨(sp)	±	plus or minus sign	+ −	
#	number sign	+ +		²	superscript 2	2 ^	
'	apostrophe	'(sp)	'(sp)	³	superscript 3	3 ^	
@	commercial at	A A		μ	micro sign	/U*	
[	opening bracket	((		¶	paragraph sign	P!	
\	backslash	// or /<		·	middle dot	. ^	
]	closing bracket	))		¹	superscript 1	1 ^	
^	circumflex accent	^(sp)	^(sp)	º	masculine ordinal	O_	
`	grave accent	`(sp)	`(sp)	››	closed angle brackets	>>	
{	opening brace	(-		¼	fraction one-quarter	1 4*	
|	vertical line	/^		½	fraction one-half	1 2*	
}	closing brace	)-		¿	inverted ?	??	
~	tilde	~(sp)	~(sp)	À	A grave	A`	`A
¡	inverted !	!!		Á	A acute	A'	'A
¢	cent sign	C/ or C|		Â	A circumflex	A^	^A
£	pound sign	L- or L=		Ã	A tilde	A ~	~A
¥	yen sign	Y- or Y=		Ä	A umlaut	A" or "A	"A
§	section sign	SO or S! or S0		Å	A ring	A* or A° (degree sign)	°A
¤	currency sign	XO or X0		Æ	A E diphthong	AE*	
©	copyright sign	CO or C0		Ç	C cedilla	C,	
ª	feminine ordinal	A_		È	E grave	E`	`E
«	open angle brackets	<<		É	E acute	E'	'E
Ë	E umlaut	E" or "E	"E	Ê	E circumflex	E^	^E
Ì	I grave	I`	`I	å	a ring	a* or a° (degree sign)	°a
Í	I acute	I'	'I				
Î	I circumflex	I^	^I	æ	a e diphthong	a e*	
Ï	I umlaut	I" or "I	"I	ç	c cedilla	c, (comma)	
Ñ	N tilde	N~	~N	è	e grave	e`	`e

Figure 1-6

THE STANDARD DIGITAL KEYBOARD □ 35

Compose Sequences for Multinational Characters

(1)		(2)	(3)[b]	(1)		(2)	(3)[b]
Ò	O grave	O `	`O	é	e acute	e'	'e
Ó	O acute	O '	'O	ê	e circumflex	e^	^e
Ô	O circumflex	O^	^O	ë	e umlaut	e" or "e	"e
Õ	O tilde	O~	~O	ì	i grave	i`	`i
Ö	O umlaut	O" or "O	"O	í	i acute	i'	'i
Œ	O E diphthong[c]	O E*		î	i circumflex	i^	^i
Ø	O slash	o/		ï	i umlaut	i" or "i	"i
Ù	U grave	U`	`U	ñ	n tilde	n~	~n
Ú	U acute	U'	'U	ò	o grave	o`	`o
Û	U circumflex	U^	^U	ó	o acute	o'	'o
Ü	U umlaut	U" or "U	"U	ô	o circumflex	a^	^o
Ÿ	Y umlaut[c]	Y" or "Y	"Y	õ	o tilde	o~	~o
β	German small sharp s	ss		ö	o umlaut	o" or "o	"o
°	degree sign `	0^		œ	o e diphthong[c]	o e*	
à	a grave	a`	`a	ù	u grave	u`	`u
á	a acute	a'	'a	ú	u acute	u'	'u
â	a circumflex	a^	^a	û	u circumflex	u^	^u
ã	a tilde	a~	~a	ü	u umlaut	u" or "u	"u
ä	a umlaut	a" or "a	"a	ÿ	y umlaut[c]	y" or "y	"y
NBSP	no break space	sp sp		´	acute accent	''	
¦	broken vertical bar	¦¦or !		¸	cedilla	, ,	
¬	logical not	-,*		¨	diaresis	" "	"(sp)
-	soft (syllable) hyphen	- -		Ý	Y acute	Y'	'Y
®	registered trademark	R O		ý	y acute	y'	'y
—	macron	-^		Þ	capital Icelandic thorn	T H	
¾	three quarters	3 4*		þ	small Icelandic thorn	t h	
÷	division sign	-:		Ð	capital Icelandic Eth	-D	
×	multiplication sign	x x		ð	small Icelandic Eth	-d	
ø	o slash	o/					

[a] (sp) = space bar.
[b] You must type the characters for these sequences in the order shown (includes all two-stroke and some three-stroke sequences).
[c] This character is available only when you use the DEC Multinational character set.
[d] These characters are available only when you use the ISO Latin-1 multinational character set.

Figure 1-6 (*continued*)

Type-Ahead Buffer
One of the features of the VAX is a special section of memory, referred to as a type-ahead buffer, that stores commands issued from the keyboard but not yet executed by the computer—typically, commands issued while the VAX was involved in processing another command. This is in effect an extension of the abilities of the terminal.

Commands enter into the type-ahead buffer after they have been sent to the computer when the Return key is struck. The commands are executed in a first-in first-out (FIFO) order.

If you have made an error in typing in a command that has not yet been executed, or if you change your mind about a command in the buffer, you can clear the type-ahead buffer by striking the Ctrl-X character combination.

USING SET-UP TO CUSTOMIZE YOUR TERMINAL

The VT200, VT300, and their compatible competitors are extremely flexible devices which can be readily adapted to specific needs of users. In addition to the standard settings locked into place as part of the hardware—screen color, screen resolution, keyboard design, and the like—the user can personalize the terminal in dozens of ways using the series of Set-Up menus.

Most VT and compatible terminals store these selections in a set of nonvolatile RAM chips which retain their instructions even when the power is turned off.

You enter into the Set-Up menus by pressing the F3 key on the LK201 keyboard. This is a toggle switch: Pressing the key once enters Set-Up and pressing the key a second time turns off the utility. Any data on the screen when the Set-Up key is pressed will disappear and a menu of customization options will appear. When the Set-Up key is pressed again, the menu will leave the screen and the data will return, unaltered. (If you are using a terminal other than a Digital VT200, read the instruction manual's section on the Set-Up menus first.)

In the ordinary communication setting for the terminal, selecting the Set-Up screen temporarily puts the terminal into an off-line mode, while halting the flow of incoming data at the host computer end (technically, the terminal disables its handshaking response to the host, causing the host to bide its time, with the data waiting for the proper XON/XOFF signal from the terminal.)

The master Set-Up screen is called the Set-Up Directory. This is the first screen that will ordinarily be displayed when the F3 key is pressed, and is also reachable from within any of the subsidiary menu screens. The Set-Up Directory is the master menu, offering access to each of the principal sub-menus as well as some important top-level customization.

Figure 1-7 is a representation of the opening Set-Up screen from an international version of the VT320, which is similar to that presented by the VT220 and other such terminals. Note that the Set-Up English and North American Keyboard options may not appear on all terminals, depending on the international capabilities included in each device.

The user steps through the selections of the Set-Up menus using the cursor keys to move a *field cursor* which highlights options.

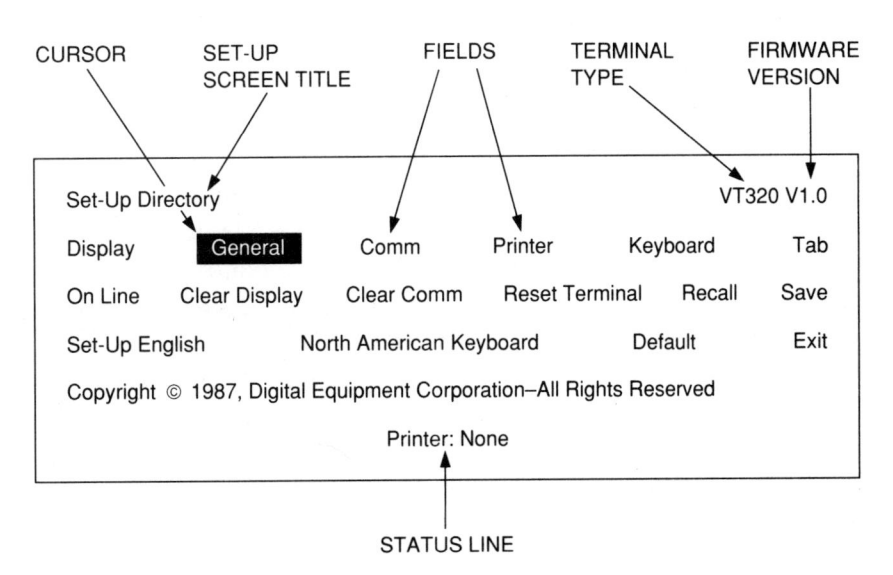

```
CURSOR    SET-UP           FIELDS      TERMINAL    FIRMWARE
          SCREEN TITLE                 TYPE        VERSION

Set-Up Directory                                    VT320 V1.0

Display      General        Comm        Printer      Keyboard      Tab
On Line      Clear Display  Clear Comm  Reset Terminal  Recall    Save
Set-Up English    North American Keyboard           Default      Exit

Copyright © 1987, Digital Equipment Corporation–All Rights Reserved

                        Printer: None

                        STATUS LINE
```

Figure 1-7 The opening set-up screen

Most screens include the following information:

- Name of the screen.
- Terminal identifier.
- Firmware version number. This indicates the date of completion of the instruction set for the Set-Up screens in use. Various terminals in an office may have different firmware and show slight differences in options.
- Status line. At the bottom of each screen, indicates the current status of the modem (if enabled), the printer, and the terminal's insert/replace mode.

    Insert/Replace: Insert. (All characters entered from the keyboard at the cursor position will move existing characters to the right. Existing characters moved past the right margin are lost.)

    Insert/Replace: Replace. (All characters entered from the keyboard at the cursor position will overwrite any existing characters on screen. This is the normal setting.)

    Printer: Ready.

    Printer: Not Ready.

    Printer: None.

    Printer: Auto. (The terminal is in the Auto Print mode.)

    Printer: Controller. (The printer is in Printer Controller mode.)

    Modem: DSR, Data. (The modem is set to send or receive data.)

    Modem: DSR, Talk. (The modem is set to allow voice communications.)

    Modem: No DSR, Data. (The modem is not available.)

    Modem: No DSR, Talk. (The modem is not available.)

- Fields

    Action. This is a direct command issuable from within the Set-Up screen. Moving the cursor to highlight the "To Directory" command will move the system to the master directory.

Parameter. This is an entry offering a selection of options, chosen by pressing the Enter key. For example, a "margin bell" can be enabled or disabled.

Text Parameter. This entry accepts direct entry of data from the keyboard. The user's keystrokes are displayed on a temporary status line at the bottom of the screen. Pressing Enter sends the data to the terminal's memory.

On current Digital models and most compatibles, the following screens are available: Display, General, Communications, Printer, Keyboard, and Tab.

A Tour Through the Set-Up Menus

The sample directory screens discussed in this section are from the VT320 terminals, and they include some features not available on previous families of terminals. Additionally, terminals from other manufacturers may have special screens or special features not represented here—these include emulation of other types of terminals, color screen attributes, and additional character fonts.

Use the arrow keys on the keyboard to move the cursor so that it highlights (makes bold or changes to reverse video) a particular feature in the menu. If the feature has more than one possible setting, use the Enter (not Return) key to move through the available settings for each feature.

Features with only one available setting are called *action fields* in that when they are selected and the Enter key pressed, the terminal performs the action. For example, "Clear Comm" and "To Next Set-Up" are acted upon immediately.

Master Set-Up Directory

Here are some of the options presented on a Master Set-Up screen:

Feature	Settings	Function
Display	Display	Displays the Display Set-Up Menu.

Feature	Settings	Function
General	General	Displays the General Set-Up Menu.
Comm	Comm	Displays the Communications Set-Up Menu.
Printer	Printer	Displays the Printer Set-Up Menu.
Keyboard	Keyboard	Displays the Keyboard Set-Up Menu.
Tab	Tab	Displays the Tab Set-Up Menu.
On Line/Local		Instructs the terminal whether to communicate with a host system or operate as a local device.
	On Line (default)	Establishes communication with the host system.
	Local	Terminal sends keyboard input to the screen alone, putting the host system on hold.
Clear Display	Clear Display	Clears the screen when the user exits from the Set-Up menu.
Clear Comm	Clear Comm	Clears communication in the following ways: ■ Stops print operations ■ Stops escape or control sequences ■ Stops the printer controller mode and returns the terminal to normal print mode ■ Clears keyboard buffers ■ Clears the receive buffer ■ Clears the transmit buffer

Feature	Settings	Function
		■ Clears an XON signal to the host
		■ Resets XOFF received flags at the printer and host
Reset Terminal	Reset Terminal	Resets many operating features of the terminal to the default settings expected by most application programs. Screen, communication, character set modes, and user-defined keys are not affected.
Recall	Recall	Resets all Set-Up features to their saved states, thereby removing any changes made since Save was last executed. (If a modem is in use, Recall will also disconnect communication with the host system.)
Save	Save	All current feature settings on Set-Up screens are saved to nonvolatile memory.
Default	Default	Returns all Set-Up features to the factory-default settings. The screen is cleared and the cursor is returned to the upper-left corner.
Exit	Exit	Exits from Set-Up

Display Set-Up Screen

Here are some of the options presented on a Display Set-Up screen:

Feature	Settings	Function
To Next Set-Up	To next Set-Up	Displays the General Set-Up Menu.
To Directory	To Directory	Displays the Master Set-Up Menu.
xx Columns	80 Columns (default)	The standard display width for a VT terminal.
	132 Columns	Selects 132-column mode for the display.
xx Controls		Instructs the terminal whether to execute or display control codes from the host system. Often used in debugging programs.
	Interpret Controls (default)	Instructs the terminal to execute received control codes without displaying them.
	Display Controls	Instructs the terminal to display received control codes without executing them.
Auto Wrap		Instructs the terminal whether to automatically wrap text down to the next line when characters reach the right margin.
	No Auto Wrap (default)	When the cursor reaches the right margin, characters do not wrap to the next line, but instead overprint each other in the last column of the line.
	Auto Wrap	When the cursor reaches the right margin, the characters continue on the next line.
xx Scroll		Instructs the terminal on how fast to display new lines of text on the screen.

Feature	Settings	Function
	Smooth Scroll (default)	Limits the speed at which new lines are displayed on the screen, producing a smooth, steady scroll.
	Jump Scroll	Puts no limit on the speed at which new lines are displayed on the screen, causing a jump scroll, which displays new lines as fast as they are received.
xx Text, xx Screen		Chooses between a normal or reverse video display.
	Light Text, Dark Screen (default)	Selects a screen display of light text against a dark background.
	Dark Text, Light Screen	Selects a reverse video display of dark text against a light background.
Text Cursor	Cursor (default)	Instructs the terminal to display the text cursor.
	No cursor	Instructs the terminal not to display the text cursor.
xx Cursor Style	Block (default)	Selects a blinking block as cursor.
	Underline	Selects a blinking underline as cursor.
xx Status Display		Instructs the terminal how and when to display the status line at the bottom of the screen.
	No Status Display (default)	The status line appears only then the Set-Up Menu is displayed.
	Indicator	The status line appears at all times.

Feature	Settings	Function
	Host Writable	Host applications are permitted to write messages to appear in place of the status line.

General Set-Up Features

Here are some of the options presented on a General Set-Up Menu screen.

Feature	Settings	Function
To Next Set-Up	To Next Set-Up	Displays the Communications Set-Up Menu.
To Directory	To Directory	Displays the Master Set-Up Directory screen.
xx Mode xx		Selects the operating mode for the terminal.
	VT300 Mode, 7-Bit Controls (default on VT320 terminals)	Supports all VT300 features, 8-bit graphic display characters, and 7-bit control characters.
	VT200 Mode, 7-bit Controls (default on VT200 terminals)	Supports all VT200 features, 8-bit graphic display characters, and 7-bit control characters.
	VT300 Mode, 8-bit Controls	Allows the terminal to use all VT320 features in an 8-bit environment with 8-bit control characters. This mode is not yet supported by most applications.
	VT100 Mode	Allows the terminal to run applications that require the more limited VT100 settings.

Feature	Settings	Function
	VT52 Mode	Allows the terminal to run applications that require the more limited VT52 settings.
Terminal ID	VT320 ID VT220 ID VT100 ID VT101 ID VT102 ID	Selects the ID that will be given by the terminal in response to a query from an application on the host system. Some older software may not recognize a VT320, for example, and in this case the terminal fools the software by calling itself a VT220.
User-Defined Keys xx		Instructs the terminal whether or not the host can change user-defined key (UDK) definitions.
	Unlocked (default)	Allows the host to define UDKs.
	Locked	Prevents the host from changing UDKs.
xx Keypad		Instructs the terminal whether the numeric keypad keys send the characters identified on their keycaps or instead send programming functions.
	Numeric (default)	The keypad keys send the characters on their keycaps.
	Application	The keypad sends programming functions as defined by an application.
xx Cursor		Instructs the terminal whether cursor keys are to control cursor movement or send application control functions.

Feature	Settings	Function
	Normal (default)	Arrow keys move the cursor up, down, left, or right as marked on key caps.
	Application	Arrow keys send application control functions.
xx New Line		Selects whether the Return key moves the cursor to a new line.
	No New Line (default)	The return key sends a carriage return only.
	New Line	The Return key sends a carriage return and a line feed.
User-Preferred Character Set		Selects one of two character sets.
	UPSS DEC Supplemental (default)	Selects the DEC Multinational set.
	UPSS ISO	Selects the ISO Latin-1 set. The difference between the two sets is their supplemental character set, called a user-preferred set.

Communications Set-Up Menu

Here are some of the options presented on the Communications Set-Up screen:

Feature	Settings	Function
To Next Set-Up	To Next Set-Up	Displays the Printer Set-Up Menu.

Feature	Settings	Function
To Directory	To Directory	Displays the Master Set-Up Directory Menu.
Transmit = xx	75 1200 110 2400 150 4800 300 9600 600 19200	Selects the baud rate used by the terminal to send data to the host. The terminal's speed for transmission must match the host's speed of reception. The VT320 is capable of transmitting at one speed and receiving at another. Default is 9600.
Receive = xx	Receive = Transmit (default) 75 1200 110 2400 150 4800 300 9600 600 19200	Selects the baud rate used by the terminal to receive data from the host. The terminal's speed for reception must match the host's speed of transmission. The VT320 is capable of transmitting at one speed and receiving at another.
XOFF xx	XOFF at 64 (default) XOFF at 128 No XOFF	Selects the number of characters the terminal can receive before sending an XOFF signal to the host to stop the transmission of data.
xx Bits	8 Bits, No Parity (default) 8 Bits, Even Parity 8 Bits, Odd Parity 8 Bits, Even Parity, No Check 8 Bits, Odd Parity, No Check 7 Bits, Even Parity No Check 7 Bits, Odd Parity No Check	Selects the protocol used to communicate with the host.

48 □ THE TERMINAL SOLUTION

Feature	Settings	Function
	7 Bits, No Parity 7 Bits, Even Parity 7 Bits, Odd Parity 7 Bits, Mark Parity 7 Bits, Space Parity	
xx Stop Bit		Selects the number of stop bits used in the communication protocol.
	1 Stop Bit (default)	Recommended.
	2 Stop Bits	For use with baud rates under 300.
Local Echo		Instructs the system whether or not to send keyboard data to the host.
	No Local Echo (default)	Sends keyboard data to the host.
	Local Echo	Sends keyboard data to the screen and to the host.
Host Port		Instructs the system whether to use limited modem control signals.
	DEC-423, Leads Only (default)	Use if a modem is not in use.
	DEC-423, Modem Control	Provides limited modem control signals for modems.
xx Transmit		Instructs whether to limit the terminal's transmit speed.
	Limited (default)	Limits the terminal to 150 to 180 characters per second transmission, regardless of the baud rate setting selected under the Transmit= feature. This selection may be requested by the system

USING SET-UP TO CUSTOMIZE YOUR TERMINAL □ 49

Feature	Settings	Function
		operator to ease the burden on the computer.
	Unlimited	Unlimited terminal transmit speed.
Auto Answerback	Auto Answerback (default)	Instructs the system whether to send the answerback message to the host.
	No Auto Answerback	
Answerback=		Allows the user to enter an answerback message of up to 30 characters.

Printer Set-Up Menu

Here are some of the options presented on a Printer Set-Up screen:

Feature	Settings	Function
To Next Set-Up	To Next Set-Up	Displays the Keyboard Set-Up Menu.
To Directory	To Directory	Displays the Master Set-Up Directory Menu.
Speed = xx	75 1200 110 2400 150 4800 300 9600 600 19200	Selects the baud rate used to send data to a printer. Default is 4800.
Printer to Host Comm		Selects whether the printer sends data to the host system.
	No Printer to Host (default)	Data is directed from host to printer only.

Feature	Settings	Function
	Printer to Host	Data is directed from host to printer and printer to host.
Print Mode		Determines how printing is performed.
	Normal (default)	Printing functions can be initiated from the keyboard.
	Auto Print	Prints the current line of text on the printer when the terminal receives a line feed, form feed, vertical tab, or autowrap.
	Controller	Data is sent directly to the printer without displaying the data on the screen.
XOFF	XOFF (default)	Instructs the terminal whether or not to use XON/XOFF flow control with the printer.
	No XOFF	
xx Bits, xx Parity		Selects a character protocol to match the printer.
	8 Bits, No Parity (default) 8 Bits, Even Parity 8 Bits, Odd Parity 7 Bits, No Parity 7 Bits, Mark Parity 7 Bits, Space Parity 7 Bits, Even Parity 7 Bits, Odd Parity	
xx Stop Bit		Selects the stop bit protocol.
	1 Stop Bit (default)	
	2 Stop Bits	

Feature	Settings	Function
Print xx		Instructs the terminal how much of the screen to print when the Print Screen key is struck.
	Full Page (default)	Prints the full screen.
	Scroll Region	Prints only the scrolling region.

Keyboard Set-Up Menu

Here are some of the options presented on a Keyboard Set-Up screen:

Feature	Settings	Function
To Next Set-Up	To Next Set-Up	Displays the Tab Set-Up Menu.
To Directory	To Directory	Displays the Master Set-Up Directory Menu.
xx Lock	Caps Lock (default)	When the Lock key on the keyboard is pressed, the alphabetic keys send their uppercase characters while other keys send the bottom character on the keycap.
	Shift Lock	When the Lock key on the keyboard is pressed, all keys send the top character on the keycap.
Auto Repeat		Instructs the terminal whether to send a character repeatedly when a key is held down.

Feature	Settings	Function
		The following keys, however, never repeat: Hold Screen, Print Screen, Set-Up, Return, Break, Lock, and Ctrl.
	Auto Repeat (default)	
	No Auto Repeat	
Keyclick		Instructs the system whether or not to generate a clicking or beeping sound as keys are pressed.
	Keyclick (default)	
	No Keyclick	
Margin Bell		Instructs the terminal whether to issue a bell tone when the text cursor approaches the right margin.
	Margin Bell (default)	
	No Margin Bell	
Warning Bell		Instructs the terminal whether to issue a bell tone when operating errors occur or when the Ctrl-G character is struck.
	Warning Bell (default)	
	No Warning Bell	
Break		Instructs the terminal whether the Break key sends a break signal. (Communications with a modem can be ended through use of the Shift-

Feature	Settings	Function
		Break key combination whether or not the Break feature has been enabled.)
	Break (default)	
	No Break	
Compose		Instructs the system whether or not the Compose character key works.
	Compose (default)	
	No Compose	

Tab Set-Up Menu

Here are some of the options presented on a Tab Set-Up Screen:

Features	Settings	Function
To Next Set-Up	To Next Set-Up	Displays the Display Set-Up Menu.
To Directory	To Directory	Displays the Master Set-Up Directory Menu.
Clear All Tabs	Clear All Tabs	Clears all tabs previously set.
Set 8 Column Tabs	Set 8 Column Tabs	Automatically sets tabs every 8 columns, starting at column 9.

Saving Your Set-Up Modifications

Any changes that you make in the Set-Up menus will be in effect immediately, and will remain so until the terminal is turned off or the setting is changed again. In order to save a setting so that it will remain a part of your terminal's default environment even when power to the terminal is shut off, move the cursor to the "Save" option and press the Enter key. The message "Done" will appear on the status line.

A Worst-Case Scenario

If you have made some changes in the Set-Up options and suddenly your application program is not working or communication has failed or the screen is garbled (any or all of these problems could be caused by the same improper setting), you have two safety nets beneath you.

First of all, if you have not yet saved your changes by moving the cursor to the Save choice of the master or top-level menu, you can revert to the previously saved settings by selecting the Recall option. (Another way to do this is to shut off the terminal and then power it back up. Do this only when you have no other option, though, since each power-up puts a strain on the terminal's electronics.)

The second level of protection lies in the use of the Default setting, which returns all Set-Up features to their factory settings. Return to General Set-Up and select "Save."

2 A Few Small Steps for VAX Users

As we've seen, a computer terminal is, at heart, little more than a high-resolution television screen and a keyboard. Although the manner in which it displays and exchanges information is highly customizable, nearly all the work it performs is under the control of a computer at the other end of a cable.

There are two basic things to understand before you undertake your first session: first, it is almost impossible to damage the computer itself by any action you might call for from the keyboard of the terminal; second, though, you must be careful not to do damage to the programs and data that are available to you as a user. Among your privileges as a user is the right to erase or change files, so you must learn about what you have to do before you plunge into your first session.

LOGGING IN

Your first task as a user is to establish a connection from your terminal to the computer. In computer terms, this is called logging in.

Turn on your terminal. (Power switches are in various locations on different kinds of terminals—consult your user manual or the system manager if the switch is not evident.) Most terminals have a green or red pilot light on the front to indicate that the power is on. Screens will typically take from 15 to 30 seconds to warm up.

The first indication of life you see may be a blinking cursor (an underscore or a small box) or a message on the screen. Many terminals automatically perform tests on their various elements. Displays for these self-tests range from complex messages to a simple notice that a test is under way.

You should get a message of some sort indicating that the test is completed and the terminal is ready. If you don't, consult the manual and then check the power cord and other connecting cables before calling the system manager or the repair service.

When the terminal is ready, hit the Return key which is located at the right-hand side of the standard typewriter-like keyboard. Note that on a VT terminal (the standard terminal for Digital VAX Computers) there is both a Return key and an Enter key. The Enter key is used in certain applications and is generally not the same thing as Return.

If you hit the Return key, you should be greeted by the sign-on message from your VAX/VMS system. (Remember that almost everything you do at the terminal end is merely notetaking until you press the Return key and send the message on the cable to the computer.) If you get no response, try typing the Ctrl-C or Ctrl-Y characters, which are obtained by using the Ctrl key as a shift key—just hold down Ctrl and then hit the C or Y key.

You should now see

Username:

The computer is asking you for the name of the account you have established. This is part of the security facility of your system—only those persons with a valid account and password are given access to the computer. (Once logged on, there are further levels of restriction in many systems, designed to protect vital files from unauthorized access.) Type in your account name and press the Return key.

Next, the computer will display

Password:

Type in your password and press the Return key. Note that the characters you type are not printed on the screen. This is to help prevent an onlooker from seeing your password.

The computer will then compare your account name and password with the secret list it maintains. If the password or account name is not on the list, you will receive the message

User authorization failure

Depending on the system, you may be granted additional attempts to sign on, or the terminal connection may shut down for a while as part of a security system to prevent unauthorized access.

If your entry is accepted by the system, you will see a welcome message. Here is a typical successful login session:

Username: **SANDLER**   <Return>
Password: **password**   <Return>

Welcome to WILLIE-CORP's VAX/VMS V4.5 System

Last interactive login on Monday, 19-AUG-87 06:01

Last non-interactive login on 19-AUG-83

You have 2 new mail message(s)

$

That last dollar sign is not your bill—it is the standard *prompt* of the DCL interpreter. A prompt is a request for a command. Later on in this book, you'll learn how to customize that prompt to make it more friendly and informative.

Remote Logins

The login session we've been discussing to this point is one that would be typical of a session in which the user is communicating with a local computer, or with one linked directly over a network such as Digital's DECnet.

It is also possible that you will be communicating from a remote location, using a modem for telecommunications over standard telephone lines or over a special leased line. Your system manager will provide you with instructions on how to use the terminal or PC to dial up the access port on your computer.

Once you have made contact with the VAX via telecommunications, you will be greeted with the same, or similar, sign-on process as with a local connection. On some systems, telecommunications users will face an additional level of security. One such system uses a *callback modem*. This is a device that queries the user for a password and then disconnects the link. It then calls back to a predetermined phone number to open communications. This arrangement adds another level of protection to the system—even if a password is compromised, the computer will make connection only to a specific location.

Consult with your system manager to determine if there are any special security requirements for your system.

Another form of remote login involves a connection from a local node to another system across interconnected networks. In such a situation, the user must first sign on to the local system and then change hosts. In many cases, using the next host will require another login process.

PASSWORDS

Why bother with passwords? Are you absolutely convinced that there is no chance that any person will ever attempt to read your confidential files or change them without your authorization? Are you certain that no untrained person will ever accidentally erase or change or damage your critical files? Then please invite the rest of us over to your place—we've never seen such perfection. For the rest of us, the best policy is: Use passwords, make them difficult or impossible to guess, and change them regularly.

The proper strategy for picking a password is not to have an obvious pattern. Don't use your nickname. Don't use your husband's or wife's name. Don't use your telephone extension. These have all been used before, and a clever hacker will try them first. Reach for a word or a combination of numbers that is outside of your public persona.

Next, try to retain the password in your head rather than writing it down. If you must write it down, don't tape it to the side of the terminal or the underside of the keyboard, and don't leave it on a slip of paper in your desk drawer or your Rolodex. Trust me—that's a bit obvious.

You might try writing it down in code—scramble every other letter by adding two letters or numbers, for example. Keep the paper in your wallet.

You should also get in the habit of changing your password every few weeks or months. Use the **SET PASSWORD** command and enter first the old password and then the new one.

And finally, you should log off your terminal any time you are going to be away from it for a length of time. An unattended, logged-on terminal is an open door to your files.

This is all a bit of trouble, but so is locking the front door of your house when you go away.

3 The Digital Command Language

It may appear that a computer speaks many different languages. In truth, it speaks only one—the language of pulses of electricity representing one of two bits of information. You can think of it as dealing only with 0s and 1s, yeses and nos, ons and offs, or any similar pair. This lowest of low-level languages is called *machine language*.

LEVELS OF COMPUTER LANGUAGE

The designers of computers and operating systems will have to, at some point in the process, deal with these binary codes, writing basic instructions in 0s and 1s to be placed directly into the computer's registers. But luckily, we users don't ordinarily have to come anywhere near this level of tedium. The typical user will work several levels away from the lowest level.

Here's a description of some of the levels of programming language in use on modern computers:

Machine language: The binary language of 0s and 1s used by all digital computers. Other, higher-level languages must be compiled or otherwise translated into binary code.

Compilers: Programs that take the instructions of higher-level languages and translate them into machine language.

Assembler language: A mid-level language that accepts English-like statements and converts them in a one-to-one correspondence to machine language.

High-level languages: An interpreter system that allows the programmer to express operations in English-like commands less directly linked to machine language. Examples of higher-level languages include BASIC, FORTRAN, and Cobol.

Operating system: Software that controls the operations of a computer, including the scheduling and initiation of jobs, the use of storage devices such as memory and disk, and the output of results to printers and video terminals. Operating systems, such as VMS used on Digital's VAX hardware, usually include a programming language that is similar to a high-level language in its use of English-like commands and grammar. Under VMS, the programming language is called DCL, for Digital Command Language.

Application programs: Most software designed to perform specific functions—word processors, databases, communication programs, and the like—includes a high-level language that may be akin to natural language or an operating system language in use.

Natural language instructions: A scheme midway between a high-level language and an artificial intelligence language. Natural language interpreters include glossaries of synonyms that allow the user to issue commands in the manner of "Display the names of all persons with outstanding balances greater than $1,000."

Artificial intelligence: A software system that includes a detailed set of rules for the computer that allows it to "reason" and make decisions based on its experience.

SOME FACTS ABOUT DCL

The Digital Command Language is the means for the user to communicate with the VAX/VMS operating system and through it to the computer itself. In the list above, it would sit within the fifth level, as an operating system language.

DCL allows the user to develop and run programs; work with files, disks, and other storage media; obtain information about the system; and modify the work environment for a custom fit between machine and user.

DCL has two modes: interactive and noninteractive. As an interactive language, the computer accepts DCL commands issued directly from the terminal. In noninteractive mode, VAX/VMS creates a new process to execute commands for you, based on a set of DCL commands included as part of a batch job or another process. A batch job is a processing technique in which similar transactions are gathered and submitted as a group. The opposite is real-time processing, in which input is processed as it is received.

As we've discussed in chapter 2, you must log in to the system in order to use a VAX/VMS system. The login procedure is partly for security reasons to make sure that only authorized users gain access to a particular system, and partly procedural, to make sure that each user is able to work with his or her own set of files and programs.

When the system accepts a user at login time, it creates an environment in which the user can issue commands—referred to as a process. The computer consults its user authorization file, set up by the system manager, to determine the allowable characteristics for each process. Such characteristics include

1. The user's account name and user identification code.
2. The default disk drive and directory name to help the system locate the user's files.
3. The privileges and quotas assigned to the user on the system.

DCL COMMANDS

A DCL command is made up of an English-like syntax using verbs, compound modifiers, and objects. Here is a full DCL command, using the names of its elements:

$LABEL: VERB PARAMETER /QUALIFIER !A COMMENT

Following are descriptions of the elements of this command:

- **$** is the default DCL prompt. As we'll learn later, this symbol can be modified by the user.
- **LABEL** is an optional element of the command. The label assigns a name or gives an explanation, but is not acted upon by the computer. VMS distinguishes the label by its trailing colon. A label is useful in writing a multiline program of DCL commands.
- **VERB** is a valid command name in the DCL dictionary.
- **PARAMETER** is the object of the action to be performed by VMS. There can be more than one parameter in a single command, but they must be separated by a space or tab.
- **QUALIFIER** is an element of the command that limits or modifies the action to be performed. For example, a qualifier can call for a full or a brief display of the result of a command. More than one qualifier can be added to a command; they are separated from each other by slash (/) characters.
- **Comments** are preceded by an exclamation point. They can be used as a reminder of the purpose of a command or information about other commands or procedures. Comments are ignored by the system.

The Abbreviated Form

Commands do not need to be spelled out completely—the computer needs to know only enough to distinguish between similar commands. For example, if you were to type

$SHOW PR   <Return>

the computer would not know whether you wanted to know about the PRinter, the PRocess, or the PRotection level. If you type

$SHOW PRO   <Return>

it is narrowed down to PROcess or PROtection, but the computer is still uncertain. Add one more character, though, and the command is suitably unique:

$SHOW PROC   <Return>

can mean nothing but **SHOW PROCESS** in DCL terminology.

Self-Prompting Commands

Although it is often easier and more direct to enter a compound sentence as an order to the computer, many of the commands in DCL will ask you for information if you don't supply enough at first.

For example, the following incomplete command would result in the prompts shown on the next two lines.

$COPY   <Return>

$_From: Enter source

$_To: Enter destination

Messages from the System

The second line in the following display is an example of a message you may see appear on your screen:

$PRINT FILENAME.EXTENSION   <Return>

Job FILENAME (queue LPA0, entry 246) started on SYS$PRINT

$

In this case, the system is notifying you of the completion of a printing job it was given earlier. The computer names the job, using the filename as source, tells which queue the job has been assigned to, gives the job a number for tracking, and confirms the name of the printer where the work will be performed.

A number of DCL commands, including PRINT, will accept as a modifier the /NOTIFY request. This will cause the system to send a message to the terminal telling the user when a job has been completed. It will help in your own scheduling. The message will appear on screen but not affect the completion of any work in progress. To clear messages off the screen and repaint the screen, use the Ctrl-W key combination. Ctrl-W works in most, but not all, applications and operating system situations. (In the case of a print job, this will tell you when the job has been dispatched from the computer to the queue waiting for the printer's attention—it does not necessarily indicate that the printing itself has been completed.)

Here is the form for a **/NOTIFY** request using the **PRINT** command:

$PRINT filename/NOTIFY   <Return>

A Few Housekeeping Essentials

Very few users have identical assignments at a computer or ways of performing the same task. You will learn in this book about many ways to customize your sessions with a VAX. The particular application program you use (a word processor, database, spreadsheet, or other such special-purpose software) should also allow adaptation to your particular needs.

In any case, users should understand a few "housekeeping" details to help in the orderly management of their account on the computer. Like most environments, a computer benefits from orderliness, including the discarding of unnecessary files, proper identification of needed files, and a logical system of organization.

Following are some basic commands. You'll find fuller explanations of these and other commands in Chapter 10.

DIRECTORY

Let's start with the organization. After you have signed on to your account, examine the catalog of files assigned to your name. This is done with the **DIRECTORY** command. Type in the following:

$DIRECTORY   <Return>

You will be greeted by a listing of files, together with some of the attributes of those files. You can find out more about the meaning of the filename attributes in Chapter 4.

DELETE

Did you see any files in the directory that you no longer need? To remove a file from your account, use the DELETE command followed by the name of the file to be removed:

$DELETE filename(s)   <Return>

You will learn later on about global characters, such as the asterisk, which will allow you to delete one or more files with the same name or filename extension.

PURGE

In the directory of files, you may have seen multiple copies of the same file, the only difference being in the number at the end of the filename, as in

SAMPLE.TXT;3
SAMPLE.TXT;2
SAMPLE.TXT;1

    This is the result of one of the VMS operating system's automatic protection schemes. Every time you add to or update a previously created file, the system will create a new version of the file and increment the *version number*, which is the final element of the filename. The previous version of the file is kept in your directory in case you need to use it. You may decide that the changes you have made were not correct or not needed; you may decide that you need the version of a file which was in effect on a previous day. Until you delete previous versions of files, they are kept by the operating system.

    Obviously, it is usually not necessary to keep all of the older versions of your files.

    Stop and think before you try this: If you do not need any of the extra copies of your files, and require only the latest version (the latest version is the file with the highest version number), use the following command:

$PURGE   <Return>

This command will automatically remove all of the extra files from your account, leaving only the highest numbered version (the most recently created file). Be careful to use this command with care and forethought.

    If there are a few files that you need to purge while retaining others, you can use the PURGE command with the file name to remove them manually:

$PURGE filename   <Return>

COPY

Suppose that you want an extra copy of one of your files, either as a backup or as a file to modify for another purpose. The solution comes with the use of the COPY command. Enter the following:

$COPY original_filename new_filename <Return>

In this usage, the computer will assume that the source file (called the input filename) is in your present directory and stored on the default or standard storage device for your account. In this usage, the destination file (output filename) will go to the same location.

It is also possible to copy a file from your directory into a subdirectory of your account or into the directory or subdirectory of another user—if you have been granted the right to make such a transfer. You'll learn more about these special transfers in Chapter 4. Here, though, is an example of how such a copy and transfer operation is performed:

$COPY [SANDLER]FISH_PRICES.TXT;3
          [WILLIE] PRICE_LIST.TXT   <Return>

In this case, we are asking the computer to copy version 3 of the file named FISH_PRICES, with the filename extension of .TXT, and place the new copy in the directory of another user named WILLIE. That new file will be given the name of PRICE_LIST.TXT. Since no version number is specified and there is no other copy of a file with the same name in WILLIE's directory, the new file will have a version number of 1.

You'll find more details about file naming conventions in Chapter 4.

APPEND

Another housekeeping chore might involve the merging of one or more files into another. For example, daily price lists might be merged into a weekly list. The command to merge files is called APPEND, since it appends one file onto the end of another.

Here is how the command looks:

$APPEND input-file-spec output-file-spec   <Return>

In use, the specified input file or files are added to the end of the specified output file. The specification (file-spec) means name, directory, and physical location of the file.

RENAME

There may also come times when you want to rename a file. For example, you may choose to maintain a regular log of activities or a price list in your directory at all times, always using the same name for the current version. In this case, you will rename outdated versions from time to time.

The syntax for renaming a file is

$RENAME input-file-spec output-file-spec   <Return>

where **input** is the present name and specification and **output** is the new name and specification. If directories are not included in either the input or output elements of the command, the computer will assume the unadorned file names are in the default directory of the user.

Here's a shortcut if you want to move a file from your directory to a subdirectory of yours (see Chapter 4) or another user's directory, and rename it in the process: **RENAME** the file and include the directory name of the new owner of the file as part of the output file specification, as in:

**$RENAME [SANDLER]FISH_PRICES.TXT;3
        [WILLIE]PRICE_LIST.TXT**   <Return>

In this instance, the file named FISH_PRICES.TXT;3 has been renamed to PRICE_LIST.TXT and made part of the directory named WILLIE. It no longer exists in the directory called SANDLER.

PRINT

The process of printing a file from within DCL is ordinarily a very simple one, although you should consult with your system manager to learn about the available printing devices and the default queues that are in use on your system. The command to print uses the verb PRINT, as in

$PRINT filename <Return>

which will send the specified file to the default printer.

Your system may have logical names available to various printing devices, in which case the command may be something like

$LASER filename <Return>

for a laser printer, or

$LINEPRINT filename <Return>

for output to a line printer.

There are a few command qualifiers you will learn about in Chapter 10, under PRINT, that will help you in specifying your needs to the computer. These include **/COPIES = x** to request more than one copy to be printed, and **/NOTIFY**, discussed earlier in this chapter.

Within an applications program such as a word processor, database, or spreadsheet, the commands and procedures for printing may vary.

Logging Out

Logging out is the final act of any session. The most important reason to log out is to preserve the security of the data and programs on your system. Once a session is logged out, it can be reactivated only with a password-protected login procedure. A secondary reason, but not unimportant, is that it frees up system resources for other users.

The logout is a simple process. Just enter

$LOGOUT <Return>

or

$LO <Return>

If you'd like to obtain more information about your session, use the command

$LOGOUT/FULL   <Return>

to yield such data as total time logged on to the account, total CPU time used, and other information.

Here is an example of a full logout:

$LOGOUT/FULL

SANDLER logged out at 23-OCT-1987 10:30:53.25

Accounting information:
Buffered I/O count:	694	Peak working set size:	929
Direct I/O count:	270	Peak page file size:	1421
Page faults:	2384	Mounted volumes:	0
Charged CPU time: 0 00:00:35.11		Elapsed time: 0 00:08:22.27	

HELP IS ALWAYS AT HAND

No matter where you are in a DCL session—and in most applications programs—you are just a keystroke away from help at all times. If you type

$HELP   <Return>

or press the F15 key on a VT200, VT300, or compatible keyboard, the screen will display a menu of help topics. Select the subject you need assistance with by typing the full name of the displayed subject, or as many characters as are needed to make your choice obvious to the computer. For example, to seek information on the **CONNECT** command you have to enter **CONN** to avoid confusion with the **CONTINUE** and **CONVERT** commands.

Here is an example of a request for help on the RENAME command:

Topic? **RENAME**   <Return>

RENAME

Changes all or part of a file specification(s).

Format

RENAME input-file-spec,... output-file-spec

Additional information available:

Parameters Qualifiers

/BACKUP /BEFORE[=time] /BY_OWNER[=uic] /CONFIRM
/CREATED (default) /EXCLUDE(=file-spec,...)
/EXPIRED/LOG
/MODIFIED /NEW_VERSION (default) /SINCE[=time]

At this point, the computer asks if the user requires any assistance on subtopics such as the BACKUP command:

RENAME Subtopic?

If you enter the name of one of the subtopics listed and press (Return), you will be given additional information, as follows:

RENAME Subtopic? **/BACKUP**   <Return>

RENAME
 /BACKUP
  /CREATED (default)
  /EXPIRED
  /MODIFIED

Selects files for the rename operation according to the dates of their most recent backups, their creation dates, their expiration dates, or the dates of their last modifications. Relevant only with the /BEFORE and /SINCE qualifiers.

Figure 3-1 shows a listing of the available Help topics on a typical VMS system.

Additional information available:

20-20	2020	ACCOUNTING	ALLOCATE	ANALYZE	APPEND	Ascii
ASSIGN	ATTACH	BACKUP	BASIC	CALL	CANCEL	CLOSE
Command_procedure		CONNECT	CONTINUE	CONVERT	COPY	CREATE
CTRAIN	DEALLOCATE	DEASSIGN	DEBUG	DECK	DEFINE	DELETE
DEPOSIT	DIFFERENCES		DIRECTORY	DISCONNECT	DISMOUNT	DSCALC
DUMP	EDIT	EOD	EXAMINE	EXIT	Expressions	
File_spec	FMS	GKS	GOSUB	GOTO	HELP	Hints
IF	IMPRINT	INITIALIZE	INQUIRE	Instructions		Kermit
Lexicals	LIBRARY	LINK	LOGOUT	MAIL	MERGE	MESSAGE
MF	MOUNT	New_Features_V44		Numbers	ON	OPEN
PRINT	Privileges	Procedures	Protection	PURGE	READ	RECALL
REMAME	REPLY	REQUEST	RETURN	RUN	RUNOFF	SEARCH
SET	SHOW	SORT	SPAWN	START	STOP	Strings
SUBMIT	Symbol_assignment		SYNCHRONIZE		TEX	THEN
Time	TYPE	UNLOCK	WAIT	WP	WPSPLUS	WRITE

Figure 3-1 A sample VMS help topic screen

Here are some of the general navigational tools of the **HELP** command under DCL:

Type **PROCEDURES** and (Return) for information on commonly performed tasks.

Type **HINTS** and (Return) if you are not sure of the name of the command or topic for which you need help.

Type **INSTRUCTIONS** and (Return) for more detailed instructions on how to use Help.

Type a question mark and (Return) to redisplay the most recently requested text.

Press the Return key one or more times to exit from Help.

You can also skip past the display of Help topics by directly querying the Help library. Just enter **HELP** followed by a topic or command:

$HELP LOGIN   <Return>

With such a direct query, you can also enter the subtopic and even a sub-subtopic from the command line:

$HELP RENAME/BACKUP/CREATED   <Return>

Help within Applications Programs

Consult the instruction manuals for your applications to determine the amount and nature of Help available to users. Or you can try pressing the Help key and see what happens.

A number of special application programs such as word processors or VT emulation packages will include on-screen displays of the keyboard to help locate any special command keys or to show how a PC keyboard has been adapted to emulate keys on the LK201 keyboard.

4 Files

At the heart of the way a computer goes about its business is its organization of information into files. Each job that a user works on is indexed and stored like a folder in a filing cabinet.

The nature of the data in the file folder is of no importance to the system—it may be text, numeric information, graphics, or a combination of data types.

The file folders may be automatically opened, updated, and closed by an application program such as a word processor, or the folders may be created and managed under the direct command of the user. Depending on the version of the operating system in use, the type of storage media used, and the limits placed on the user by the system operator, each user can have hundreds or even thousands of files readily accessible at any one time.

If you think of all of these files residing in a large box, mixed in with the thousands of other files from other users and from the system itself, you can see the importance of having a logical and uniform identification and storage scheme.

FILE SPECIFICATIONS

On a VMS system, the identification system is called a *file specification*. The full specification can include as many as six elements. Here is a file specification for a word processing file from Bluefish Industries:

NODE_NAME:DEVICE_NAME :[DIRECTORY]
FILE_NAME.EXTENSION;VERSION

- Node Name: If the system you are signed on to is part of a network of other computer systems, it operates as a "network node" and uses a Node Name, which can be up to six characters in length. Depending on the privileges granted your system and each user, you may be able to access files from other systems on the network.

    If your system is not part of a network, the VAX will not expect a node name. If your system is part of a network, but you do not specify a node name in the description of a file you wish to create or modify, the computer will assume the file will be located within your own node.

- Device Name: This is the physical location of the file, usually on a disk drive, but also possibly on a tape drive, a cartridge drive, or other device. The name itself consists of a combination of four characters to identify the type of device and the controller hardware involved.

    If you do not specify a device name, the system will look on the default device, as defined in the definition of your account or as modified in a DCL command since the last sign-on.

- Directory: Within the hardware storage device, this is the name of the directory or subdirectory where the file is stored. Directory names can contain up to nine characters.

    If no directory is specified, the system will look in the default directory as indicated at sign-on or as modified in a DCL command since the last sign-on. For additonal information on directories and subdirectories, see the last section in this chapter.

- Filename: This is the title of the file. You can use as many as 39 characters as the file name. Certain application programs will automatically create file names, while others have some specific limitations on names or alphanumeric characters employed.

    The following characters may be used in file names and file types:

    A through Z

    a through z

0 through 9

underscore (_)

hyphen (-)

The dollar sign can also be used, although Digital has reserved this character for many special purposes. The system will interpret lowercase letters as the same as uppercase; therefore TESTFILE.TXT is the same as testfile.txt or Testfile.Txt.

No two files can carry the exact same file specifications, although there can be thousands of files with the same name but with different version numbers.

- File type: Also called a filename extension, this is a code of up to 39 alphanumeric characters used to indicate the type of file. Typical extensions include TXT for text, DTA for data, COM for a command procedure, and TMP for a temporary file. Some application programs will assign their own file types to filenames. If you do not specify a file type, the computer will assume that the filename has no extension.
- Version number: Each time a file is changed or another version created, the file version number is increased by one. The highest number, therefore, indicates the most recently modified file.

You can access and edit any existing version of a file. And in creating a file, you can give it any version number you want (up to five digits in the range between 1 and 32,767).

Style Conventions for Filenames

You can use any standard alphanumeric character in naming a file. Several punctuation marks and special computer characters, however, serve other purposes and can therefore not be used.

No blank spaces are accepted as part of a file name. However, the user can substitute an underscore for a space for the same effect. Here is an example:

DAILY_CATCH_FIGURES.DTA

Defaults in File Specifications

The VMS system does not require the user to enter all the file specification information each time a file is called for. If the file is in the directory identified to the computer as the primary source, and if the file is stored on the expected hardware device, all the computer requires is the filename and extension. In this case, the operating system will fill in the blanks with the default information of directory and disk.

The operating system will always choose the latest version of a file for editing, unless the user adds a version number to the file specification. For example, to read the seventh and latest version of the file DAILYCATCH.DTA, you would enter

$TYPE DAILYCATCH.DTA <Return>

which would be the same as entering **DAILYCATCH.DTA; 7**.

To read the sixth version, you could enter DAILYCATCH.DTA; 6 or use a negative number for the version number, which causes the computer to count backwards from the latest version; for example,

$TYPE DAILYCATCH.DTA;-1 <Return>

would yield the sixth version if the seventh is the latest one on file.

GLOBAL CHARACTERS

One shortcut to many VMS operations involves the use of the asterisk (*) and percent sign (%) as global, or wildcard, characters. With these, you can apply a single DCL command to a specified set of files rather than just a single file at a time.

The asterisk tells the computer to accept any alphanumeric characters from the position of the asterisk to the right end of a particular element of the file specification. For example, assume you have the following files in your default directory:

BLUEFISH.DTA;1
CATFISH.DTA;1
CATFISH.DTA;2
DAILY_CATCH.DTA;1
DAILY_CATCH.DTA;2
DAILY_CATCH.DTA;3
DAILY_EXPENSES.SPD;1
DAILY_REVENUES.SPD;1
DAILY_REVENUES.SPD;2
DOGFISH.DTA;1
DRAGNET_ORDER.TXT;1
MAILING_LIST_CUSTOMERS.LIS;1

If you entered

$DIR DAILY_CATCH.DTA <Return>

you would receive a listing of all three of the versions with that name in the directory.

Suppose instead that you wanted a listing of all of the files that began with the word DAILY for comparison. If you were to enter

$DIR DAILY*.* <Return>

you would receive a listing of all files that begin with DAILY and have anything else in the filename. The use of the second asterisk would extend the definition to any filename extension. This would be your yield:

DAILY_CATCH.DTA;1
DAILY_CATCH.DTA;2
DAILY_CATCH.DTA;3
DAILY_EXPENSES.SPD;1
DAILY_REVENUES.SPD;1
DAILY_REVENUES.SPD;2

Suppose you wanted just a listing of spreadsheet (.SPD) files beginning with DAILY. The following instruction would do that:

$DIR DAILY*.SPD   <Return>
DAILY_EXPENSES.SPD;1
DAILY_REVENUES.SPD;1
DAILY_REVENUES.SPD;2

If, instead, you wanted to see the names of all files of any name, but only those ending in the DTA extension, the command and response would be

$DIR *.DTA   <Return>
BLUEFISH.DTA;1
CATFISH.DTA;1
CATFISH.DTA;2
DAILY_CATCH.DTA;1
DAILY_CATCH.DTA;2
DAILY_CATCH.DTA;3
DOGFISH.DTA;1

The global characters can be used in many DCL operations, including DIRECTORY, PRINT, COPY, RENAME, and DELETE. (Obviously, you should handle a global delete command with great respect—it is quite easy to make a minor mistake in a DCL DELETE command and end up with a major headache.)

You'll find that as you become more adept at using global characters you may add your own special filenaming conventions to make it easier to retrieve and manipulate particular types of files. For example, in our fishing company here, we might want all files dealing with specific types of fish to begin with F-, all daily catch reports with C-, and all reports on income and expenses to begin with an A- for accounting. The new subdirectory would include

A-DAILY_EXPENSES.SPD;1
A-DAILY_REVENUES.SPD;1
A-DAILY_REVENUES.SPD;2
A-DRAGNET_ORDER.TXT;1
A-MAILING_LIST_CUSTOMERS.LIS;1
C-DAILY_CATCH.DTA;1
C-DAILY_CATCH.DTA;2

C-DAILY_CATCH.DTA;3
F-DOGFISH.DTA;1
F-BLUEFISH.DTA;1
F-CATFISH.DTA;1
F-CATFISH.DTA;2

Then, to look at all accounting files, no matter what the filename or extension, you would enter this instruction:

$DIR A-*.* <Return>

To find just the A- files with a SPD extension, the command would be

$DIR A-*.SPD <Return>

Now, let us suppose that we want to be even more selective; we want to look at just those files that deal with DAILY information, whether they begin with A- or C- prefixes. Here is where the % global character comes into play. The percent mark identifies just a single position as a *wildcard* spot.

If you were to enter the following instruction:

$DIR %-DAILY*.* <Return>

you would be telling the computer to look for any file in the default directory that has any character in the first position of its name, a dash character in the second position, the word DAILY in the third through seventh spots, anything else from that point in the filename on, and any filename extension. Here is the yield from the previous instruction:

A-DAILY_EXPENSES.SPD;1
A-DAILY_REVENUES.SPD;1
A-DAILY_REVENUES.SPD;2
C-DAILY_CATCH.DTA;1
C-DAILY_CATCH.DTA;2
C-DAILY_CATCH.DTA;3

The number of permutations of searches using wildcards is enormous when you include all the elements of the filename and specifications.

FILE MANIPULATION

As with any filing cabinet storage system, the "owner" of a group of electronic files can make copies, rename, throw away, or merge information into new folders.

COPY

To make a copy of a file, use the command **COPY** as a verb, followed by the location and name of the original file and the location and name of the new file. For example:

$COPY C-DAILY_CATCH.DTA
        DAILY_CATCH.ARCHIVE   <Return>

Since no location is given for the original and new files, the system assumes they are located in the default directory (in this case, the example directory from the previous section). There the computer will find the file called C-DAILY_CATCH.DTA and make a copy in the same directory called DAILY_CATCH.ARCHIVE.

Let us suppose instead that we want to make a backup copy of the daily catch file but want to store that backup in a different (previously created) subdirectory, called ARCHIVE. The command would be

$COPY C-DAILY_CATCH.DTA
        [ARCHIVE]DAILY_CATCH.ARCHIVE   <Return>

As with almost every other DCL command, you can use global characters to perform multiple operations. For example, let's look at our full default directory again:

A-DAILY_EXPENSES.SPD;1
A-DAILY_REVENUES.SPD;1
A-DAILY_REVENUES.SPD;2
A-DRAGNET_ORDER.TXT;1
A-MAILING_LIST_CUSTOMERS.LIS;1

C-DAILY_CATCH.DTA;1
C-DAILY_CATCH.DTA;2
C-DAILY_CATCH.DTA;3
F-DOGFISH.DTA;1
F-BLUEFISH.DTA;1
F-CATFISH.DTA;1
F-CATFISH.DTA;2

When you issue the command

$COPY %-DAILY*.* [ARCHIVE]*.ARCHIVE   <Return>

you instruct the computer to make a copy (from the default directory) of all files beginning with any letter, followed by a hyphen (-) and the word DAILY, followed by any other letters or words in the filename, and ending with any extension. The second half of the command says that the new files are to be placed in the ARCHIVE subdirectory, and will be given the same filename the original had, with a new filename extension of .ARCHIVE.

The command would select the following files:

A-DAILY_EXPENSES.SPD;1
A-DAILY_REVENUES.SPD;1
A-DAILY_REVENUES.SPD;2
C-DAILY_CATCH.DTA;1
C-DAILY_CATCH.DTA;2
C-DAILY_CATCH.DTA;3

and would create the following new files in the ARCHIVE subdirectory:

[ARCHIVE]A-DAILY_EXPENSES.ARCHIVE;1
[ARCHIVE]A-DAILY_REVENUES.ARCHIVE;1
[ARCHIVE]A-DAILY_REVENUES.ARCHIVE;2
[ARCHIVE]C-DAILY_CATCH.ARCHIVE;1
[ARCHIVE]C-DAILY_CATCH.ARCHIVE;2
[ARCHIVE]C-DAILY_CATCH.ARCHIVE;3

DELETE

To remove a file, use the verb **DELETE** followed by the location of the file and the filename and extension. If no location is given, the system assumes the file is located in the default directory. It is also necessary to indicate the version number.

If you were to issue the command:

$DELETE A-DAILY_REVENUES.SPD;1   <Return>

that file would be removed, but version 2 of that same file would not be erased.

You can use a global command with a delete instruction, but please exercise great care. A slip of the finger could remove many, or even all, of the files in your directory. Here are two delete commands using global characters:

$DELETE *.SPD.*   <Return>

$DELETE %-*.L*;2   <Return>

The first command would delete all files with the filename extension of SPD, in all versions. The following files, then, would be deleted:

A-DAILY_EXPENSES.SPD;1
A-DAILY_REVENUES.SPD;1
A-DAILY_REVENUES.SPD;2

The second command is more complex. It deletes any file that begins with any letter, is followed by a hyphen (-) and then with any other letters or words, with a file extension that begins with the letter *L*, but only with a version number of 2. In this case, the computer will not even erase

A-MAILING_LIST_CUSTOMERS.LIS;1

because it is version 1.

APPEND

To append one file to another, use the command **APPEND** as a verb. The system will query for the name of the file to be copied into the original file, as in

$APPEND <Return>
_From: **A-DAILY_REVENUES.SPD;1** <Return>
_To: **A-DAILY_EXPENSES.SPD;1** <Return>

This will yield a new file, with the same filename of A-DAILY_EXPENSES.SPD;1, containing the original contents of that file, followed by the contents of the REVENUES file.

It is important to note two things about this command:

1. The APPEND command does not erase the file that is copied onto the tail of the new file.
2. The command does not create a new version number of the appended file, but instead keeps the same filename and version number for the now-combined file.

RENAME

To give a file a new name, use the command **RENAME** as a verb, followed by the original filename and the new filename. If no location is stated in the command, the computer will assume that either or both files are located in the default directory.

To rename your appended file (see above), issue the command

**$RENAME A-DAILY_EXPENSES.SPD;1
A-DAILY_EXP_AND_REV.SPD;1** <Return>

The **RENAME** command can also be used with global characters. For example, the command

$RENAME *.SPD *.SPREADSHEET <Return>

would give all files with the filename extension of SPD a new filename extension of SPREADSHEET. The files would keep their original filenames, as in

A-DAILY_EXPENSES.SPREADSHEET;1
A-DAILY_REVENUES.SPREADSHEET;1
A-DAILY_REVENUES.SPREADSHEET;2

TYPE

If you want to examine the contents of a file, there are several routes. One is to load the file from within a word processor or through use of the VMS EDT program.

A more direct way is to **TYPE** a file from the VMS prompt. The command uses TYPE as a verb followed by the filename, as in:

$TYPE A-DAILY_EXPENSES.SPREADSHEET <Return>

PURGE

We have noted that each time the user creates a new version of a file, the computer increments the version number that is part of the filename. In most instances, the computer will retain all previous copies of a file under their original version numbers.

After you have carefully considered whether there are any earlier versions of files you need to retain, you should purge your directory of unneeded files to free up disk space.

The basic command is the verb **PURGE**. The computer will then delete all but the latest versions of all files.

You can also use the PURGE command to remove a specific file, as in

$PURGE A-DAILY_REVENUES.SPREADSHEET;1 <Return>

If you want to delete some but not all versions of files, you might find it useful to use the **/KEEP** qualifier, as in

$PURGE/KEEP=3 <Return>

or

$PURGE/KEEP=3 A-D*.*;* <Return>

The first command will purge all files in the directory, but will keep the most recent version as well as the two previous versions of each file. The second command will do the same for any file beginning with A-D.

DIRECTORIES AND SUBDIRECTORIES

Over the course of time–probably a lot sooner than you would expect–you will end up with a large collection of files. Although the system will automatically list those files in alphabetical order, it is still quite easy to end up with a collection of several hundred files.

The solution to this information overload is to subdivide your cabinet of files into smaller, more specific pieces. The central file is called your directory, also called a *root* or top-level directory; these secondary divisions are called *subdirectories*.

VMS allows as many as seven levels of subdirectories beneath the root directory. The presence of a subdirectory is indicated in the directory above it by a directory file. This file bears the name of the subdirectory as its filename and .DIR as the filename extension.

To create a subdirectory, use the command **CREATE** as a verb and **/DIRECTORY** as a specification filed by the name of the subdirectory enclosed in square brackets.

Assume you are in your root directory, BLUEFISH, and want to create a subdirectory called ARCHIVE in which to keep archive copies of revenue and expense reports. To create the file, type the command

$CREATE/DIRECTORY [.ARCHIVE]　　　　　　　　　　<Return>

In order to move into the subdirectory, use the command **SET** as a verb to change the DEFAULT, as in

$SET DEFAULT [.ARCHIVE]　　　　　　　　　　<Return>

Once inside the subdirectory, you can create deeper levels of directories with further **CREATE/DIRECTORY** instructions. Here is a command to create a 1988 subdivision within the ARCHIVE subdirectory:

$CREATE/DIRECTORY [.1988]　　　　　　　　　　<Return>

If you issue a **DIR** command, you will obtain the listing of files within whatever directory or subdirectory you are located—

determined by the most recent **SET DEFAULT** instruction if one has been issued. **SET** commands issued during a session remain in effect only for the duration of that session. *Exception*: commands made part of a LOGIN.COM file, which are put into effect at log-in.

An alternate way to examine the contents of a subdirectory is to include the directory and subdirectory names in the DIR command, as in

$DIR [BLUEFISH.ARCHIVE.1988] <Return>

Finally, you can ask for a directory that includes all of your files, wherever they are located; just use an ellipsis within the square brackets:

$DIR [. . .] <Return>

5 Symbolic Logic

When you're finishing up a Sunday drive, you may say to your companion, "Let's go home," and that is all the communication necessary. *Home* is understood to be your place of residence, a place different from where you are, and a short notation for a specific address in a specific neighborhood of a specific town, reached by taking one of several predefined routes.

If you tell your trusted and experienced secretary to "Put this in the safe, please," you should not have to define what a safe is, explain its location, specify the combination and the rules for opening the lock, and issue a reminder to lock the door and spin the wheel once done—this has all been explained before.

In these examples, *home* and the concept of *put this in the safe* can be thought of as simple equivalences, or shorthand notations for more complex instructions.

In DCL, there are two very valuable methods of shorthand notation that can be used to allow brief, to-the-point "conversations" with the computer. One is through the use of *symbols* as substitutes for character strings or integer values; the second is the use of *logical names* as equivalences for file specifications. (Logical names will be discussed in Chapter 6.)

Expressions are values or groups of values that are intended to be evaluated, with the result of the expression assigned a symbol. You'll find more details about creating expressions in Chapter 7.

Here are some of the uses of symbols:

- To equate with a command string, allowing use of the symbol as a synonym or equivalent to a command.

- As variables in a DCL expression.
- As variables in a DCL command procedure.
- To pass parameters to command procedures.
- To refer to data records when combined with commands such as **READ, WRITE,** and **INQUIRE.**
- To define foreign commands.

When a symbol is used in a DCL expression, the operating system replaces the symbol with its value before the expression is executed.

REAL SYMBOLIC EXAMPLES

We've seen the logic of the directory and subdirectory structure of VMS. But even a speedy typist will find it cumbersome (and make an occasional mistake) to type in a command like this every time he or she signs on to the system:

$SET DEFAULT [.ARCHIVE.1988] <Return>

There are many other repetitive commands you may regularly issue. For example, it may be your practice to make copies of all files each day and place them in an ARCHIVE subdirectory. For example:

$COPY *.* [.ARCHIVE.1988]*.ARCHIVE <Return>

The solution is to use a symbol which assigns a shorter name to a DCL command. The symbol can also be used to define a string of characters or numbers. Here is a definition of a symbol to change the default directory:

$ARCHIVE == "SET DEFAULT [.ARCHIVE.1988]"<Return>

The use of the doubled equal sign indicates to the operating system that this is a definition of a symbol.

Just as the operating system parses a command, you can instruct the computer to expect an even shorter form of command where appropriate. By using an asterisk at a point in a symbol definition, the computer will treat all letters to the right of the asterisk as optional. You should take great care not to create ambiguous symbol names. Here is an example of the short form:

$AR*CHIVE == "SET DEFAULT [ARCHIVE.1988]"   <Return>

Once this is done, the computer will accept **AR**, **ARCHIVE**, or any entry in between (e.g., **ARCH**) as a definition calling for the **SET DEFAULT** instruction. For example, the symbol CALENDAR could be assigned as follows:

$C*ALENDAR = "CALENDAR"   <Return>

As shown above, using the asterisk an abbreviation symbol will cause the full symbol CALENDAR to be sent to the operating system when any of the following is entered at the DCL prompt: **C, CA, CAL, CALE, CALEN, CALEND, CALENDA,** or **CALENDAR**.

Be careful not to accidentally redefine a symbol through the use of an abbreviated symbol that contains within it the full name of another symbol.

In order to create as a symbol our complex **COPY** backup command, we could use this definition:

$BAK == COPY *.* [.ARCHIVE.1988]*.ARCHIVE <Return>

It is important, in this instance, to use a symbolic name other than **BACKUP** or **COPY**, each of which exists as a predefined DCL command.

You can keep track of any symbol redefinitions by using the **SHOW SYMBOL** command.

All your work in redefining symbols thus far, though, is temporary and will be removed from the system when you next log off the system. The way to make your symbols a permanent part of your way of doing business with the VAX is to include them in your LOGIN.COM file, part of every user's ordinary identification to the system.

First, locate your LOGIN.COM file in your root directory. You could issue the following command:

$DIR*.COM   <Return>

which might yield the followng:

$LOGIN.COM;4

Examine the contents of the file by using a **TYPE** command, or use your text editor to open it for reading and altering. Each line of the LOGIN.COM file will begin with a $ prompt. If the dollar sign is followed by an exclamation point, the line is intended as a comment or explanatory note.

You should proceed carefully and in a step-by-step manner when making modifications to the LOGIN.COM file. Make just one change at a time, then sign off and sign back on to make the file effective and to see if the system is performing as you would like. Consult your system manager to verify the changes you make.

Using the EDT editor or other text editor, simply add a symbol definition line or lines to LOGIN, as in

$! LOGIN.COM
$! [OTHER INSTRUCTIONS WILL GO HERE]
$!
$BAK == COPY *.* [.ARCHIVE.1988]*.ARCHIVE
$AR*CHIVE == "SET DEFAULT [ARCHIVE.1988]"
$!

CREATING YOUR OWN SYMBOLS

Symbols are created with the Assignment Statement command, which uses the following form:

SYMBOL_NAME = EXPRESSION

Here is an example of an integer value assigned to a symbol:

$COUNTER = 0

For the COUNTER symbol, the 0 is evaluated as an integer. Decimal integers are assumed. To specify a number as a nondecimal integer, use a radix (base) operator before the number. The following radix operators are available:

%X hexadecimal
%D decimal (default)
%O octal

Here is an example:

$COUNTER = %O10
$SHOW SYMBOL COUNTER

$COUNTER = 8 Hex = 00000008 Octal = 00000000010

When a symbol with an integer value is used as part of an expression, the symbol's value is substituted for the symbol. For example:

$COUNTER = 8
$COUNTER_ADD = COUNTER + 1
$SHOW SYMBOL COUNTER_ADD
COUNTER_ADD = 9 Hex = 00000009 Octal = 00000000011

Here is an example of a string value assigned to a symbol:

$TEST = "This is a test symbol."   <Return>

In this example, the symbol is assigned to a character string, signified to the system by its enclosure in double quote marks (").

An alternate means of defining a symbol as a character string is through the use of a colon and equal sign, as follows:

$TEST := this is a test symbol.   <Return>

Note that by using this means of assigning a symbol, the quote marks are not required around the string. However, the system will automatically convert the string to all uppercase letters, and leading, trailing, and multiple internal spaces are all removed.

To continue a long character string over two lines, a plus sign for string concatenation or a hyphen for continuation are required. Here is an example:

$TEST : = This is a lengthy character string -   \<Return\>
$that is continued to a second line in definition.   \<Return\>

$SHOW SYMBOL TEST   \<Return\>

TEST = "THIS IS A LENGTHY CHARACTER STRING THAT IS CONTINUED TO A SECOND LINE IN DEFINITION."

Another way to create a long character string for a symbol is to concatenate several symbols. First create the separate symbols, and then create an additional symbol that combines the previous symbol names with a plus sign, as in

$TEST1 : = This is the first part of the symbol,   \<Return\>
$TEST2 : = and this is the second part.   \<Return\>
$TEST3 : = TEST1 + TEST2
$SHOW SYMBOL TEST3   \<Return\>

TEST3 = "This is the first part of the symbol, and this is the second part."

Symbol names can range from 1 to 255 characters, and must begin with a letter, an underscore, or a dollar sign. After the first character, any alphabetic or numerical character can follow, as well as underscores and dollar signs. In order to use a quotation mark as a character, it must be entered twice consecutively.

To display symbols, use the command SHOW SYMBOL as follows:

$SHOW SYMBOL/ALL   \<Return\>

This will display all currently defined symbols. To get information about a particular symbol, use that symbol as a parameter:

$SHOW SYMBOL COUNTER <Return>
COUNTER = 0 Hex = 00000000 Octal = 00000000000

For symbols that are assigned to character strings, the response from the system is as follows:

$SHOW SYMBOL TEST <Return>
TEST = "This is a test symbol."

LOCAL AND GLOBAL SYMBOLS

Symbols can be made to be local or global. Local symbols, defined as shown in the examples above with a single equals sign, are available to the current command level and to command procedures executed from that current level. Global symbols, defined with two equal signs (**COUNTER == 0**) are available to all command levels.

Local symbols are maintained in the local symbol table, global symbols in the global symbol table. To delete a symbol, use the **DELETE/SYMBOL** command. To remove a symbol from the global table, the command **SET SYMBOL/COPE = NOGLOBAL** can be used.

When the DCL command interpreter seeks the value of a symbol, it searches symbol tables in the following order: 1) the local symbol table set for the current command level; 2) the local symbol tables for previous command level, working backward from the current level, and 3) the global symbol table.

The computer will accept any changes to globals and will also accept ambiguous symbols. However, error messages are issued when these symbols are called into use.

The system also maintains three reserved global symbols, as follows:

- **$STATUS** Holds the condition code returned by the most recently executed command.
- **$SEVERITY** Holds the severity level of the condition code returned by the most recently executed command,

the three low-order bits of **$STATUS**. **$SEVERITY** can have one of the following values:

0 Warning

1 Success

2 Error

3 Information

4 Severe (fatal) error

- **$RESTART** Holds the value TRUE if a batch job was restarted after being interrupted by a system crash; otherwise holds the value FALSE.

LEXICAL FUNCTIONS

A special type of symbol is the *lexical function*, which is a means of requesting information about a particular item. For example, the lexical function F$DIRECTORY() returns the name of the current default directory in which a process is running.

The way to use a lexical function with a symbol is to assign a symbol name to the lexical function and then perform an operation on the symbol. For example,

$CURDIR = F$DIRECTORY() <Return>

$SHOW SYMBOL CURDIR <Return>

CURDIR = "[SANDLER]"

For a list of lexical functions available for use with DCL commands, see *Lexical Functions* in Chapter 10 (pages 192-195).

6 Logical Names

We've seen in our early explorations of DCL the very basic operations we need as part of the housekeeping of our accounts. In this chapter, we'll explore some of the more advanced features of DCL, which are aimed at making our computing lives a bit simpler as we attempt more and more complex operations.

In DCL, the user is permitted to use *logical names* as equivalences for any valid group of characters. These equivalence strings (a string is a computer term meaning a connected group of characters that can be interpreted as data) can include file specifications, device names, or other logical names. The system will translate a logical name to its corresponding equivalence string and execute the command.

Some examples include defining HOME or ROOT as a logical name for the user's default disk or directory, or CALENDAR as a logical name for a continuously updated schedule listing.

Logical names can also be used as substitutes for physical devices. Two different printers can be renamed as MICKEY and MINNIE instead of their more complex (and more easily forgotten) system names.

CREATION OF LOGICAL NAMES

There are two ways to create logical names under DCL: the **ASSIGN** command and the **DEFINE** command.

DEFINE associates an equivalence name with a logical name. If you specify an existing logical name, the new equivalence name replaces the existing equivalence name.

The format is

$DEFINE <logical name> [<equivalence name>,...]<Return>

If you **DEFINE** a logical name as more than one equivalence name, you can create a *search list*, which will be discussed in the last section of this chapter.

ASSIGN performs the same task, although its syntax is the opposite. The format for an ASSIGN command is

$ASSIGN [<equivalence name>,...] <logical name><Return>

To **DEFINE** a logical name, use the verb **DEFINE** followed by the new logical name and then the equivalence name. For example,

$DEFINE SCHED $DISK1:[SANDLER.CALENDAR]
              TODAYS_SCHEDULE   <Return>

will establish a logical name called SCHED and equate it to the file within the subdirectory [SANDLER.CALENDAR] called TODAYS_SCHEDULE.

From this point on, the logical name SCHED can be used as the object of a DCL verb, as in

$PRINT SCHED   <Return>

or

$DIR SCHED   <Return>

or

$COPY SCHED NEWFILENAME   <Return>

The logical name does not require a full file specification, but could instead use the default specifications. For example, the logical name assignment,

$DEFINE PRICES PRICELIST_1988   <Return>

assumes that the file PRICELIST_1988 is in the current directory and uses the current set of devices.

A logical name can also be applied to a part of a filename specification, rather than to a specific file. For example,

$DEFINE ROOT [SANDLER]   <Return>

equates the name ROOT to the directory [SANDLER]. You could call for a directory of [SANDLER] by entering

$DIR ROOT   <Return>

You could also use ROOT as part of a file specification, identifying the directory as such:

$EDIT ROOT:PRICELIST   <Return>

In addition, logical names can be combined; for example,

$EDIT ROOT:PRICES   <Return>

calls forth the logical names ROOT and PRICES, just as if the command had instead read:

$EDIT [SANDLER]PRICELIST_1988   <Return>

Here's another example:

$DEFINE CALENDAR BLUEFISH:[SANDLER.SCHEDULE]
         CALENDAR.TXT   <Return>

From this point on, the word CALENDAR is interpreted by the system as the file CALENDAR.TXT, which is located on node BLUEFISH in the subdirectory SCHEDULE of the directory SANDLER. You could, for example, edit that file from anywhere in your session by entering:

$EDIT CALENDAR   <Return>

A logical name can also be assigned to just an element of the file specification. For example, SCHEDULE could be defined to stand in place of [SANDLER.SCHEDULE] with the command

$DEFINE SCHEDULE [SANDLER.SCHEDULE] <Return>

After that point, the logical name SCHEDULE can be employed in uses such as

$EDIT SCHEDULE:1988CAL <Return>

To delete a logical name, apply the DEASSIGN command. To remove CALENDAR, for example, enter

$DEASSIGN CALENDAR <Return>

KEEPING TRACK OF WHAT GOES WHERE

How do you keep track of logical name assignments? Two DCL commands—**SHOW LOGICAL** and **SHOW TRANSLATION**—will display any such redefinitions currently in effect.

The general command, **SHOW LOGICAL**, will yield a listing of all current logical names in any of the four tables. For example,

$SHOW LOGICAL <Return>

might yield a display such as:

(LNM$PROCESS_TABLE)

   "STAFF" = "SYS$MANAGER:STAFF.DIS"
   "BL" = "BLUEFISH:"

(LNM$JOB_802B5BD0)

   "SYS$LOGIN" = "$DISK1:[SANDLER]"
   "SYS$LOGIN_DEVICE" = "$DISK1:"
   "SYS$SCRATCH" = "$DISK1:[SANDLER]"

(LNM$GROUP_000300)

(LNM$SYSTEM_TABLE)

   "$CONSOLE" = "_OPA0:"
   "$DISK1" = "_BLUEFISH$DUB3:"
   "$FLOPPY1" = "_DUA1:"
   "$FLOPPY2" = "_DUA2:"
   "$PRINTER1" = "LPA0:"
   "$PRINTER3" = "_TXA2:"
   "$TAPE1" = "_MUA0:"
   "$TERMINAL0" = "_TXA0:"

You can learn more about the meaning of this listing in the next section of this chapter.

You can also ask for a more specific listing of a logical name; for instance

$SHOW LOGICAL STAFF　　　　　　　　　　　　　　　　　　　　　<Return>

might yield

"STAFF" = "SYS$MANAGER:STAFF.DIS"
　　　　　　　　　　　　　　　　　(LNM$PROCESS_TABLE)

In this instance, the system is responding to the request for information about the logical name STAFF by showing the equivalence string and the fact that the logical name is located in the process logical name table.

If your logical name includes within it other logical names, and therefore more than one translation is performed by the system before it comes up with the final equivalence string, **SHOW LOGICAL** will display the translation in multiple lines. The second and following lines will include a level number, with level 1 being the second level of translation, level 2 the third, and so on. Here is an example in which one logical name has been defined to include another:

$DEFINE BASE BLUEFISH:ROOT　　　　　　　　　　　　　　　　　<Return>

$SHOW LOGICAL BASE　　　　　　　　　　　　　　　　　　　　　<Return>

"BASE" = "BLUEFISH:ROOT" (LNM$PROCESS_TABLE)

$DEFINE TEST2 BASE <Return>

$SHOW LOG TEST2 <Return>

"TEST2" = "BASE" (LNM$PROCESS_TABLE)

1"BASE" = "BLUEFISH:ROOT" (LNM$PROCESS_TABLE)

LOGICAL NAME TABLES

This section is not of direct value to most users, but may help you understand more about the way the computer and the operating system go about their business.

The system stores logical names in special files called logical name tables. Some of these tables are made available only to the current process or subprocesses while others are open for use by anyone on the system. Logical name tables include the following:

- System table: Includes logical names available to any user of the system.
- Group table: Includes logical names available to all users in the current UIC group.
- Job table: Includes logical names available to the current process and any subprocesses created under it.
- Process table: Includes logical names available only to the current process.

The VMS system includes a series of logical names it uses for the needs of the DCL command line interpreter. These system logical names can be identified by the prefix SYS$.

The user cannot redefine a default system logical name, but the names can be used as part of command procedures.

Here are some of the default system logical names in the process table and their equivalences:

- SYS$COMMAND The initial file or input stream, from which the DCL command line interpreter reads data.

- **SYS$DISK** The user's default disk, as assigned in the User Authorization File set up by the system manager, or as changed by a **SET DEFAULT** command.
- **SYS$ERROR** The target of any error or informational messages produced by the system. By default, errors are displayed on the terminal used in an interactive session. If the session is instead in batch mode, errors are directed to the batch job log file.
- **SYS$INPUT** The default file or input stream used by the DCL command line interpreter or programs under execution for data or commands. By default, in an interactive session SYS$INPUT looks to the terminal; in a batch session, to the batch job stream or command procedure.
- **SYS$NET** Defined only during task-to-task communication as part of a DECnet-VAX communication. SYS$NET is the source process that invokes a target process.
- **SYS$OUTPUT** The default file or output stream to which command responses or program output are written by the DCL command line interpreter or a program under execution. By default, in an interactive session SYS$OUTPUT sends to the terminal; in a batch job to the batch job log file.
- **TT** The default device name for terminals.

The job table includes logical names available to the current process and any of its subprocesses. At login, the operating system creates a number of default job logical names:

- **SYS$LOGIN** The home directory and device indicated at login.
- **SYS$LOGIN_DEVICE** The device element of SYS$LOGIN.
- **SYS$REM_ID** When a job is initiated through a DECnet network connection, SYS$REM_ID represents the identification of the process on the remote node where the job originated.
- **SYS$REM_NODE** When a job is initiated through a DECnet network connection, SYS$REM_NODE represents the name of the remote node from which the job originated.

- SYS$SCRATCH The default directory and device where temporary files are written.

The system table includes logical names available to all users in the system. In addition to names added on a system basis by the system manager the following default system logical names are available:

- DBG$INPUT The default input stream for the VAX/VMS Debugger.
- DBG$OUTPUT The default output stream for the VAX/VMS Debugger.
- SYS$COMMON The device and directory name for the common element of SYS$SYSROOT.
- SYS$ERRORLOG Device and directory name for the error log data files.
- SYS$EXAMPLES Device and directory name for the system examples.
- SYS$HELP Device and directory names for the system help files.
- SYS$INSTRUCTION Device and directory names for the system instruction files.
- SYS$LIBRARY Device and directory names for the system libraries.
- SYS$MAINTENANCE Device and directory names for the system maintenance files.
- SYS$MANAGER Device and directory names for the system manager files.
- SYS$MESSAGE Device and directory names for the system message files.
- SYS$NODE If DECnet-VAX is in use, the network node name of the local system.
- SYS$SHARE Device and directory names for system shareable images.
- SYS$SPECIFIC Device and directory names for the node-specific part of SYS$SYSROOT.
- SYS$SYSDEVICE The system disk with system directories.
- SYS$SYSROOT Device and directory names for the system directories.

- SYS$SYSTEM   Device and directory names for the operating system programs and procedures.
- SYS$TEST   Device and directory names for the User Environment Test Package files, if present.
- SYS$UPDATE   Device and directory names for the system update files.

SEARCH LISTS

VMS includes a special type of logical name called a search list. A search list is a logical name with more than one equivalence string assigned.

For example, the user could define the logical name WORK to refer to two commonly used subdirectories, [SANDLER.CALENDAR] and [SANDLER.PRICE_LIST], with the following command:

$DEFINE WORK DISK1:[SANDLER.CALENDAR],DISK1: [SANDLER.PRICE_LIST]   <Return>

If you were to look at this logical name with the **SHOW LOGICAL** command, the following would be displayed:

$SHOW LOGICAL WORK   <Return>

"WORK" = "DISK1:[SANDLER.CALENDAR]"
        (LNM$PROCESS_TABLE)
      = "DISK1:[SANDLER.PRICE_LIST]"

When a search list is the object of a command, the system will apply the command to each equivalence string in the search list. For example, to see a directory listing of every file with a .TXT extension in [SANDLER.CALENDAR] and [SANDLER.PRICE_LIST], the two subdirectories listed as equivalence strings in the WORK search list, the command

$DIR WORK:*.TXT   <Return>

might yield

Directory DISK1:[SANDLER.CALENDAR]
MAY_CAL.TXT;1
JUN_CAL.TXT;8
JUN_CAL.TXT;9
Total of 3 files.

Directory DISK1:[SANDLER.PRICE_LIST]
BLUEFISH_PRICES.TXT;1
SWORDFISH_PRICES.TXT;3
Total of 2 files.

Grand total of 2 directories, 5 files.

The search is made on the equivalence strings in the order in which they are included in the search list. If there is no result from the command as applied to a particular element of the search list, no result is displayed. For instance, in the previous example, if one of the subdirectories had contained no files with the filename extension of .TXT, that subdirectory would not have appeared in the on-screen report.

7 DCL Expressions

A DCL expression is a value or group of values that are intended to be evaluated. The result of that expression is assigned to a symbol.

There are two types of DCL expressions: character string expressions and integer expressions.

CHARACTER STRING EXPRESSIONS

A character string expression is an expression that will evaluate as a string value, created in the following format:

<**symbolname**> =[=] <**string expression**>

The string expression can include character strings, lexical functions that can be evaluated as character strings, or symbols that have string values. Another form will include groups of string operands connected by operators to perform string operations.

Here are examples of character string expressions as they are equated to symbols:

$ **PRICES** = "TODAYS_PRICES.DAT"
$ **REMINDER** = "REMEMBER TO BACKUP PRICES BEFORE UPDATE"

$ PRICELIST_TOTAL = "TOTAL NUMBER OF PRICE
                    LISTS = " +F$STRING(COUNT_LISTS)

The first expression is a simple assignment of a string to a symbol, which will allow use of the shorter symbol to make reference to a particular file.

The second expression assigns a message to a symbol, allowing for the easy calling of that message from a command procedure or other operation.

The third expression combines a string ("The total number of price lists = ") with an integer that is derived by instructing the lexical function F$STRING to convert the COUNT_LISTS integer to a symbol. The plus sign serves to concatenate the two operands.

INTEGER STRING EXPRESSIONS

An integer expresssion is an expression that evaluates to an integer, created in the following format:

<symbolname> =[=] <integer expression>

An integer expression can include integers, lexical functions that will evaluate as integers, or symbols that have integer values.

OPERATIONS

Figure 7-1 shows the operators that can be used in expressions. Operators with a higher precedence (right-hand column of Figure 7-1) are performed before operators below them; operators with identical levels of precedence are performed from left to right as they appear in the command string. Parentheses can be used to override the order of precedence; operators within parentheses are evaluated first.

Logical and comparison operators must be preceded and terminated by a period without blank spaces. Any number of spaces or tabs can be placed between operators and operands.

Operator	Description	Precedence
+	Positive number	7
−	Negative number	7
*	Multiplies a pair of numbers	6
/	Divides a pair of numbers	6
+	Adds a pair of numbers, or concatenates two character strings	5
−	Subtracts one number from another, or reduces two strings	5
.EQS.	Tests if two character strings are equal	4
.GES.	Tests if the first string is greater than or equal to the second	4
.GTS.	Tests if the first string is greater than the second	4
.LES.	Tests if the first string is less than or equal to the second	4
.LTS.	Tests if the first string is less than the second	4
.NES.	Tests if two strings are not equal	4
.EQ.	Tests if two numbers are equal	4
.GE.	Tests if the first number is greater than or equal to the second	4
.GT.	Tests if the first number is greater than the second	4
.LE.	Tests if the first number is less than or equal to the second	4
.LT.	Tests if the first number is less than the second	4
.NE.	Tests if two numbers are not equal	4
.NOT.	Logically negates a number	3
.AND.	Combines two numbers with a logical AND	2
.OR.	Combines two numbers with a logical OR	1

Figure 7-1 Operators and their precedences

STRING OPERATIONS

Strings can be operated upon by the system in a manner similar to that of arithmetic operations.

Character strings can be reduced or concatenated into a new character string; integer strings can become part of calculations to result in a new integer value.

The two operator symbols for character string operations are

+ String concatenation
− String reduction

Both operands of a concatenation or reduction operation must be character strings in order for the result to be a new character string; otherwise both operands will be converted to integers and the result will be an integer.

The concatenation operation, using the plus sign between two strings enclosed within quotation marks, adds the second string to the first; for example,

EXAMPLE1 = "PRICE_LIST" + ".TXT"

assigns the string "PRICE_LIST.TXT" to EXAMPLE 1.

The reduction operation, using a minus sign between two strings enclosed within quotation marks, removes from the first operand the first occurrence of the second string; for example,

EXAMPLE2 = "PRICE_LIST.TXT" − "_LIST"

assigns the string "PRICE.TXT" to EXAMPLE 2. If the string following the minus sign occurs more than once in the first string, only the first occurrence is removed.

Symbol names can be included within a string operation. For example, we could have

EXAMPLE3 = "ORIGINAL_"

and then concatenate the symbols, as in

EXAMPLE4 = EXAMPLE3 + EXAMPLE2

and "ORIGINAL_PRICE.TXT" would be assigned to EXAMPLE 4.

STRING TO INTEGER CONVERSION

Character strings are converted to integers as follows:

- Strings (identified as such by quotation marks) that are numbers are changed to their integer values. For example, the character string "4628" would be converted to the integer 4628.
- Alphabet strings are converted to the integer 1 if the string begins with the letters T, t, Y, or y, (as a test for a "True" or "Yes" response). The string is converted to the integer 0 if it begins with any other letter.

In most cases, where an expression contains both an integer and a string value, DCL will convert the string values to integers before an operation is performed. The exception is a string comparison, where DCL will convert the expression to strings before undertaking the comparison.

Here are some examples:

String	Integer	
"4462"	4462	
"44SJ7"	0	(false)
"True"	1	(true)
"T"	1	(true)
"Tomato"	1	(true)
"Yes"	1	(true)
"Y"	1	(true)
"Yellow"	1	(true)
"False"	0	(false)
"Fruit"	0	(false)
"Willie"	0	(false)

Integer to String Conversion

Integers are converted to character strings as follows:

Integer	String
4462	"4462"
0	"0"
1	"1"

Arithmetic Operations

With integer strings, the following arithmetic operations are allowed. Any nondecimal values are converted to decimal integer values before the operations. As an integer operation, all fractional values are dropped off and the result of all operations is an integer.

+ Arithmetic sum
− Arithmetic difference
+ Arithmetic conversion plus
− Arithmetic conversion negate
* Arithmetic product
/ Arithmetic division (integer quotient)

Logical Operations

Logical operations, based on Boolean syntax, can be applied to integer values or expressions. The result of all logical operations is an integer (0 or 1). The following logical operators can be used:

.AND.   Logical AND
.OR.   Logical OR
.NOT.   Logical complement

Arithmetic Comparisons

Arithmetic comparison operators can be used to compare integer values, with the result an integer 1 for true or the integer 0 for false.

The comparison operation expects to be dealing with integer strings. If a character string is presented as an operand, it is converted to an integer value before the comparison is undertaken—character strings beginning with a T, t, Y, or y are converted to the integer 1 and character strings beginning with any other letter are converted to the integer 0. If, however, the character string consists entirely of numbers that are equivalent to a valid integer, the string is converted to that integer equivalent.

Figure 7-2 shows some examples of the results of arithmetic comparisons of strings:

Expression	Value	Explanation
4.GT.54	0 (false)	4 is not greater than 54
4.LE.54	1 (true)	4 is less than or equal to 54
4 + 54 .EQ. 62	0 (false)	4 plus 54 is not equal to 62
"TRUE".EQ.1	1 (true)	"TRUE" is evaluated as the integer 1 since it begins with the letter "T"
"FIGS".EQ.0	1 (true)	"FIGS" is evaluated as the integer 1 since it begins with the letter "F"

Figure 7-2 Some arithmetic comparisons

String Comparisons

String comparisons can be used to compare character strings. The system compares the strings by looking at the characters as strings of ASCII values and comparing those binary values. The result of a string comparison is a binary 0 or 1.

Comparisons are made on a character-by-character basis, not on the combined ASCII value of the string. The comparison is ended as soon as two characters do not match. If one string is shorter than the other, the shorter string is padded out with null characters, which will result in a value of 0 (false) for the comparison. Also, lowercase letters have higher numeric values than uppercase letters, and are therefore not equivalent to them. See Figure G–1 on page 341 for a list of ASCII characters.

If a character string is not enclosed within quote marks, the system assumes the string to be a symbol name and will issue an error message if the symbol is not defined.

The following operators can be used in a string comparison:

.EQS.	String equal to
.GES.	String greater than or equal to
.GTS.	String greater than
.LES.	String less than or equal to
.LTS.	String less than
.NES.	String not equal to

Figure 7-3 shows some examples of string comparisons:

Expression	Result	Explanation
"PRICES".LTS."prices"	1 (true)	The ASCII value of P, the first character compared, is less than that of P in the second operand, and therefore the expression is evaluated as true.
"APRICES".LTS."BPRICES"	1 (true)	The ASCII value of A, the first character compared, is less than that of B in the second operand, and therefore the expression is evaluated as true.
"APRICE".GTS."APRICES"	0 (false)	The expression is evaluated as false once the system reaches the null character placed in the rightmost position of the shorter, first operand.

Figure 7-3 Some string comparisons

EVALUATION OF AN EXPRESSION

DCL has a set of predetermined rules for evaluating an expression as either an integer or string. The operating system will examine the type of value used in the expression and the operations assigned to the expression. Here are the rules:

Expression	Mode and Value Type
Integer value	Integer
String value	String
Integer lexical function	Integer
String lexical function	String
Integer symbol	Integer
String symbol	String
+, −, or .NOT. any value	Integer
Any value .AND. or .OR. any value	Integer
String + or − string	String
Integer + or − any value	Integer
Any value + or − integer	Integer
Any value * or / any value	Integer
Any value <string comparison> any value	Integer
Any value <arithmetic comparison> any value	Integer

In this system, if *any value* is a character string value, it is converted to an integer value before operations are performed. An exception is the string comparison expression; in such cases, if *any value* is an integer, it is converted to a string value before the string comparison is performed.

DCL also includes a pair of lexical functions, F$INTEGER and F$STRING, which enable the user to explicitly change the type of an expression. F$INTEGER converts a string expression to an integer value while F$STRING changes an integer to a string. The F$TYPE lexical function will display the current value type of a symbol.

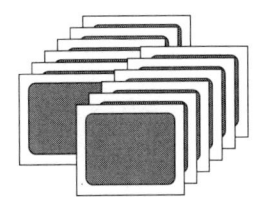

8 Your Electronic Postman

Neither rain, nor snow, nor time of day, nor location of user can slow VMS Mail, an extremely useful utility that links every VMS user for the purposes of exchanging messages, text files, or data.

Every user has a mail account for sending mail and a "mailbox" to receive incoming information. The mailbox name is generally that of the account user. Messages can be created and sent from within the Mail program, or they can be prepared beforehand using any VMS application, including a word processor, and transmitted as mail.

If there is new mail waiting for you in your mailbox, you will see a notice when you sign on to the system, as in

You have 2 new messages.

If someone sends you a message while you are signed on to VMS, a note will appear on screen; for example,

New mail on node BLUEFISH from TESSA

or

New mail from TESSA

READING YOUR MAIL

You must enter the Mail program to read and respond to your mail. The command **MAIL** will bring you from the VMS prompt to the Mail program:

$MAIL   <Return>

The program will respond with its own prompt:

MAIL>

If there are any messages in your account that you have not yet read, you will see a message such as

You have 4 new messages.

To read the messages in a first-in, first-out order (oldest messages first), simply press the Return key, or type

READ   <Return>

You can then step through the messages, one by one, using the return key, or by typing

NEXT   <Return>

Consulting the Directory

To learn something about the messages in your mailbox before you read them, examine the Mail directory first. The command format is

MAIL>**DIRECTORY [foldername]**   <Return>

which yields a display that lists the messages in the current mail file, including the sender's name, the date the message was sent, a subject line if used by the sender, and a message number.

If *foldername* is not included in the command, VMS Mail will assume the user seeks information about the currently selected folder and will display a directory of messages in that folder. If there is no currently selected folder, MAIL displays a directory of the NEWMAIL folder (if there are any unread messages) or the MAIL folder for previously read mail.

Here is an example of a directory command and response:

MAIL>**DIRECTORY**   <Return>

#	From	Date	Subject
1	TESSA	6-JUL-87	Travel plans
2	RECEPTION	6-JUL-87	Telephone messages
3	JANICE	7-JUL-87	Budget reconciliation
4	TESSA	8-JUL-87	Bluefish futures

At this point you can choose to read all of your messages, by typing the return key or READ, or you can select individual messages, as in

MAIL>READ 3   <Return>

This command will place you at position 3 in your current directory of unread messages. If you were to type a Return key or the command **NEXT** after reading message 3, you would move on to the fourth message.

You can also select a message by merely typing its directory number, as in

MAIL>**3**   <Return>

There are a number of command parameters and qualifiers that can be used to make the directory command more specific. The parameter **foldername** in

MAIL>**DIRECTORY [foldername]**   <Return>

will yield a listing of the messages in a particular folder, which is a subdirectory of messages within the mail program.

Qualifiers of the DIRECTORY command include

MAIL>**DIRECTORY/BEFORE** = **date**   <Return>

in the form

MAIL>**DIRECTORY/BEFORE** = **6-JUL**   <Return>

to display mail messages received before the specified date.

MAIL>**DIRECTORY/FOLDER**   <Return>

will display a listing of all of the folders in the current mail file.

MAIL>**DIRECTORY/FULL**   <Return>

will yield a listing of mail messages that will tell you the number of records in each message and whether you have replied to each message.

MAIL>**DIRECTORY/NEW**   <Return>

will yield a display of any new or unread messages in the current folder.

MAIL>**DIRECTORY/SINCE** = **date**   <Return>

in the form

MAIL>**DIRECTORY/SINCE** = **6-JUL**   <Return>

will display a listing of all messages received since the specified date.

MAIL>**DIRECTORY/START** = **start**   <Return>

serves as a wild card to specify a directory listing of those messages that begin with the number or letter specified.
  If the qualifier is stacked with the /FOLDER qualifier, as in

MAIL>**DIRECTORY/FOLDER/START** = **A**   <Return>

the directory will list those folders with names that begin with the letter A.

Using Folders to Organize Your Mail

The Mail program can subdivide your mail messages into folders, in much the same manner as the subdirectories within VMS.

When you first begin using your Mail account, you will have a folder called MAIL. As soon as you receive an incoming message, the system will create a folder called NEWMAIL. New and unread messages are automatically routed into the NEWMAIL folder; once read, they are automatically moved into MAIL. When the contents of the NEWMAIL directory have been read, that folder is removed until it is needed again.

If you delete a message, it is placed in a folder called WASTE-BASKET, which is cleaned out when you **EXIT** from the program or issue a **PURGE** command from within Mail. If you accidentally delete a mail message, you can retrieve it if you have not yet exited from MAIL or purged your mail account. Set the folder to WASTEBASKET, obtain a directory, and then **FORWARD** or **SEND** the deleted message to another folder.

There is no limit on the number of folders that can be created. The system will inform you of the name of the current folder with a message displayed at the top right corner of the screen when you enter a **READ** or **DIRECTORY** command. The command **DIRECTORY/FOLDER** will yield a display of the existing folders in the current mail file.

Folders are automatically removed when all the messages within them have been deleted or moved. The creation of a folder is automatic when you direct the Mail program to **FILE** or **MOVE** a message.

Your MAIL account is organized by VMS as follows:

Personal Mail Utility (MAIL)

mail file   {[+ + + + +][+ + + + +][+ + + + +]}
    folder   [+ + + + +]
        message   +

Most accounts will have just one mail file and multiple folders with multiple messages in each folder.

Moving Messages

After you have read a message about the budget reconciliation, for example, you could move it from NEWMAIL to a folder called BUDGET with the following command:

MAIL>**MOVE BUDGET**   <Return>

or

MAIL>**FILE BUDGET**   <Return>

If you attempt to move or file a message to a nonexistent folder, the system will query you to see if you want to create a folder with that name. Here is an example of such a conversation, in this case using the self-prompting feature of VMS:

MAIL>**MOVE**   <Return>
_Folder:**BUDGET**   <Return>
_File: <Return>
Folder BUDGET does not exist.

Do you want to create it (Y/N, default is N)? **Y**   <Return>

%MAIL-I-NEWFOLDER, folder BUDGET created

A command qualifier can be added to eliminate the query about new folders. In such usage, the system will automatically create a new folder if the specified one does not exist:

MAIL>**MOVE BUDGET/NOCONFIRM**   <Return>

When you **MOVE** or **FILE** a mail message, that message is deleted from its previous folder before being moved to a new folder.

If you enter the **MOVE** command, supply a foldername, and then decide that you do not want to move the message, enter Ctrl-Z to abort the operation and keep you within MAIL.

Copying a File

In order to send a copy of a mail message to another folder while keeping a copy in the original folder, use the **COPY** command:

MAIL>**COPY foldername**   <Return>

If the folder name as specified does not exist, the system will create the new folder.

If you need to copy a message to a sequential file outside of MAIL, such as an EDT file for editing, use the **EXTRACT** command.

If you enter the **COPY** command, supply a foldername, and then decide that you do not want to copy the message, enter Ctrl-Z to abort the operation and keep you within MAIL.

A Short Note About Long Mail Messages

You may notice in your directory one or more file listings with a combination of alphanumeric characters and a .MAI extension, as in:

MAIL$nnnnnnnnnnnnnnnnnn.MAI

This is a temporary file created by the Mail program to hold a mail message of more than three blocks in size. (See Glossary.) This file will be automatically deleted when you delete the message from within Mail. If you delete the file yourself from the VMS prompt, you will still find the message listed in your Mail directory, and you will receive an error message for trying to read a file that has been deleted from outside of MAIL if you attempt to read the file.

SENDING A MESSAGE

At the heart of the MAIL utility, of course, is the ability to send a message. There are two interchangeable commands: **MAIL** and **SEND**.

If you enter only the command **SEND** or **MAIL**, the system will prompt you for the name of the user or users to receive the message. If the user is within your local network, just enter the account name. Otherwise, it will be necessary to enter a nodename for transfer to connected systems. You can also use a distribution list of names, which will be explained later.

Here is the form for mailing addresses:

[[nodename::]username,...] [,] [@ listname]

The MAIL program will next ask for the subject of the mail. If you want to skip the "Subj:" prompt, specify the **/SUBJECT** qualifier with the MAIL command.

You can include a file specification with the MAIL command, and the text in that file will be sent to the specified user or group of users.

If no file is specified, MAIL will prompt the user for the text of a message. At this point, you have access to a line-by-line editor. Messages created within MAIL itself do not wrap at the end of the line; it is necessary to hit the Return key somewhere before the 80th character position on the screen (or the 132nd if you are in 132-column mode.) Once you have pressed Return on a particular line, there is no way to get back to that line to edit it.

When you have entered your complete message, press Ctrl-Z to transmit it. If you decide to abandon a message before it has been sent, but want to stay within MAIL, type Ctrl-C. To abandon a message and exit from MAIL, type Ctrl-Y.

Sending a File by Mail

You can use MAIL to send a copy of a file from one user to another. This is a good way to send prepared documents, or you can use the facilities of a word processor or other program to produce and edit a lengthy file for the MAIL program.

The command is simple:

MAIL>**SEND**[filename]   <Return>

The system will then prompt you for the name of the user to receive the file.

It is also possible to include all of the elements of the command in a single line, as in:

MAIL>**SEND** Filename Username   <Return>

from within MAIL.

And, in an even more convenient method, you can do the whole job from the DCL prompt without entering the MAIL program, as in

$MAIL Filename Username <Return>

For example,

$MAIL MEETING_DATES.TXT BLUEFISH::TESSA <Return>

will send the file called **MEETING_dATES**.TXT to the user named Tessa in the node Bluefish. The nodename is optional, required only when the recipient is not in your default node. Signify the use of a nodename by employing double colons as shown. The system will assume that the file you are specifying exists in your default directory; otherwise you will need to specify its location.

It is also possible to include a short message identifying the nature of the mail you are sending. Here is an example of such a command:

**$MAIL[/subject = "August's meeting schedule"]
 MEETING_DATES.TXT TESSA** <Return>

Sending an Electronic Chain Letter

You can send one message to multiple users by stringing their mailbox names together with commas, as in

_To: **TESSA,WILLIAM,JANICE**

You can also create your own list of mailbox names to allow you to send a single message to a group of accounts. You need to create a file with the filename extension of .DIS (for distribution). You do so by using the **CREATE** command from DCL or under the EDT text editor. Here is an example using **CREATE**:

$CREATE STAFF.DIS <Return>
TESSA <Return>
WILLIAM <Return>

JANICE	\<Return\>
ARLENE	\<Return\>
HERBERT	\<Return\>
SONYA	\<Return\>
DAN	\<Return\>
Ctrl-Z or F6	\<Return\>

If it would help you to remember the purpose of a particular distribution list, you can add comments to the file. A comment is a line of text that begins with an exclamation point. Here is a commented version of STAFF.DIS:

$CREATE STAFF.DIS	\<Return\>
!Boston office staff:	\<Return\>
TESSA	\<Return\>
WILLIAM	\<Return\>
JANICE	\<Return\>
ARLENE	\<Return\>
HERBERT	\<Return\>
SONYA	\<Return\>
DAN	\<Return\>
^Z or F6	\<Return\>

To send a memo to the members of the STAFF.DIS listing, precede the name of the .DIS file with an @ sign in place of an ordinary mailbox name. Here's an example:

$MAIL	\<Return\>
MAIL\>**MAIL**	\<Return\>
_Subj: "**4Q 1987 Sales figures**"	\<Return\>
_To: **@STAFF**	\<Return\>
_Text: "**Enter text here . . .**"	\<Return\>
^Z	\<Return\>

The filename extension of .DIS is assumed by the system and does not have to be entered.

Let's suppose you have a second distribution list, with office staff in your San Francisco branch on node SWORDFISH as well as a group of secretaries on your default node. Here's another list:

$CREATE SUPPORT_STAFF.DIS	<Return>
!San Francisco branch and Home office support	<Return>
!San Francisco:	<Return>
SWORDFISH::KEEFE	<Return>
SWORDFISH::SANDLER	<Return>
!Boston support staff:	<Return>
NEIL	<Return>
STEVEN	<Return>
^Z	<Return>

Distribution lists can also be mixed in with ordinary account names, as in

_To:**KENNEDY, @STAFF**	<Return>

The distribution list must be at the end of the command.

It is not possible to include more than one distribution list in a single mailbox command. However, you can *nest* one distribution list within another, as in

$CREATE ALL_STAFF.DIS	<Return>
@STAFF	<Return>
@SUPPORT_STAFF	<Return>
^Z or F6	<Return>

If you mix ordinary mailbox account names with nested distribution lists, the distribution lists must be at the end of the main distribution list file. You might, for example, have three separate lists of names for different departments in your company, and one master list that nests the smaller lists for company-wide distribution.

Extending the Powers of the SEND Command

There are three useful command qualifiers to the **MAIL** or **SEND** commands: **EDIT**, **SELF**, and **SUBJECT**.

MAIL>**MAIL/EDIT**	<Return>

allows the use of the EDT text editor for composing a message. It is also possible to change the default text editor—see your system manager for details.

MAIL>**MAIL/SELF** <Return>

sends a copy of the current message to your own folder.

MAIL>**MAIL/SUBJECT**="text" <Return>

specifies a subject for use in the heading to the message. If the text is more than one word in length, it must be enclosed in quote marks. Here is an example:

MAIL>**MAIL/SUBJECT**="Your vacation schedule"
                          FILENAME.EXT <Return>

USING THE KEYPAD FOR COMMANDS IN MAIL

The Mail program includes a set of predefined commands assigned to the keypad of the LK201 keyboard used on VT220s and imitated by most terminals designed to be compatible with the VT220. Most of the keys have two functions—one given by merely pressing the key, and the secondary function issued by first pressing the Gold key (PF1) and then striking the keypad key.

Figure 8-1 shows the default key assignments, with the primary assignment listed first, and the secondary assignment, which must be preceded by the Gold key, listed second.

These assignments, however, are not necessarily binding on you, the user. The Mail program allows you to redefine any of the keys on the keypad to personalize commands in as many groupings as you'd like, using the **DEFINE/KEY** command and parameter.

The format for a key definition is:

MAIL>**DEFINE/KEY keyname string** <Return>

PF1 GOLD	PF2 HELP DIR/FOLDER	PF3 EXTRACT MAIL EXTRACT	PF4 ERASE SELECT MAIL
7 SEND SEND/EDIT	8 REPLY REPLY/EDIT/EXT	9 FORWARD FORWARD/EDIT	— READ/NEW SHOW NEW
4 CURRENT CURRENT/EDIT	5 FIRST FIRST/EDIT	6 LAST LAST/EDIT	, DIR/NEW DIR MAIL
1 BACK BACK/EDIT	2 PRINT PRINT/PR/NOTIF	3 DIR DIR/STAR 99999	ENTER
0 NEXT NEXT/EDIT		FILE DELETE	SELECT:

Figure 8-1 Keypad commands in Mail

The keyname is the name of the key to be redefined; the string is the command to be assigned to that key.

The following keys are available for redefinition within Mail:

Keyname	LK201 (VT200)	VT100	VT52
PF1	PF1	PF1	blue key
PF2	PF2	PF2	red key
PF3	PF3	PF3	gray key
PF4	PF4	PF4	n/a
KP0–KP9	keypad 0–9	keypad 0–9	keypad 0–9
PERIOD	period key	period key	period key
COMMA	comma key	comma key	comma key
MINUS	minus key	minus key	minus key
ENTER	Enter key	Enter key	Enter key
E1	Find key	n/a	n/a
E2	Insert key	n/a	n/a
E3	Remove key	n/a	n/a
E4	Select key	n/a	n/a

Keyname	LK201 (VT200)	VT100	VT52
E5	Previous screen	n/a	n/a
E6	Next screen	n/a	n/a
HELP	Help (15)	n/a	n/a
DO	Do (16)	n/a	n/a
F17–F20	function keys	n/a	n/a

Note that you cannot redefine the arrow keys or function keys 1 through 14.

For example, to redefine the PF3 function key to issue the **READ/NEW** command, enter the following command line:

MAIL>**DEFINE/KEY PF3 "READ/NEW"**   <Return>

A valuable command qualifier is the **/TERMINATE** instruction, which tells the computer to immediately execute the command associated with a particular key. This is equivalent to pressing the special key and then hitting the Return key to call for execution. Here is an example:

MAIL>**DEFINE/KEY PERIOD
         "DIRECTORY"/TERMINATE**   <Return>

You can also turn off the display of a command when a special key is struck, with the command qualifier **/NOECHO**, as in

MAIL>**DEFINE/KEY COMMA
         "FORWARD"/NOECHO**   <Return>

You can have an unlimited number of key redefinitions if you subdivide your new choices into *states* for various purposes. For example, you could have a keypad redefinition for use during an editing session while retaining a basic mail command set and an advanced mail set.

There are three qualifiers here. **/IF_STATE**=**state_list** specifies a list of states, one of which must be **SET** to enable use of a redefined key. If this qualifier is not used, the current state is assumed. **/LOCK_STATE** makes the default state the state specified by the most recent **/SET_STATE** qualifier until a new state is specified. **/SET_STATE** = **state** associates a state with the key being defined.

For example

MAIL>**DEFINE/KEY F17 "SET"**
    /SET STATE = ADVANCED_MAIL <Return>

will have the F17 function key on the LK201 keyboard issue a **SET** command and change the current state to ADVANCED_MAIL.

MAIL>**DEFINE/KEY F18 "FORWARD"**
/TERMINATE /IF_STATE = ADVANCED_MAIL <Return>

Under these two redefinitions, if the F17 key is pressed, followed by the F18 key, the Mail program will know to use the ADVANCED_MAIL redefinition of the F18 key.

Keypad reassignments made during a mail session will not be retained by the computer when you exit from the Mail program. In order to retain these redefinitions, it is necessary to create a file in your top-level (root) directory with the definitions and then add a pointer to that file in your LOGIN.COM command file.

Here is an example of how to create such a file of keypad redefinitions, starting from the VMS prompt:

$CREATE MAIL$KEYS.DEF   <Return>
DEFINE/KEY PF1 "MAIL"   <Return>
DEFINE/KEY PF3 "READ/NEW"   <Return>
DEFINE/KEY PERIOD "DIRECTORY"   <Return>
DEFINE/KEY COMMA "DIRECTORY/FOLDER" <Return>
^Z or F6   <Return>

Next, you must add to your LOGIN.COM file the following statement:

$DEFINE MAIL$INIT
    SYS$LOGIN:MAIL$KEYS.DEF <Return>

The list of redefinitions will be read into the computer and made active as part of the Mail program the next time the LOGIN.COM file is read at login.

READING A MAP OF MAIL

It is valuable to know about one command that will display the current state of any keyboard definitions, as well as other qualifiers, including *terminate, echo* and *state*.

MAIL>**SHOW KEY [keyname]** <Return>

will tell you the definition given to a particular key.

MAIL>**SHOW KEY/ALL** <Return>
MAIL>**SHOW KEY/ALL/STATE = (state,state,....)** <Return>

will yield a full list of all key definitions in the default state, or if a state or states are specified, the definitions of those states. Note that as states are specified, they are listed within parentheses and are separated by commas.

MAIL>**SHOW KEY/BRIEF** <Return>

displays only key definitions, leaving out other qualifiers.

MAIL>**SHOW KEY/DIRECTORY** <Return>

identifies the names of all states for which keys have been identified.

EVERYTHING YOU NEED TO KNOW ABOUT YOUR MAIL ACCOUNT

After you have completed—or before you have begun—the customization of your Mail account, issue the following simple command:

MAIL>**SHOW ALL** <Return>

This instruction will yield the following:

The name of the mail file directory.

The current mail file and folder.

The name of the WASTEBASKET folder if adjusted by **SET WASTEBASKET_NAME** command.

The amount of deleted message space.

The number of new (unread) messages.

The forwarding address for mail, if set with **SET FORWARD** command.

The personal name, if set with **SET PERSONAL_NAME** command.

Whether the user will receive copies of mail messages under **SEND** or **ANSWER**, as set by **SET COPY_SELF** command.

Whether Mail will empty the WASTEBASKET when **EXIT** or **SET FILE** commands are used.

HELP IS IN THE MAIL

Mail has a full set of Help messages and explanations of commands, available whenever the Mail program is being used.

The form to ask for help is

MAIL>**HELP** <Return>

for a prompted help session, or

MAIL>**HELP** * <Return>

for information about all Mail commands, or

MAIL>**HELP** [topic] <Return>

for instructions about a specific command or topic. The list of available subjects is displayed with a basic **HELP** command.

The following is a list of Help topics under Mail in a typical system:

/EDIT	ANSWER	ATTACH	BACK	COMPRESS	Convert_files		
COPY	CURRENT	DEFINE	DELETE	DIRECTORY	EDIT	ERASE	
EXIT	EXTRACT	FILE	FIRST	Folders	FORWARD		
GETTING_STARTED	HELP	KEYPAD	LAST	MAIL	MOVE		
NEXT	PRINT	PURGE	QUIT	READ	REPLY	SEARCH	
SELECT	SEND	SET-SHOW	SPAWN	Syntax	V4_CHANGES		

A MAIL DICTIONARY

Following are definitions and examples of use of some of the most important Mail commands.

ANSWER

Allows the user to send a message to the originator of the message currently being read, or the one last read. **ANSWER** and **REPLY** are interchangeable. The command can include the name of a prepared file to be sent to the originator, as in

MAIL>**ANSWER Filename.Ext**   <Return>

or you can wait for the system to prompt you for the text of a message.

The following command qualifiers are available for use with the ANSWER or REPLY command.

MAIL>**ANSWER/EDIT**   <Return>

calls for the EDT editor to allow editing of the reply you compose. When you **EXIT** from EDT, the message is automatically sent (to cancel sending of the message, use the EDT command **QUIT**.)

MAIL>**ANSWER/EXTRACT**   <Return>

calls for the EDT editor to allow you to edit the text of the message you are currently reading.

MAIL>**ANSWER/LAST**   <Return>

tells the system that the last message that was sent is to be used as the text for the reply.

MAIL>**ANSWER/SELF** <Return>

tells Mail to send a copy of the response to you so that you can retain a record.

COPY

Places a duplicate of an existing file in another folder within the Mail program. (If you want to copy a mail message to a program outside of Mail, use the **EXTRACT** command.) The command uses the current file.

The form for the command is:

MAIL>**COPY foldername [filename]**

For example

MAIL>**COPY PHONECALLS** <Return>

will make a copy of the current message and place it in the folder called PHONECALLS within the Mail program.

Note: If the specified folder name does not exist, it will be created by the system, following a request for confirmation.

MAIL>**COPY PHONECALLS/NOCONFIRM**

eliminates the confirmation request by the system and automatically creates a new folder if an unknown folder is requested.

MAIL>**COPY PHONECALLS/ALL**

tells the system to copy all messages (see **SELECT** on page 140) to the specified folder. If the **selected/ALL** switch is not used, only the current message is copied.

As with most commands, the system will also prompt the user for information, as in

MAIL>**COPY** <Return>
_Folder: **foldername** <Return>

_File: <Return>
MAIL>

CURRENT

Displays the beginning of the message currently being read, an easy way to reexamine the top of a lengthy message:

MAIL>**CURRENT**   <Return>

To move to the top of the current message and then invoke the EDT editor, enter

MAIL>**CURRENT/EDIT**   <Return>

DELETE

Deletes the message currently being read, or the message most recently read. The form is

MAIL>**DELETE**   <Return>

to remove the current or most recently read message.

MAIL>**DELETE [message number]**   <Return>

deletes a specific message as listed in the directory.

MAIL>**DELETE/ALL**   <Return>

will delete those messages that have been specified by a **SELECT** command.

Note: Messages are not immediately erased, but are placed into the WASTEBASKET folder that is a part of every Mail account. The WASTEBASKET folder is automatically emptied when an **EXIT** or **PURGE** command is issued.

If you want to recover a message accidentally deleted but not yet purged, **SELECT** the WASTEBASKET folder, call for a **DIRECTORY** to see the message numbers in that folder, **READ** the message you wish to retain, and then **MOVE** it to another folder.

EDIT

This command invokes the EDT editor to allow editing of a message before it is sent. See the VAX EDT Reference Manual for details on EDT commands themselves.

The command qualifier **/EDIT** is available for a number of Mail commands, automatically calling forth EDT for such uses as **FORWARD** and **ANSWER**.

As a command on its own, **EDIT** has the following form:

MAIL>**EDIT [filename]**   <Return>

The command also has a number of command qualifiers.

MAIL>**EDIT/COMMAND**=**ini-filename**   <Return>

invokes EDT and calls an EDT startup command file (EDTINI). See details in the VAX EDT Reference Manual. If the user does not call for a special startup command file, the default file of EDTINI.EDT is automatically called.

MAIL>**EDIT/CREATE**   <Return>

tells Mail to invoke the EDT editor and create a file. If a filename is not included in the **EDIT** command line, the editor will prompt the user for a filename.

ERASE

A simple command to clear the screen during a Mail session, it uses no qualifiers:

MAIL>**ERASE**   <Return>

EXIT

MAIL>**EXIT**   <Return>

To leave the Mail program, enter the command **EXIT**, or type Ctrl-Z. When you exit the program, all messages in the WASTEBASKET folder are deleted, unless the **SET NOAUTO_PURGE** command has been issued. (See **SET** on page 146.)

EXTRACT

One of the more useful capabilities of MAIL is the opportunity to take a file out of MAIL and work on it under other programs, archive it, or place it in a database. The key is to *extract* it from MAIL, a process that creates a separate file under VMS that can later be retrieved and worked on. The form of the command is

MAIL>**EXTRACT filename-spec**

The **EXTRACT** verb applies to the current message, and the filename-specification is used to specify a name for the output file. The default file specification of .TXT is used unless a different extension is given.

The following command qualifiers are among those available for the **EXTRACT** command:

MAIL>**EXTRACT/ALL**   <Return>

Copies all files chosen with the **SELECT** command to a single file.

MAIL>**EXTRACT/APPEND**   <Return>

adds the current or selected message or messages to the end of a specified, existing file. If the filename does not exist, a new file with that name is created.

MAIL>**EXTRACT/NOHEADER**   <Return>

extracts a message file, removing the header information (To:, From:, and Subject:) from the mail message.

FILE

FILE and **MOVE**, which are interchangeable commands, move the current message to the specified folder. If you enter the **FILE** command, supply a foldername, and then decide that you do not want to file the message, enter Ctrl-Z to abort the operation and stay within Mail.

The format for the command is

MAIL>**FILE foldername [filename]**

FORWARD

Sends a copy of the current message to a user or group of users. The system will prompt you for the mailbox names of addressees. The form is

MAIL>**FORWARD**   <Return>

To edit a file, enter:

MAIL>**FORWARD/EDIT**   <Return>

to invoke the EDT file editor to allow changes to the current message before it is forwarded.

MAIL>**FORWARD/NOHEADER**   <Return>

strips off the header information (To:, From:, and Subject:) before a message is forwarded.

MOVE

Interchangable with **FILE**.

PRINT

To send a copy of the current message to a printer, use the **PRINT** command, in the form

MAIL>**PRINT**   <Return>

The files are not ordinarily released to the printer until the user exits from Mail, so that all files are printed at the same time. The default print queue for Mail is SYS$PRINT. Five command qualifiers are available.

MAIL>**PRINT/ALL**   <Return>

prints all the messages indicated by a **SELECT** command.

MAIL>**PRINT/COPIES = n** <Return>

orders the specified number of copies of a file to be printed.

MAIL>**PRINT/NOTIFY** <Return>

calls for a message to be sent to your account when your printing request has been completed.

MAIL>**PRINT/PRINT** <Return>

releases messages queued by previous **PRINT** commands without the need for an **EXIT** command. **PRINT/PRINT** will not order a print of the current message.

MAIL>**PRINT/QUEUE = queuename** <Return>

orders printing of a file or files on a print queue other than the default **SYS$PRINT**. For example, if your system has a laser printer with a queue called **SYS$LASER**, the command would be

MAIL>**PRINT/QUEUE = SYS$LASER** <Return>

PURGE

As we've seen, files deleted from MAIL folders are not immediately erased from the system but are instead placed within the WASTEBASKET folder. The files in that folder are automatically discarded when the user exits from Mail. The **PURGE** command is used to remove files from that folder while remaining within MAIL.

The form of the command is

MAIL>**PURGE** <Return>

The following command qualifiers are available.

MAIL>**PURGE/RECLAIM** <Return>

releases space from deleted messages back to the VAX Record Management Services for reuse. *Note* that while a PURGE/RECLAIM operation is underway, you will not be able to receive new mail, and users sending mail during that time will receive an error message.

MAIL>**PURGE/STATISTICS** <Return>

gives a report on the amount of space reclaimed.

QUIT

To leave Mail without clearing the WASTEBASKET folder, the **QUIT** command is available. The form is

MAIL>**QUIT** <Return>

A Ctrl-Y key combination performs the same command.

READ

The verb to display messages, in the form

MAIL>**READ [foldername] [message-number]**

Pressing the Return key with Mail in most instances is interpreted by the system as equivalent to a request to **READ** the current message.

To display a list of available messages in the current directory, along with the message numbers, use the **DIRECTORY** command.

If the **READ** command is entered without parameters or a file specified, Mail will display the oldest message in the NEW-MAIL (unread mail) folder. If there are no messages in that folder, Mail will display the oldest message in the MAIL folder.

If you enter a message number that is higher than the last message in a folder, the system will display the last message in the folder. This gives you a quick way to get to the end of a folder without knowing the message numbers—simply specify a very large number that you know is larger than the number of messages in a folder.

The following command qualifiers are available.

MAIL>**READ/BEFORE**=date

displays messages received before the indicated date, as in

MAIL>**READ/BEFORE** = 19-JUL <Return>

If no date is indicated in the command, all messages before the current date are displayed.

MAIL>**READ/EDIT**

invokes the EDT editor with your **READ** command.

MAIL>**READ/NEW**

displays any new mail messages received while you are using Mail.

MAIL>**READ/SINCE** = **date**

displays messages received after the indicated date, as in

MAIL>**READ/SINCE** = 06-JUL <Return>

REPLY

Interchangeable with **ANSWER**.

SEARCH

If you accumulate a large folder of files, it may become difficult to find previous messages. The **SEARCH** command will look through the files in the current folder for the first occurrence of a particular string of characters among your messages. The form is

MAIL>**SEARCH** search-string <Return>

Here is an example:

MAIL>**SEARCH Bluefish futures** <Return>

SELECT

Identifies a set of messages that can be acted upon as a group. The selected group is acted upon as if it were in a separate folder.

The following commands can be applied to a set that has been selected:

COPY
DELETE
DIRECTORY
EXTRACT
FILE
MOVE
READ
SEARCH

If no foldername is indicated in the command, the current folder is used.

The following command qualifiers are available.

MAIL>**SELECT/BEFORE**=**date**   <Return>

chooses all messages dated before the indicated date, as in

MAIL>**SELECT/BEFORE**=**06-JUL**   <Return>

To choose only new, unread messages, enter

MAIL>**SELECT/NEW**   <Return>

The **SINCE** qualifier chooses all messages dated since the indicated date, as in

MAIL>**SELECT/SINCE**=**19-JUL**   <Return>

SEND

Operates identically to **MAIL** command, defined earlier in this chapter.

Navigational Commands within Mail Files

Another class of commands within MAIL is navigational. They can be used in the selection or manipulation of files within the folders of Mail.

BACK

Entered at the **MAIL>** prompt, **BACK** displays the message preceding the current or most recently read message. If the most recent command was **DIRECTORY**, issuing a **BACK** command displays the preceding screen of the directory. The form is

MAIL>**BACK**   <Return>

Another option with **BACK** is:

MAIL>**BACK/EDIT**   <Return>

which performs as above and also invokes the EDT editor to work on the displayed message.

FIRST

Selects as the current message and then displays the first message in the current file. The form is

MAIL>**FIRST**   <Return>

Another way to invoke the command is

MAIL>**FIRST/EDIT**   <Return>

which displays the first message and invokes the EDT file editor.

LAST

Selects as the current message and then displays the last message in the current folder. The form is:

MAIL>**LAST**   <Return>

Another way to use this command is

MAIL>**LAST/EDIT**   <Return>

which invokes the EDT editor and then displays the last message in the current folder.

NEXT

Moves on to the next message in a directory of Mail messages. The form is

MAIL>**NEXT**   <Return>

If you are reading a message and are at the bottom of that message, hitting the Return key will move on to the next message automatically; the **NEXT** command is most useful, then, in moving through long messages.

MAIL>**NEXT/EDIT**   <Return>

moves to the next message and invokes the EDT text editor.

System Commands within Mail

SPAWN

Allows you to create a subprocess from the current process. The context of the subprocess is copied from the current VMS process. You can use the **SPAWN** command to leave Mail temporarily, perform other functions (such as displaying a directory listing or printing a file), and then return to Mail.

Going in the other direction, while editing a file you can **SPAWN** a subprocess to read a new mail message, and then **ATTACH** back to the editing process. The **ATTACH** command switches control between processes created using the **SPAWN** command.

Be aware that your system configuration and the load of users and processes on your system may combine to make the **SPAWN** command an attractive but unworkable concept because of loss of speed. Consult your system manager for instructions about your system.

The **SPAWN** command uses the following form:

MAIL>**SPAWN [command]**

For example, you can use

MAIL>**SPAWN PHONE** <Return>

to temporarily exit Mail and conduct a Phone session.
 The following command qualifiers are available.

MAIL>**SPAWN/INPUT**=**filename** <Return>

tells the program to use an input file containing one or more DCL command strings to be executed within the context of the subprocess created by the **SPAWN** command. If a command string is specified along with the name of an input file, the program processes the string first before moving on to the command file.

MAIL>**SPAWN/LOGICAL_NAMES** <Return>

instructs the system to copy the logical names of the parent process to the spawned subprocess. The default is **/LOGICAL_NAMES**. To block passage, use **/NOLOGICAL_NAMES**.

MAIL>**SPAWN/SYMBOLS** <Return>

instructs the system to pass DCL global and local symbols to the subprocess. The default is **/SYMBOLS**. To block passage, use **/NOSYMBOLS**.

MAIL>**SPAWN/PROCESS**=**subprocessname** <Return>

allows the user to specify the name of the subprocess to be created. If this qualifier is not used, the default name is the Username and an incremented number, as in USERNAME_n.

MAIL>**SPAWN/OUTPUT**=**filename**=**spec** <Return>

tells the Mail program to direct output of a **SPAWN** subprocess to the indicated file. This command should be used in conjunction with the **/NOWAIT** qualifier.

MAIL>**SPAWN/WAIT** <Return>

instructs the system to wait until a subprocess is completed before allowing further commands to be specified.

MAIL>**SPAWN/NOWAIT** <Return>

allows the user to specify new commands while the subprocess is running. This command qualifier should be used with **/OUTPUT=file-spec** to direct the output to a file instead of the screen.

It is also possible to **SPAWN** a Mail session from the DCL command level. Here is an example:

$SPAWN MAIL
%DCL-S-SPAWNED, process XXXXXXNAME_1 spawned
%DCL-S-ATTACHED, terminal now attached to
                                  process XXXXXNAME_1
MAIL>

To return from Mail, use the following command:

MAIL>**ATTACH XXXXXNAME_1**   <Return>

%DCL-S-RETURNED, control returned
                                  to process XXXXXXNAME

ATTACH

Allows you to move between processes created with the **SPAWN** command. For example, while editing a file, the user can **SPAWN** a subprocess (MAIL) to read a new mail message and later **ATTACH** back to the editing session. The form is

ATTACH [/PARENT] [processname]   <Return>

COMPRESS

Compresses ISAM mail files so that they take up less space in disk storage. ISAM, Indexed Sequential Access Method, is a procedure for storing and retrieving files using sets of indexes that describe where records are on disks.

When a file is compressed, a temporary file named MAIL_nnnn_COMPRESS.TMP is created. (nnnn is a unique four-digit number.) The contents of the file to be compressed are then copied to the temporary file and compressed. The original (uncompressed) file is renamed with a file type of OLD. Finally, the newly compressed file is renamed from MAIL_nnnn_COMPRESS.TMP back to its original name.

The form is:

MAIL>**COMPRESS** [filename]

SET; SHOW

The **SET** command allows for customization of some of the features of Mail, and the **SHOW** command displays the current state of those commands. Some examples follow.

MAIL>**SET NOAUTO_PURGE** <Return>

instructs the system not to automatically purge the contents of the WASTEBASKET folder when an **EXIT** or **SET FILE** command is given. With this instruction in place, the user must enter a **PURGE** command to clean out the WASTEBASKET folder. To turn the automatic purge back on, issue the command

MAIL>**SET AUTO_PURGE** <Return>

To display the current state of the AUTO_PURGE default, issue the command

MAIL>**SHOW AUTO_PURGE** <Return>

To determine the default instruction for the **SEND** or **REPLY** command to deliver or withhold a copy of a message to the sender, use

MAIL>**SET COPY_SELF** <Return>

To display the current state of the **COPY_SELF** default, issue the command

MAIL>**SHOW COPY_SELF** <Return>

The command

MAIL>**SET FILE** [filename] <Return>

establishes or opens another file as the current mail file.

MAIL>**SHOW FILE** <Return>

displays the current file.

MAIL>**SET FOLDER [foldername]** <Return>

establishes or opens another folder as the current mail folder.

MAIL>**SHOW FOLDER** <Return>

displays the current folder.
    The **SET FOLDER** command has the following command qualifiers. Use

MAIL>**SET FOLDER/BEFORE**=**date** <Return>

or

MAIL>**SET FOLDER/SINCE**=**date** <Return>

to set the folder and select messages within it that are either before or since the indicated date. Use

MAIL>**SET FOLDER/NEW** <Return>

to select the NEWMAIL folder with unread mail.
    To establish a default forwarding address for mail, use

MAIL>**SET FORWARD address** <Return>

This default stays in effect until a **SET NOFORWARD** command is given. To determine what the default forwarding address is, issue the command

MAIL>**SHOW FORWARD** <Return>

    You can personalize your mail's return address label with the following command:

MAIL>**SET PERSONAL_NAME "text string"** <Return>

This command adds a string of characters to the "From:" field of a message, allowing personalization of messages with information beyond that of the account name. Character strings can be no more than 127 characters in length. Here is an example:

MAIL>**SET PERSONAL_NAME "The man who signs your paycheck"** <Return>

This will yield the following on-screen message at a recipient's terminal when a message is sent:

New mail on node SWORDFISH from BLUEFISH::SANDLER "The man who signs your paycheck"

On a less frivolous note, the message could also include a short note such as

MAIL>**SET PERSONAL_NAME "Urgent update on prices."**

To display any personal names, use the command

MAIL>**SHOW PERSONAL_NAME** <Return>

To cancel personal names, issue the following:

MAIL>**SET NOPERSONAL_NAME** <Return>

Another command allows personalization of the name of the folder ordinarily named WASTEBASKET. The form is

MAIL>**SET WASTEBASKET_NAME foldername** <Return>

The contents of the WASTEBASKET, if any, are transferred to the new file.

MAIL>**SHOW WASTEBASKET_NAME** <Return>

will display the name of the WASTEBASKET folder.

9 The Million-Dollar Phone Call

Forget about all of the fancy number-crunching, database management and computerized graphics and design capabilities of your VAX system: Here's a really neat use of your million-dollar system—as a telephone.

Well, it's not quite as simplistic an option as that. The VAX/VMS system includes within it a facility called *Phone*, which allows for direct, interactive written text communication between users across the network already in place.

Like any modern telephone system, VMS Phone has a whole set of sophisticated features that Alexander Graham Bell never envisioned, including conference calls, hold buttons, and facsimile transmission. Here is one way in which the system might work:

> You are signed on to your VAX from a distant branch office and are reading your mail when you realize that you need some help from a user in the headquarters office. You make a quick check of the names of the users signed on to the system and find that the account of the person you want is currently active. You "phone" him on-line and discuss with him the files you need. He informs you that a coworker on another VAX system, tied into the network but located overseas, has a current file with the information you need. You put your first call on hold, dial up the European users, reconnect the first party and then the three of you watch the information stream into your account and then hold a short, three-way conversation.

When you enter the VMS Phone facility, your screen will split into three parts, with a command input line at the top, a *viewport* section with your node and user name for the display of messages you type into the system, and a viewport section for the response from the user you have dialed. If you engage in a conference call, the screen will be subdivided further for additional users.

PHONE COMMANDS

In order to enter a command from within the Phone program, you must begin with the command character. The default character is the percent sign; Phone will allow you to redefine the command character if necessary.

$PHONE <Return>

enters the Phone program and displays the Phone command screen.

At this point, commands require a percent sign as the first character. To call another user, for example, enter

%DIAL BLUEFISH <Return>

An alternate way to enter the Phone program and place an immediate call is to enter the following from the VMS prompt:

$PHONE BLUEFISH <Return>

This command enters the Phone program and dials the user named BLUEFISH in one instruction.

The **PHONE** verb has several available qualifiers that allow you to customize your account

$PHONE/NOSCROLL <Return>

determines how new lines of text are displayed on the screen as the viewing section of the screen becomes full. If the **/NO-SCROLL** qualifier is used, text lines are wrapped and new text appears at the top line of the viewport. If **/SCROLL** is specified (it is the default), new text appears at the bottom of the viewport, and the text is scrolled up and off the screen each time a new line of text is entered.

$PHONE/SWITCH_HOOK = "character" <Return>

allows you to select your own *switch hook* or command character to precede each command. The character can be any nonalphanumeric character. The default character is the percent mark. Here is an example of use of the command:

$PHONE/SWITCH_HOOK = "&" <Return>

changes the switch hook character to an ampersand.

$PHONE/VIEWPORT_SIZE = n

allows the user to choose the number of lines in a viewport, within the range of 3 to 10, with a default size of 10.

DIALING A CALL

Placing a call to another VAX user is about as simple as can be. Just use the verb **DIAL** or the verb **PHONE** followed by the name of the user account you seek to communicate with. If the user is on your default node, you do not need to add that information to the command. If, however, you need to speak with a user in another node, just add that information and add a pair of colons before the user name. Here are two examples:

PHONE KENNEDY <Return>

or

DIAL BLUEFISH::TESSA <Return>

A third way to place a call is to merely enter the name of a user at the Phone command prompt. In such a case, the system assumes the verb **PHONE** and places the call.

When you issue the **DIAL** or **PHONE** command, the computer will *broadcast* a message to the party you are calling to indicate that you are phoning. The message will flash on the recipient's screen every ten seconds until

- the recipient of the message answers the phone;
- the recipient rejects the incoming call; or
- the sender cancels the call by pressing any key on the keyboard.

CONFERENCE CALLS

You can add as many as four other VAX users to your conversation in a conference call.

In setting up the conference, one participant who is already on-line serves as the operator, calling other users and adding them to the conversation. If you call someone who is already involved in a phone conversation with one or more participants, only the direct recipient of your call can be added to your conference.

To add new parties to a conversation, just use the **DIAL** or **PHONE** command, preceded by the switch hook character, as in

%PHONE KENNEDY   <Return>

DIRECTORY ASSISTANCE

Since the Phone utility is an on-line, interactive means of communication (as opposed to the send-and-hold design of VMS Mail), the user you seek to communicate with must be signed on to the system and willing to accept a call in order for you to communicate. There are three ways to determine who is available for a phone conversation. First, you can just place a call to the party you seek and let the system inform you with a message if no such account name is presently on-line. Second, you can issue a **SHOW USER** command from the VMS prompt and read the names of the accounts presently signed on. This will not tell you whether a particular user is willing to accept a broadcast message, and it requires you to exit Phone, issue the **SHOW USER** command, and then re-enter Phone. The most direct way to obtain a listing of available users is to use the **DIRECTORY** command within the Phone utility. This command is

%**DIRECTORY** <Return>

for the default node, or

%**DIRECTORY BLUEFISH** <Return>

for a specific node on the system.

The directory will list the following information for each user:

Process name
User name
Terminal device name
Phone status

The Phone status indicator will tell you whether a particular user has issued the command **SET BROADCAST=NONE** from the VMS prompt. If such a command has been given, all classes of messages, including VMS Mail and VMS Phone, are screened out from that terminal. The **SET** command also allows the user to selectively screen out phone calls, with a **SET NOPHONE** command.

ANSWERING THE CALL

When you receive a broadcast message that you are being called, go to the VMS prompt and enter the Phone program by typing:

$**PHONE** <Return>

Once inside the Phone program, type

%ANSWER <Return>

to complete the link to your caller.

If you are already within the Phone program when a broadcast message comes in, simply type **ANSWER** (Return) as a command.

HANGING UP

There are three ways to end a Phone conversation.

%EXIT <Return>

ends a conversation with an automatic **HANGUP** command, and then exits the Phone program and returns the user to the VMS prompt. Ctrl-Z when there is no ongoing conversation is equivalent to issuing the **EXIT** command. Typing Ctrl-Z during a conversation merely ends the conversation and is equivalent to the **HANGUP** command.

%HANGUP <Return>

disconnects all current links, including active conversations, calls on hold, and any caller who has placed you on hold. You will stay, however, within the Phone program.

SENDING A FILE

The **FACSIMILE** command allows you to include the contents of a file in a conversation, sending it to all current participants. The transmission of the file continues until the end of the file is reached or until the sender presses any key on the keyboard. The format is

%FACSIMILE filename <Return>

Phone will continue to send the file until it reaches the end of the file or until you type any key at your keyboard.

HOW TO PHONE FOR HELP

VMS maintains a file of Help messages within the Phone program. To obtain assistance, issue the following command:

%**HELP** <Return>

The system will display a list of available help topics, with a typical selection including

| ANSWER | Characters | DIAL | DIRECTORY | EXIT | | FACSIMILE | HANGUP |
| HELP | HOLD | MAIL | REJECT | Switch_hook | | | UNHOLD |

A more direct route to obtaining help is to issue a specific command, as in

%**HELP FACSIMILE** <Return>

Here is an example of the system's response to the **HELP FACSIMILE** request:

VAX/VMS Phone Facility

Press any key to cancel the help information and continue.

FACSIMILE

The **FACSIMILE** command allows you to include the contents of a file into your conversation. It requires a file specification, and proceeds to send the contents of that file to everyone in the conversation. Thus the complete syntax is:

FACSIMILE file-spec

PHONE continues to send the file until it reaches end of file or until you type any key at your keyboard.

PLACING A CALL ON HOLD

The user can temporarily suspend the link to current participants in a one-on-one or conference call by issuing the **HOLD** command. A message is sent to each terminal announcing that it has been put on hold. The user can place calls to other users while a previous conversation is on hold.

To place a conversation on hold, issue the command

%HOLD <Return>

To resume a conversation, issue the command

%UNHOLD <Return>

THE COMPUTER AS AN ANSWERING MACHINE

From within the Phone program, you can leave a message another user. This facility is useful if you call someone who is not on-line, or if a user has rejected your incoming Phone call.

The command is as follows:

%MAIL [node::]user "message" <Return>

The use of the node is optional and necessary only if the recipient is not on your default node. The message itself can be no longer than one line. Here is an example:

%MAIL TESSA "Please Phone me when you are available." <Return>

REJECTING AN INCOMING PHONE CALL

While you are signed on to Phone, you can reject an incoming request for a conversation. Adding the optional verb **EXIT** after the command will return you to the VMS prompt after you have rejected a call. For example,

%REJECT <Return>

tells the calling party that her request for a Phone conversation has been rejected. The sender of the Reject command will remain within the Phone program.

%REJECT EXIT <Return>

will reject a call and then immediately exit the Phone program and return the user to the VMS prompt.

Contrast this to the **SET BROADCAST=NONE** command which signifies your account as off-line for Phone messages.

EFFECTS OF KEYBOARD CHARACTERS

Here is an explanation of some of the effects of keyboard characters input during a Phone session:

Delete: Deletes the previous character from your screen and from the viewport displaying your side of the conversation at the receiving end or ends of your call.

Line Feed: Deletes the previous word from your screen and receiving viewports.

Return: Starts a new line.

Tab: Advances to the next tab stop.

Ctrl-G: Sounds the beeper at your terminal and at the terminal of any users linked to the current Phone conversation.

Ctrl-L: Clears all text in the viewport.

Ctrl-Q: Reopens your viewport to the receipt of text, negating a Ctrl-S.

Ctrl-S: Freezes your viewport to block further characters.

Ctrl-U: Clears the current line of the viewport.

Ctrl-W: Refreshes (redraws) the entire screen.

Ctrl-Z: A **HANGUP** command if used during a conversation; an **EXIT** command if used when no conversation is underway.

10 A Dictionary of Selected DCL Commands and Statements

This chapter presents a highly selective dictionary of DCL commands and statements for the ordinary user. Excluded from this list are most of the technical commands employed by the system operator or programmer in the set-up and modification of the system itself. The intent of this section is to help you customize your working environment and understand the overall picture of a VAX/VMS system. Commands are in alphabetical order, with the symbols =, :=, and @ occurring at the beginning.

= (Assignment Statement)

symbol-name=[=]**expression**

An assignment statement allows you to define a symbolic name for a character string, extending and personalizing the Digital Command Language.

The symbol name must begin with an alphabetic character, an underscore, or a dollar sign and be between 1 and 255 characters in length.

Using a single equal sign between the symbol name and the expression creates a local symbol, for use only in the current command level. Using a double equal sign creates a global symbol.

Strings are enclosed within quote marks, and are retained in the form in which they are entered, including upper- and lowercase letters and extra spaces if used.

The assignment statements remain active only for the duration of the current session, disappearing when the user signs off. To make the assignment statements permanent, include them as statements within the LOGIN.COM file which is invoked each time you sign on to the system.

Here are examples of use:

$US == "Show user" <Return>

$ROOT == "SET DEF [SANDLER]" <Return>

In the first assignment statement, the short symbolic name US will now be equivalent to entering the "SHOW USER" command; the second statement will make ROOT call upon the system to change the default directory from its present assignment to the identified directory, in this case the author's root directory.

:= (String Assignment)

symbol-name:=[=]string

A string assignment allows the user to define a symbolic name for a character string or an integer.

The string assignment does not require use of quote marks around the string; it therefore automatically converts lowercase letters to uppercase for consistency and removes any leading and trailing spaces and tabs. Multiple spaces and tabs between characters are compressed to a single space. To avoid these changes, use quote marks or use the assignment statement.

Using a single equal sign between the symbol name and the string creates a local symbol, for use only in the current command level. Using a double equal sign creates a global symbol.

Here is an example of use:

$ROOT :== SET DEF [SANDLER] <Return>

@ (Execute Procedure)

@ file-spec [p1 [p2 [... p8]]]

executes a command procedure. The @ command can execute a command procedure containing DCL command lines or data, qualifiers, or parameters for a specific command line.

The **file-spec** is used to identify either the command procedure to be executed or the device or file that is to provide input for the preceding command. If a file type is not specified, the system will assume the default file type of .COM. p1 [p2 [... p8]] specifies from one to eight optional parameters to be passed to the command procedure.

Your system manager may include system-wide command procedures, such as **@DIAL** or **@PLOT** to call, for example, communications or plotting procedures.

Command Qualifiers

/OUTPUT = file-spec

instructs the system to direct all output to the file or device specified.

APPEND

APPEND input-file-spec[,input-file-spec,input-file-spec...] output-file-spec

A means to add the contents of a file or files to the end of an existing output file. **APPEND** might be used to update a list or maintain a log of events, or to concatenate several text files.

The **input-file-spec** is the name of the source file. If you use more than one input file, separate the names with commas or plus signs. Multiple files are appended in the order specified at the end of the output file. The **output-file-spec** is the name of the file to which input files will be appended.

Command Qualifiers

/BEFORE[= time]
/SINCE[= time]

Select only those files dated before or since the time specified in the command qualifier. The time can be a date, in the form of **06-JUL**, or it can be one of the keywords **TODAY**, **TOMORROW**, and **YESTERDAY**. If no time is specified in the command, DCL assumes **TODAY**.

/CONFIRM
/NOCONFIRM (default)

Tell the system whether to query the user before each APPEND operation is performed. The following are proper responses to such queries:

TRUE 1	Positive responses.
NO FALSE 0 (Return)	Negative responses.
QUIT CTRL-Z	Call for an end to processing the command.
ALL	Calls for a continuation of processing without further prompts.

Figure 10-1

ASSIGN

ASSIGN equivalence-name[,...] logical-name[:]

Creates a logical name and assigns an equivalence string, or list of strings, to that name. Similar to **DEFINE** command, except in syntax.

The **equivalence-name[,...]** is the source string that is to be assigned to the new logical name. The equivalence name can be from 1 to 255 characters in length. If it contains anything other than alphanumeric characters, the dollar sign, or the underscore character, the string should be enclosed in quote marks. If the equivalence string includes a file specification, include the punctuation marks (colon, brackets, or periods) that would ordinarily be used.

The **logical-name** is the name to be created. The logical name can have from 1 to 255 characters. If it contains anything other than alphanumeric characters, the dollar sign, or the underscore character, the string should be enclosed in quote marks. The [:] is optional and is ignored by the system.

To delete a logical name from a table, use the **DEASSIGN** command.

Here is an example of use of **ASSIGN**:

$ASSIGN DUMMY:[SALES_FIG]BLUEFISH_COST
BLUECOST   <Return>

$PRINT BLUECOST   <Return>

In this instance, the system is told to equate the logical name BLUECOST with a particular file on a particular disk in a specified directory. When the print command is issued using the logical name, the system will search out the file on the basis of the equivalence name.

Logical names can be assigned to files, devices, and commands.

ATTACH

ATTACH [process-name]

Allows switching control from the current process to another process, when used in conjunction with the **SPAWN** command.

When the **ATTACH** command is issued, the source, or *parent* process, is put into hibernation, available for later use but not active. You cannot **ATTACH** to a process if it does not exist, if it is your current process, or if the process is not part of your current job.

See **SPAWN** for further instructions.

Contrast with **CONNECT**.

CONNECT

CONNECT virtual-terminal-name

Connects your physical terminal to a virtual terminal connected to another process.

The process is a separate one, as opposed to the subprocess created and used by the **SPAWN** and **ATTACH** commands.

One use for the **CONNECT** command is in telecommunications, to reconnect to a process broken off because of communication problems.

CONNECT cannot be used unless the system manager has enabled the virtual terminal feature.

Command Qualifiers

/CONTINUE
/NOCONTINUE (default)

Determines whether the **CONTINUE** command is executed as part of the current process before a new connection is made to another process, allowing an interrupted image to continue processing. This command is not compatible with the **/LOGOUT** command qualifier.

/LOGOUT (default)
/NOLOGOUT

Determines whether the current process is logged out when a new connection is made to another process using a virtual terminal. The **/LOGOUT** qualifier is required if you issue a **CONNECT** command from a process not connected to a virtual terminal. This command is not compatible with the **/CONTINUE** command qualifier.

CONTINUE

CONTINUE
C

Resumes the execution of a command, program, or command procedure that has been interrupted by a Ctrl-Y or Ctrl-C key combination.

COPY

COPY input-file-spec output-file-spec
COPY input-file-spec[,...] output-file-spec

Copies the contents of one file to another.

The **input-file-spec** represents the names of one or more source files to be copied. If you list more than one input file, separate them with commas or plus signs. Wildcard characters can be used as part of the file specifications (see Chapter 4). The **output-file-spec** represents the name of the output file to which the input files will be copied. Wildcard characters can be used here as well.

If more than one file is included as an input file, the system will copy all of the files into a single output file, starting with the first file listed as an input and appending other files to the end. The longest file should be listed first in the input file specification list.

If no version numbers are included in the file specifications, the **COPY** command will assign a version number to output files—either the version number of the input file or a version number one greater than the highest version number of an existing file with the same filename and file specification.

Command Qualifiers

/BACKUP

Selects files for a **COPY** command on the basis of their most recent backup. This qualifier is used in conjunction with the **/BEFORE** or **/SINCE** qualifier. It is incompatible with the **/CREATED**, **/EXPIRED**, or **/MODIFIED** command qualifiers.

/BEFORE[= time]
/SINCE[= time]

Select only those files dated before or since the time specified in the command qualifier. The time can be a date, in the form of **06-JUL**, or it can be one of the keywords **TODAY**, **TOMORROW**, and **YESTERDAY**. If no time is specified in the command, DCL assumes **TODAY**.

/CONCATENATE (default)
/NOCONCATENATE

Determine whether a single output file is to be created from multiple input files included in a **COPY** command when a wildcard character is used in any field of the output file specification. When files are concatenated from most current VAX/VMS systems (Files-11 Structure Level 2), the files are placed in alphanumeric order in the output file. Files coming from older, Files-11 Structure Level 1 disks result in an output file with files in random order. In either case, if you use a wildcard character in the file version field, files are copied in descending order of version number.

/CONFIRM
/NOCONFIRM (default)

Tell the system whether to query the user before each COPY operation is performed. Proper responses are shown in Figure 10.1 on page 161.

/CREATED (default)

Instructs the system to select files based on their dates of creation. This command qualifier is used in conjunction with the **/BEFORE** or **/SINCE** qualifier. It is not compatible with the **/BACKUP**, **/EXPIRED**, or **/MODIFIED** command qualifiers.

/EXPIRED

Instructs the system to select files based on their expiration dates. This command qualifier is used in conjunction with the **/BEFORE** or **/SINCE** qualifier. It is not compatible with the **/BACKUP**, **/CREATED**, or **/MODIFIED** command qualifiers. **/CREATED** is the default specification for **COPY** commands.

/LOG
/NOLOG (default)

Determine whether the system will display on screen the file specifications of each file as they are copied. When the **/LOG** qualifier is enabled, the following information is shown:

- The file specifications of the input and output files.
- The number of blocks or number of records copied.
- The total number of new files created.

/MODIFIED

Instructs the system to select files based on their date of last modification. This command qualifier is used in conjunction with the **/BEFORE** or **/SINCE** qualifier. It is not compatible with the **/BACKUP**, **/CREATED**, or **/EXPIRED** command qualifiers. **/CREATED** is the default specification for **COPY** commands.

/PROTECTION = (code)

Determines a level of protection to be applied to the output file.

/REPLACE
/NOREPLACE (default)

If a file already exists with the same file specification as the specified output file, these instructions tell the system whether to delete the existing file and replace it with the new file. If the **/REPLACE** command qualifier is not specified, the system will create a new file of the same name with a version number one higher.

/SINCE[= time]

See **/BEFORE**.

CREATE

CREATE file-spec[,...]

Creates one or several sequential disk files. The contents of the file consist of whatever you input after the command line. When the file contains the necessary information, use the Ctrl-Z key combination to close the file.

If more than one file is specified, the system will accept data for the first output file until it receives a Ctrl-Z command, then open the second file, and so on.

Command Qualifiers

/LOG
/NOLOG (default)

Determine whether the system will display on the screen the file specifications of each file that has been created.

/PROTECTION = (code)

Determines the level of protection to be assigned to the new file. If no protection level is specified, the system will use the current default protection level.

CREATE/DIRECTORY

CREATE/DIRECTORY directory-spec[,...]

Creates a directory or subdirectory, part of a structure for cataloging files in a logical organization. Several subdirectories can be created at once within the same **CREATE/DIRECTORY** command.

The creation of a first-level directory for each user is generally reserved to the system operator.

Command Qualifiers

/LOG
/NOLOG (default)

Determine whether the system displays the directory specification of each directory after creating it.

/PROTECTION = (code)

Determines the level of protection to be assigned to the new directory. If no protection level is specified, the system will use the protection level in effect for the next–higher-level directory.

/VERSION_LIMIT = n

States that no more than a particular number (**n**) versions of each file created in the new directory are to be kept. Whenever the directory reaches the limit, the lowest-numbered version is erased before any new versions are created.

If the user changes the version limit setting after a directory has been created, the new limit will apply only to files created after that time; older files will have whatever version limit was in effect at the time they were created.

DEFINE

DEFINE logical-name equivalence-name[,...]

Creates a logical name and assigns an equivalence string, or a list of strings, to that name. Similar to the **ASSIGN** command except in syntax.

The **logical-name** is the name to be created. It can have from 1 to 255 characters. If it contains anything other than alphanumeric characters, the dollar sign, or the underscore character, the string should be enclosed in quote marks. If a colon is specified at the end of a logical name, the colon is saved as part of the logical name.

The **equivalence-name[,...]** is the source string that is to be assigned to the new logical name. The equivalence name can be from 1 to 255 characters in length. If it contains anything other than alphanumeric characters, the dollar sign, or the underscore character, the string should be enclosed in quote marks. If the equivalence string includes a file specification, include the punctuation marks (colon, brackets, or periods) that would ordinarily be used.

To delete a logical name from a table, use the **DEASSIGN** command.

Here is an example of use of **DEFINE:**

$DEFINE BLUECOST
        DUMMY:[SALES_FIG]BLUEFISH_COST   <Return>

$PRINT BLUECOST   <Return>

In this instance, the system is told to equate the logical name BLUECOST with a particular file on a particular disk in a specified directory. When the print command is issued using the logical name, the system will search out the file on the basis of the equivalence name.

Logical names can be assigned to files, devices, and commands.

DEFINE/KEY

DEFINE/KEY keyname equivalence-string

Allows redefinition of function and special-purpose keys on the keyboard for the particular needs of the user. Note that there is an equivalent facility within the MAIL program.

The **keyname** is the name of the key to be redefined. The **equivalence-string** is the command to be assigned to that key.

The following keys are available for redefinition as indicated:

Keyname	LK201 (VT220, VT300)	VT100	VT52
PF1	PF1	PF1	blue key
PF2	PF2	PF2	red key
PF3	PF3	PF3	gray key
PF4	PF4	PF4	n/a
KP0–KP9	Keypad 0–9	Keypad 0–9	Keypad 0–9
PERIOD	Period key	Period key	Period key
COMMA	Comma key	Comma key	n/a
MINUS	Minus key	Minus key	n/a
ENTER	Enter key	Enter key	Enter key
LEFT	Left arrow	Left arrow	Left arrow
RIGHT	Right arrow	Right arrow	Right arrow
Find (E1)	Find key	n/a	n/a
Insert Here (E2)	Insert key	n/a	n/a
Remove (E3)	Remove key	n/a	n/a
Select (E4)	Select key	n/a	n/a
Prev Screen (E5)	Previous screen	n/a	n/a
Next Screen (E6)	Next screen	n/a	n/a
HELP (F15)	Help (F15)	n/a	n/a
Do (F16)	Do (F16)	n/a	n/a
Function keys F6–F14; F17–F20	Function keys	n/a	n/a

Note that you cannot redefine function Keys 1 through 5. Not all of the above keys are available for redefinition at all times.

You must issue **SET TERMINAL/APPLICATION** or **SET TERMINAL/NONUMERIC** in order to use KP0 through KP9, PERIOD, COMMA, or MINUS.

Some keys are ordinarily reserved for command line editing. You must issue **SET TERMINAL/NOLINE_EDITING** in order to redefine LEFT, RIGHT, or F6–F14. You can also use the Ctrl-V command to enable F7 through F14. (The arrow keys and F6 are not affected by Ctrl-V.)

For example, to redefine the PF3 function key to issue the **DIRECTORY** command, enter the following command line:

DEFINE/KEY PF3 "DIRECTORY" <Return>

Command Qualifiers

/TERMINATE
/NOTERMINATE (default)

Tell the computer whether to immediately execute the command associated with a particular key. This is an equivalent to pressing the special key and then hitting the return key to call for execution. Here is an example:

DEFINE/KEY PERIOD
 "DIRECTORY"/TERMINATE <Return>

/ECHO (default)
/NOECHO

Turn on or off the display of a command when a special key is struck:

DEFINE/KEY COMMA "FORWARD"/NOECHO <Return>

States of Key Definitions: You can have an unlimited number of key redefinitions if you subdivide your new choices into *states* for various purposes. For example, you could have a keypad redefinition for use during an editing session while retaining a basic DCL command set and an advanced editing set.

Command Qualifiers

/IF_STATE = state_list

Specifies a list of states, one of which must be **SET** to enable use of a redefined key. If this qualifier is not used, the current state is assumed.

/NOIF_STATE

Tells the system to utilize the current state definitions.

/LOCK_STATE
/NOLOCK_STATE (default)

/LOCK_STATE makes the default state the state specified by the most recent **/SET_STATE** qualifier, until a new state is specified.

/SET_STATE = state
/NOSET_STATE (default)

/SET_STATE associates a state with the key being defined. **/NOSET_STATE**, or the omission of a **/SET_STATE** command qualifier, causes the current state to remain in effect.

Here are some examples of the use of **STATE** commands:

DEFINE/KEY F17 "SET" /SET STATE = ADVANCED_EDIT   <Return>

will cause the F17 function key on the LK201 keyboard to issue a **SET** command and change the current state to ADVANCED_EDIT. This command, followed by

DEFINE/KEY F18 "DIR *.W20" /TERMINATE /IF_STATE = ADVANCED_EDIT   <Return>

will result in the following sequence: If the F17 key is pressed, followed by the F18 key, VMS will immediately use the ADVANCED_EDIT redefinition of the F18 key, which is a call for a directory of files with the .W20 file specification.

Keypad reassignments made during a VMS session will not be retained by the computer when you exit from the system. In order to retain these redefinitions, you must create a file in your top-level (root) directory with the definitions and then add a pointer to that file in your LOGIN.COM command file, or make them a permanent part of your LOGIN.COM file.

To add them to the LOGIN.COM file, use EDT to load and edit the file, and add definitions in this form:

$DEFINE/KEY PF1 "MAIL"	<Return>
$DEFINE/KEY PF3 "SHOW USERS"	<Return>
$DEFINE/KEY PERIOD "DIRECTORY"	<Return>
$DEFINE/KEY COMMA "DIRECTORY *.W20"	<Return>

and so on.

Finally, it is valuable to know about one command that will display the current state of any keyboard definitions, as well as other qualifiers, including terminate, echo, and state.

$SHOW KEY [keyname] <Return>

will tell you the definition given to a particular key.

$SHOW KEY/ALL <Return>

$SHOW KEY/ALL/STATE = (state,state,.....) <Return>

will yield a full list of all key definitions in the default state, or if a state or states are specified, the definitions of those states. Note that if states are specified, they are listed within parentheses and are separated by commas.

Here is an example of a **SHOW KEY/ALL** request:

$SHOW KEY/ALL <Return>
DEFAULT keypad definitions:
F18 = "DIRECTORY"
F19 = "CALENDAR"
F20 = "DSCALC"
6-AUG-1987 08:11:09

To display only key definitions, leaving out other qualifiers, use

$SHOW KEY/BRIEF <Return>

To see the names of all states for which keys have been identified, use

$SHOW KEY/DIRECTORY <Return>

DELETE

DELETE file-spec[,...]

Deletes one or more specified files from storage.

The **file-spec** is the name of the file to be deleted. If a disk volume and/or directory is specified, the system will go to that location to delete a file. If no special instructions are included, the system will assume the file to be deleted is located on the default volume and directory. Wildcard characters can be used in any field of the command.

Here are some examples of use:

$DELETE BLUECOST.W20;7   <Return>

deletes the specific file BLUECOST.W20 with the specific version number of 7. If other versions of the file are on the volume, they will not be removed.

$DELETE BLUECOST.W20;*   <Return>

will delete all versions of that BLUECOST.W20.

$DELETE BLUECOST.*;*   <Return>

or

$DELETE BLUECOST..   <Return>

will remove all versions of all files that have the name BLUE-COST and any file specification.

Command Qualifiers

/BACKUP

Selects files for a **DELETE** command on the basis of their most recent backup. This qualifier is used in conjunction with the **/BEFORE** or **/SINCE** qualifier. It is incompatible with the **/CREATED**, **/EXPIRED**, or **/MODIFIED** command qualifiers. **/CREATED** is the default.

/BEFORE[= time]
/SINCE[= time]

Select only those files dated before or since the time specified in the command qualifier. The time can be a date, in the form of **06-JUL**, or it can be one of the keywords **TODAY**, **TOMORROW**, and **YESTERDAY**. If no time is specified in the command, DCL assumes **TODAY**.

/CONFIRM
/NOCONFIRM (default)

Tell the system whether to query the user before each **DELETE** operation is performed. Proper responses are shown in Figure 10-1 on page 161.

Here is an example of use of the **DELETE/CONFIRM** command:

$DELETE LEN.LOG.*/CONFIRM   <Return>
$DISK1:[SANDLER]LEN.LOG;2, delete? [N]:**y**

The **y** response will cause the file to be deleted.

/CREATED (default)

Instructs the system to select files based on their dates of creation. This command qualifier is used in conjunction with the **/BEFORE** or **/SINCE** qualifier. It is not compatible with the **/BACKUP**, **/EXPIRED**, or **/MODIFIED** qualifiers.

/ERASE
/NOERASE (default)

ERASE instructs the system to write over the space formerly occupied by a deleted file with a special pattern. Ordinarily, a deleted file is not actually erased but is returned to the system and made available as a storage place for later files. If no new files are created or old files updated, then deleted files remain unchanged on the disk. The /ERASE command, then, is a means of ensuring the security of DELETED files.

/EXPIRED

Instructs the system to select files based on their expiration dates. It is used in conjunction with the **/BEFORE** or **/SINCE** qualifier. It is not compatible with the **/BACKUP**, **/CREATED**, or **/MODIFIED** qualifiers. **/CREATED** is the default specification.

/LOG
/NOLOG (default)

Determine whether the system will display on screen the file specifications of each file as it is deleted.

/MODIFIED

Instructs the system to select files based on their date of last modification. It is used in conjunction with the **/BEFORE** or **/SINCE** qualifier. It is not compatible with the **/BACKUP**, **/CREATED**, or **/EXPIRED** qualifiers. **/CREATED** is the default specification.

/SINCE[=time]

See **/BEFORE**.

DELETE/KEY

DELETE/KEY [keyname]

Deletes key redefinitions that have been put into effect by a **DEFINE/KEY** command.

The **keyname** is the name of the key whose definition is to be removed.

Command Qualifiers

/ALL

Instructs the system to remove all key redefinitions in the specified state. If no state is specified, all key redefinitions in the current state are removed.

/LOG (default)
/NOLOG

Determine whether the system displays on-screen messages indicating that the specified key redefinitions have been removed.

/STATE = (statename[,...])
/NOSTATE (default)

Instruct the system whether to apply the **DELETE/KEY** command to a specific state or states.

DELETE/SYMBOL

DELETE/SYMBOL [symbol-name]

Removes a symbol definition from the local or global symbol table, or removes all symbol definitions from the specified table.

Command Qualifiers

/ALL

Instructs the system to remove all key redefinitions in the specified symbol table. If **/LOCAL** or **/GLOBAL** is not specified, all symbols defined at the current command level are removed.

/GLOBAL

Instructs the system to delete the specified symbol name from the global symbol table of the current process.

/LOCAL (default)

Instructs the system to delete the specified symbol name from the local symbol table of the current process.

/LOG (default)
/NOLOG

Determine whether the system displays on-screen messages indicating that the specified symbol definitions have been removed.

DIRECTORY

DIRECTORY [file-spec[,...]]

Produces a list of files matching the file specification included in the command.

The **file-spec[,...]** identifies to the system the files to be listed. Wildcard characters can be used in constructing any field of a DIRECTORY command. If no file specification is included in the command, the system will provide a list of all files in the current default directory. If a filename, file type, or version number is included in the command, files that match that description will be listed. If you choose to specify more than one file, separate the file specifications with commas or plus signs.

Here are some examples of use of the basic **DIRECTORY** command:

$DIRECTORY <Return>

will yield a list of all files in the current default directory.

$DIRECTORY *.W20 <Return>

will yield a list of all files with the .W20 file type, in any version number, in the current default directory.

$DIRECTORY *.*;7 <Return>

will list only those files—with any filename or file type—that have a version number of 7.

$DIRECTORY BLUECOST.W20,FISHHEADS.* <Return>

will list all versions of the file named BLUECOST with the file type of .W20 and all files with the file name FISHHEADS with any file type.

Command Qualifiers

/ACL

Determines whether the Access Control List (ACL) for each file is displayed as part of the directory.

/BACKUP

Selects files for a **DIRECTORY** listing on the basis of their most recent backup. This qualifier is used in conjunction with the **/BEFORE** or **/SINCE** qualifier. It is incompatible with the **/CREATED**, **/EXPIRED**, or **/MODIFIED** qualifiers. **/CREATED** is the default.

/BEFORE[=time]
/SINCE[=time]

Select only those files dated before or since the time specified in the command qualifier. The time can be a date, in the form of **06-JUL**, or it can be one of the keywords **TODAY**, **TOMORROW**, and **YESTERDAY**. If no time is specified in the command, DCL assumes **TODAY**.

/BRIEF (default)

Calls for a directory listing only the filename, file type, and version number of each file. Files are in alphabetical order, from left to right on each line, in descending order of version number. The **/BRIEF** qualifier is overridden when one of the following qualifiers is used: **/ACL, /DATE, /FILE-ID, /FULL, /NOHEADING, /OWNER, /PROTECTION, /SECURITY,** or **/SIZE**.

/COLUMNS=n

Instructs the system on the construction of the directory. By default, the number of columns on each line of the display is four; with this command qualifier, the number can be set.

The number of columns that can be displayed is controlled by the **/WIDTH** setting and the amount of information requested to be displayed on screen. The system will automatically adjust the number of columns, regardless of the **/COLUMNS** specification, if there is not sufficient room for the requested number.

The **/COLUMNS** qualifier is not available for use when the **/ACL** or **/FULL** command qualifier has been specified.

/CREATED (default)

Instructs the system to select files based on their dates of creation. This command qualifier is used in conjunction with the **/BEFORE** or **/SINCE** qualifier. It is not compatible with the **/BACKUP**, **/EXPIRED**, or **/MODIFIED** command qualifiers.

/DATE[= option]
/NODATE

Instruct the system whether to include date information about a file in the directory. The following options are available:

> **ALL** lists all four date types—CREATED, MODIFIED, EXPIRED, and BACKUP.
> **BACKUP** lists the date of the last backup for each file.
> **CREATED** lists the date of creation of each file.
> **EXPIRED** lists the expiration date of each file.
> **MODIFIED** lists the date a file has last been modified.

If no instructions are given with a **/DATE** command qualifier, the system will provide **CREATED** information in the directory.
Here are some examples of use of the **DIRECTORY/DATE = option**:

$DIRECTORY *.W20/DATE = ALL   <Return>

Directory $DISK1:[SANDLER]

```
1987BUD-APP1.W20;1    14-NOV-1986 10:03 15-JUL-1987
                 10:57 <None specified> 29-JUL-1987 13:08
1987BUD1.W20;3         6-NOV-1986 18:51 6-NOV-1986
                 18:51 <None specified> 29-JUL-1987 13:08
1988EDITCAL.W20;7     30-JUL-1987 17:03 30-JUL-1987
                 17:03 <None specified> <No backup done>
```

Total of 3 files.

$DIRECTORY S*.W20/DATE = MODIFIED   <Return>

Directory $DISK1:[SANDLER]

```
SAL.W20;7       23-MAR-1987 14:15
SAL2.W20;2      15-JUL-1987 10:56
SAL3.W20;2      20-APR-1987 10:14
```

Total of 3 files.

/EXPIRED

Instructs the system to select files based on their expiration dates. This qualifier is used in conjunction with the **/BEFORE** or **/SINCE** qualifier. It is not compatible with the **/BACKUP**, **/CREATED**, or **/MODIFIED** qualifiers. **/CREATED** is the default specification.

/FILE_ID

Determines whether the file identification of each file is displayed in the directory. The default is no display, except as part of a **/FULL** directory.

/FULL

Yields a directory of specified files with the following information:

> Filename
> File type
> Version number
> Number of blocks used
> Number of blocks allocated
> Date of creation
> Date of last backup
> Date last modified
> Date of expiration
> File owner's UIC
> File protection
> File identification number
> File organization
> Other file attributes
> Record attributes
> Record format
> Access Control List

Here is an example of a **DIRECTORY/FULL** command, in this case examining a specific file:

$DIR TESSA.PRICES/FULL   <Return>

Directory $DISK1:[SANDLER]

TESSA.PRICES;2   File ID: (14133,3,0)
Size: 21/21   Owner: [BOSS,SANDLER]
Created: 29-JUL-1987 16:41   Revised: 09-AUG-1987 16:41 (2)
Expires: <None specified>   Backup: <No backup done>
File organization: Sequential
File attributes: Allocation: 21,   Extend: 0, Global
   Global buffer count: 0
                       No version limit
Record format: Variable length, maximum 53 bytes
Record attributes: Carriage return carriage control
Journaling enabled: None
File protection: System:RWED, Owner:RWED, Group:RE, World:
Access Cntrl List: None

Total of 1 file, 21/21 blocks.
   26-AUG-1987 08:12:01

/MODIFIED

Instructs the system to select files based on their date of last modification. It is used in conjunction with the **/BEFORE** or **/SINCE** qualifier. It is not compatible with the **/BACKUP**, **/CREATED**, or **/EXPIRED** qualifiers. **/CREATED** is the default specification.

/OUTPUT[=file-spec]
/NOOUTPUT

/OUTPUT determines where the output of the **DIRECTORY** command will be sent. If this command qualifier is not used, the output is sent to the current process default output stream or device. If a file specification is included, a file will be created and the output of the **DIRECTORY** command will be channeled into that file. The ordinary filename and specification for such a listing is **DIRECTORY.LIS**. This command is useful if you want to produce a hard (printed) copy of your directory or if you want to send another user a copy of your directory.

/OWNER
/NOOWNER (default)

Determine whether the file owner's UIC is listed in the directory.

/PRINTER

Sets the **DIRECTORY** output for printing. If it is used in conjunction with the **/OUTPUT** command, the job is sent under the name used with that command. If it is used by itself, the **/PRINTER** command qualifier creates a file called DIRECTORY.LIS, sends that file to the default printer queue for printing, and then deletes the file after the job is completed.

/PROTECTION
/NOPROTECTION (default)

Determine whether the file protection level for each file is listed in the directory.

/SECURITY

Determines whether file security attributes are listed in the directory. Use of this command qualifier yields the same information as if the **/ACL**, **/OWNER**, and **/PROTECTION** command qualifiers were individually specified.

/SELECT = (keyword[,...])

Instructs the system to select files for listing in a directory on the basis of **/SELECT** keywords, as follows:

/SELECT = SIZE = MAXIMUM = n lists only files that take up fewer blocks than the specified **n** parameter.

/SELECT = SIZE = MINIMUM = n lists only files that take up more blocks than the specified **n** parameter.

/SELECT = SIZE = (MAXIMUM = n,MINIMUM = n) sets up a range for files with block sizes between the minimum and maximum parameters specified.

/SINCE[= time]
/SIZE[= option]
/NOSIZE (default)

Instruct the system whether to list the file size in blocks used or allocated for each file. If **/SIZE** is specified without an option, the listing provides the file size in blocks used.

The following options are available:

ALL lists file size in blocks used and blocks allocated.
ALLOCATION lists file size in blocks allocated.
USED lists file size in blocks used.

/VERSIONS = n

Determines whether the latest **n** versions of files are listed in the directory. If the **/VERSIONS** command qualifier is not used, the directory will list all versions of files.

/WIDTH = (keyword[,...])

Allows the format of the directory to be altered according to four options: filename field width, entire display width, owner field width, and file size field width:

DISPLAY = n sets the total width for the DIRECTORY display, in the range of 1 to 255. The default value is 0, which instructs the system to set the display width to the terminal width. If the total width of the display is wider than the terminal width, information is truncated.

FILENAME = n sets the width of the filename field. The default value of **n** is 19. Filenames that exceed the **n** value will wrap to the next line.

OWNER = n sets the width of the owner field. The default value of **n** is 20. If the UIC of the owner exceeds the value of **n**, the information is truncated.

SIZE=n sets the width of the file size field. The default value of **n** is 6. If the file size exceeds the value of **n**, the information will be truncated.

DISCONNECT

DISCONNECT   <Return>

Disconnects a physical terminal from a virtual terminal connected to a process. After the disconnection, both the virtual terminal and its process remain on the system. (To terminate a process, use the **LOGOUT** command.)
   DISCONNECT is used in conjunction with the **CONNECT** command.

Command Qualifiers

/CONTINUE
/NOCONTINUE (default)

Determine whether the **CONTINUE** command is executed in the current process immediately before connection to another process. Doing so permits an interrupted image to continue processing even after the user has connected to another process.

EDIT/EDT

EDIT file-spec

Invokes the EDT text editor. The **/EDT** qualifier is not needed when the EDT text editor is the default editor.
   The **file-spec** is the name of the file to be created or edited. If the file does not exist, the EDT program will create it.
   For full details on using the EDT editor, consult the VAX EDT Reference Manual.

Command Qualifiers

/CREATE (default)
/NOCREATE

If you specify a filename to EDT for editing, it will ordinarily retrieve a file by that name if it can find such a file; otherwise it will create a new file. If the **/NOCREATE** qualifier is used, EDT will reject a call to edit a file it cannot locate.

/JOURNAL[=journal-file]
/NOJOURNAL

Control the creation of a journal file during an EDT session. The journal file captures all activity in an editing session until a file is closed; its value comes if it is necessary to recover a file damaged by a system crash or other unusual event.

A journal file is ordinarily created for all editing sessions. **/NOJOURNAL** will prevent EDT from keeping a record of an editing session.

The **/JOURNAL[=journal-file]** allows the user to select the name of the journal file. Ordinarily, the journal file has the same filename as the edit file, adding .JOU as file type.

For example,

$EDIT/JOURNAL=LIFESAVER TEST.TXT   <Return>

will open EDT for a file called TEST.TXT and create a journal file called LIFESAVER. Because no file type was included in the instruction, the default file type of .JOU will be used as the extension.

$EDIT/NOJOURNAL TEST.TXT   <Return>

will open the TEST.TXT file but suppress creation of a journal file.

/READ_ONLY file-spec
/NOREAD_ONLY (default)

To limit the user from making any changes to a text file while allowing access, use the **/READ_ONLY** qualifier. No journal or output file is created. The default, **/NOREAD_ONLY**, is the ordinary editing state for EDT.

/RECOVER file-spec
/NORECOVER (default)

Use **/RECOVER** so that the EDT program can use a journal file as the input file for editing, processing commands in that file and reconstructing an edited text file.

Here is an example of use:

$EDIT/RECOVER PRICES.TXT <Return>

If the journal filename was changed from the default name, the user must add a **/JOURNAL=filename** qualifier, followed by the original EDT text filename, as in

**$EDIT/RECOVER/JOURNAL=LIFESAVER.JOU
                    PRICES.TXT** <Return>

EDIT/TECO

EDIT/TECO [file-spec]

Invokes the TECO interactive text editor. Since EDT is the default editor under VMS, the **/TECO** qualifier is required.

The **file-spec** is the name of the file to be created or edited. If the file does not exist, the EDT program will create it.

For full details on using the TECO, consult the PDP-11 TECO Editor Reference Manual.

Command Qualifiers

/COMMAND[=file-spec]
/NOCOMMAND

Instruct the system whether to use a startup command file with TECO. If no **/COMMAND** qualifier is used, TECO looks for the TEC$INIT logical name assignment; if there is no such definition, no startup commands are executed. Use of the **/NOCOMMAND** qualifier blocks TECO from using a startup command file, even if one exists.

/CREATE (default)
/NOCREATE

If you specify a filename to TECO for editing, it will ordinarily retrieve a file by that name if it can find such a file; otherwise it will create a new file. If the **/NOCREATE** qualifier is used, TECO will reject a call to edit a file it cannot locate.

/EXECUTE = command-file [argument]

Instructs the system to invoke TECO and call a TECO macro.

/MEMORY (default)
/NOMEMORY

If the file specification is omitted in the **EDIT/TECO** command, the program will call up for editing the last file edited with TECO. That file is identified by the logical name TEC$MEMORY. The use of the **/NOMEMORY** command qualifier turns off this feature.

/READ_ONLY
/NOREAD_ONLY (default)

To keep the user from making any changes to a text file while that user has access, use the /READ_ONLY qualifier. No output file is created. The default, /NOREAD_ONLY is the ordinary editing state for TECO.

EDIT/TPU

EDIT/TPU [file-spec]

Invokes the VAX Text Processing Utility. The default interface for VAXTPU is the Extensible VAX Editor (EVE). To use VAXTPU with the EDT Keypad Emulator interface, it is necessary to issue a new logical definition, as follows:

$DEFINE TPUSECINI EDTSECINI <Return>

The **file-spec** identifies the file to be created or edited under VAXTPU. If the file does not exist, TPU creates a buffer for the file.

For details on using the VAXTPU editor, consult the VAX Text Processing Utility Reference Manual.

Command Qualifiers

/COMMAND[= file-spec]
/NOCOMMAND

Instruct the system whether to use a user-written command file at the initialization of VAXTPU. If no **/COMMAND** qualifier is used, TPU looks for the TPUINI.TPU file in the default directory. Use of the **/NOCOMMAND** qualifier blocks TPU from using a startup command file, even if one exists.

/CREATE (default)
/NOCREATE

If you specify a filename to TPU for editing, it will ordinarily retrieve a file by that name if it can find such a file; otherwise it will create a new file. If the **/NOCREATE** command qualifier is used, TPU will reject a call to edit a file it cannot locate.

/JOURNAL[= journal-file] (default)
/NOJOURNAL

Control the creation of a journal file during a TPU session. The journal file captures all activity in an editing session until a file is closed; its value comes if it is necessary to recover a file damaged by a system crash or other unusual event.

A journal file is ordinarily created for all editing sessions. **/NOJOURNAL** will prevent EDT from keeping a record of an editing session.

The **/JOURNAL[= journal-file]** allows the user to select the name of the journal file. Ordinarily, the journal file has the same filename as the edit file, adding .TJL as file type. (See **EDIT/JOURNAL** for further details.)

/READ_ONLY file-spec
/NOREAD_ONLY (default)

To keep the user from making any changes to a text file while allowing access, use the **/READ_ONLY** qualifier. No journal or output file is created. The default, **/NOREAD_ONLY**, is the ordinary editing state for TPU.

/RECOVER file-spec
/NORECOVER (default)

The TPU program can use a journal file as the input file for editing, processing commands in that file and reconstructing an edited text file.

EXIT

EXIT

Ends the processing of the current command procedure, or if a command procedure is not being executed, the **EXIT** command will end the current image.

F$

See Lexical Functions.

GOSUB

GOSUB label

Part of a command procedure, **GOSUB** transfers control to a labeled subroutine. The **label** is a title of 1 to 255 alphanumeric characters appearing as the first item on a command line.

GOTO

GOTO label

Part of a command procedure, **GOTO** transfers control to a labeled statement. The **label** is a title of 1 to 255 alphanumeric characters appearing as the first item on a command line.

HELP

HELP [keyword...]

Provides access to the library of Help screens and definitions that are part of the VMS system.

The **keyword** is the name of the topic or subtopic about which the user seeks information. If an ellipsis (three periods) is used after a primary keyword, Help will display information about the keyword and then list available information one level below in subtopics.

Information within HELP is arranged in hierarchical levels on the basis of keywords:

- No keyword—Help will explain the **HELP** command and list the topics that are available in the root or top-level library.
- Topic-name—If the **HELP** command includes a topic, Help will provide information on the topic from the root directory or other library. The screen will also list keywords for additional information on this topic.
- Topic-name subtopic—If the **HELP** command includes a topic and subtopic, Help will go directly to the definition of the subtopic.
- @file-spec, @file-spec with topic-name, or @file-spec with topic-name and subtopic—If the **HELP** command includes a nonstandard Help library, the system will seek a definition from that new library.

If an asterisk is used in place of any keyword, Help will display all information available at the level indicated. For example,

$HELP MAIL *   <Return>

will yield a list of subtopics available under the topic MAIL.

To exit from a standard Help session, use a Ctrl-Z key combination or hit the Return key until the program finishes with its prompts for further queries and returns you to the DCL command level.

Command Qualifiers

/INSTRUCTIONS (default)
/NOINSTRUCTIONS

Determine whether Help gives instructions on how to use the Help program as well as the list of available topics. If the **/NOINSTRUCTIONS** qualifier is used, the program will only list the topics available.

/LIBLIST (default)
/NOLIBLIST

Determine whether a list of additional HELP libraries is included in the topic level list.

/LIBRARY = file-spec
/NOLIBRARY

Determine whether an alternate Help library is used. **/NOLIBRARY** is used to block use of the alternate library if it exists.

/PAGE (default)
/NOPAGE

Determine whether the screen display will stop after each full page of information is shown. If the **/NOPAGE** qualifier is used, output to the screen will continue until the file reaches the end.

/PROMPT (default)
/NOPROMPT

Determine the handling of additional **HELP** requests. If the **/NOPROMPT** qualifier is specified, Help returns the user to the DCL command level after it has responded to a single query. Help could then be requested again.

If the default **/PROMPT** is in effect, the Help program will ask if further information is sought on a topic or subtopic.

IF

IF expression THEN [$] command

Part of a command or a command procedure, **IF** tests the value of an expression and executes the command following the **THEN** keyword only if the result of the test is true or positive.

The **expression** is the test to be performed. The **command** is the action to follow if the expression is valued as true. **[$]** is used if the procedure is testing the value of a reserved global symbol that the system recognizes by the inclusion of a $ as its first character.

The **IF** command considers an expression to be true if the result of a test has an odd integer value; has a character string value that begins with Y or y (for *yes*), or T or t (for *true*); or has an odd numeric string value. The **IF** command considers an expression to be false if the result of a test has an even integer value; has a character string value that begins with any letter except Y, y, T, or t; or has an even numeric string value.

If the expression is evaluated as false, the **THEN** command is not executed and the procedure continues to the next command line.

INQUIRE

INQUIRE symbol-name [prompt-string]

Part of a command procedure, **INQUIRE** instructs the system to request from the user a value for a local or global symbol.

The **symbol-name** is a symbol consisting of 1 to 255 alphanumeric characters. The **prompt-string** is the prompt that will be displayed on the terminal where the **INQUIRE** command is executed. If no prompt string is specified, the command interpreter will display the symbol name as a prompt for a value.

Command Qualifiers

/GLOBAL

Instructs the system to place the symbol in the global symbol table. If **/GLOBAL** is not included in the command, the symbol is placed in the local symbol table.

/LOCAL (default)

Instructs the system to place the symbol in the local symbol table for the current command procedure.

Lexical Functions

F$function-name([arguments,...])

Used as part of a command procedure, a lexical function returns information about character strings and attributes of the current process. Lexical functions can substitute in any situation in which symbols or expressions are ordinarily used. As part of a command procedure, lexical functions can be used to translate logical names, manipulate character strings, or determine the current processing mode of a procedure.

F$ tells the system that the string that follows is a lexical function. The **function-name** specifies the name of the functions to be evaluated. The **arguments** must be enclosed within parentheses.

Function	Description
F$CVSI	Extracts bit fields from character string data and converts the result to a signed integer.
F$CVTIME	Retrieves information about an absolute, combination, or delta time string.
F$CVUI	Extracts bit fields from character string data and converts the result to an unsigned integer.
F$DIRECTORY	Returns the current default directory string.
F$EDIT	Edits a character string based on specified edits.
F$ELEMENT	Extracts an element from a string when the elements are separated by a specified delimiter character.
F$ENVIRONMENT	Obtains information about the DCL command environment.
F$EXTRACT	Extracts a substring from a character string expression.
F$FAO	Invokes the $FAO system service, which converts the specified control string to a formatted ASCII output string.
F$FILE_ATTRIBUTES	Returns information about the attributes of the specified file.
F$GETDVI	Invokes the $GETDVI system service to obtain the specified item of information about a specified device.

Function	Description
F$GETJPI	Invokes the $GETJPI system service to return accounting, status, and identification information about a process.
F$GETSYI	Invokes the $GETSYI system service to return status and identification information about the local system, or about a node in the local cluster, if a cluster is in use.
F$IDENTIFIER	Converts an identifier in named format to its integer equivalent, or an integer to its identifier equivalent.
F$INTEGER	Returns the integer equivalent of the expression specified in the command.
F$LENGTH	Returns the length of a specified string.
F$LOCATE	Locates a character or substring of characters within a string and returns its offset value.
F$LOGICAL	Translates a logical name and returns its equivalence name string.
F$MESSAGE	Returns the message text associated with the specified system status code.
F$MODE	Shows the mode in which the process is executing.
F$PARSE	Invokes the $PARSE service in RMS (Record Mangement Services, facilities for file management) to parse a file specification. Returns either the expanded file specification or the file specification field requested in the command.
F$PID	Returns the next process identification number.
F$PRIVILEGE	Answers TRUE or FALSE depending on whether the current process privileges match the privileges listed in the argument.
F$PROCESS	Returns the current process name string.
F$SEARCH	Invokes the $SEARCH service of RMS to search for a directory file. The full file specification is returned.

Function	Description
F$SETPRV	Sets the specified privileges and returns a list of keywords identifying the previous state of these privileges for the current process.
F$STRING	Returns the string equivalent of the result of the expression specified in the command.
F$TIME	Returns the current date and time, in the format dd—mm-yy hh:mm:ss.cc.
F$TRNLNM	Translates a logical name. Returns either the equivalence name string or the requested attributes of the logical name.
F$TYPE	Determines the data type of a symbol.
F$USER	Returns the current user identification code.
F$VERIFY	Examines the current command procedure verification state. Returns the integer 2 if command procedure verification is set on; returns the integer 0 if verification is set off. The function can also be used to set new verification states.

Login

(Ctrl-C)
(Ctrl-Y)
(Return)

Initiates an interactive terminal session, signaling to the system the user's need to access the system. Login can begin with any of three inputs from the keyboard– Ctrl-C, Ctrl-Y, or the Return key. The system will then prompt for the user name and password or passwords, and then validate the responses to determine if you are a legitimate user of the system. The system then establishes the default characteristics of your terminal session, as indicated in the authorization file created by the system operator. Next, it will execute the command procedure files at the system level and/or the command procedure files in your default directory.

Command qualifiers are entered on the Username line, immediately following the name of the user, as in

(Return)
Username: **SANDLER/NOCOMMAND**
Password:

Command Qualifiers

/CLI = command-language-interpreter

Specifies an alternate command language interpreter (CLI), replacing the default DCL interpreter.

/COMMAND[= file-spec]
/NOCOMMAND

Determine whether the system will execute the default command procedure at login. The **/COMMAND** qualifier can be used to specify an alternate procedure to the default; the **/NOCOMMAND** qualifier is used to tell the system not to execute any command procedure.

/DISK = device-name[:]

Overrides the default SYS$DISK device listed in the authorization file and specifies a new disk device. [:] can be used for an optional node.

/TABLES = (command-table[,...])

Gives an alternate CLI table to override the default. The default device and directory is SYS$SHARE, with a default file type of EXE.

LOGOUT

LOGOUT <Return>

Entered at the DCL prompt, **LOGOUT** terminates an interactive terminal session.

Command Qualifiers

/BRIEF

Instructs the system to acknowledge the termination of the session with a brief message with the name of the user and the date and time logged out. For interactive sessions, the default is **/BRIEF**.

/FULL

Instructs the system to acknowledge the termination of the session with the long form of the **LOGOUT** message, with a summary of accounting information. For batch jobs, the default is **/FULL**.

Information returned includes the name of the user and logout time, as well as CPU usage. Here is an example of use of the **LOGOUT/FULL** command:

$LOGOUT/FULL
SANDLER   logged out at 15-AUG-1987 17:32:36.32

Accounting information:
Buffered I/O count:	938	Peak working set size:	933
Direct I/O count:	493	Peak page file size:	1553
Page faults:	2487	Mounted volumes:	0
Charged CPU time:	00:00:23.76	Elapsed time:	0 00:13:21.9

/HANGUP
/NOHANGUP

When used with a dialup terminal, these qualifiers specify whether the phone will hang up at logout.

MAIL

MAIL [file-spec] [recipient-name]

Invokes the VMS Mail program to send messages or files to other users. For more details see Chapter 8.

The **[file-spec]** is an optional element of the **MAIL** command that specifies the name of a message file or other file to be sent to another user. If no file specification is listed in the command, the Mail program will prompt the user for a message. The [recipient-name] is an optional element of the **MAIL** command that identifies the intended target of the mail. If no recipient name is included in the command, the Mail program will prompt the user for a recipient.

MERGE

MERGE input-file-spec1, input-file-spec2[,...] output-file-spec

Invokes the VAX Sort Utility to combine two or more similarly sorted files into a single output file. Input files must be in sorted order. As many as 10 input files can be merged in one command.

For more information, see the VAX/VMS Sort/Merge Utility Reference Manual.

MESSAGE

MESSAGE file-spec[,...]

Invokes the VAX Message Utility to compile a file, or several files, of message definitions.

For more information, see the VAX/VMS Message Utility Reference Manual.

ON

ON condition THEN [$] command

Within a command procedure, **ON** defines the default responses when a command or program executed within a command procedure encounters an error condition or is interrupted by a Ctrl-Y.

The **condition** identifies the severity level of an error or interrupt. The following keywords are available:

WARNING
ERROR
SEVERE_ERROR

The default error condition is **ON ERROR THEN EXIT.** The **command** specifies the response to be given. Any valid command line can be used after the keyword **THEN.** The user can choose to precede the command line with a dollar sign to indicate a global symbol as a command.

OPEN

OPEN logical-name[:] file-spec

Within a command procedure, this command opens a file for reading or writing. The **OPEN** command assigns a logical name to the file and places the name in the process logical name table.

The **logical-name[:]** is the logical name to be assigned to the file. The **file-spec** is the name of the file or device to be opened. The default file type is .DAT. You can supply a different file type as part of the file specification.

If you specify a file that does not exist, it is necessary to use the /**WRITE** qualifier to create a new sequential file.

More than one **OPEN** command can be issued for the same file, with different logical names, if the /SHARE qualifier is used the first time the file is opened.

Command Qualifiers

/APPEND

Instructs the system to open an existing file for writing, with the record pointer at the end-of-file marker. Any new records are therefore added at the end of the file. The /**APPEND** and /**WRITE** qualifiers are mutually exclusive.

/READ

Instructs the system to open the file for reading. /**READ** is the default if no /**READ** or /**WRITE** qualifier is used. If the /**READ** qualifier is used without the /**WRITE** qualifier, an existing file must be specified.

/SHARE[= option]

Instructs the system to open the specified file as a shareable file, allowing other users read or write access. If the /**SHARE = READ** qualifier is specified, users are allowed read access only. If the

/SHARE=WRITE qualifier is used, or if the option is omitted, users are allowed read and write access.

/WRITE

Instructs the system to open the file for writing. If the /WRITE qualifier is used without the /READ qualifier, the system will allow the user to open and create a file that does not exist. The /READ qualifier can be used with the /WRITE qualifier to open an existing file, with the pointer positioned at the beginning of the file. The /WRITE and /APPEND qualifiers are mutually exclusive.

PHONE

PHONE [phone-command]

Invokes the VAX/VMS Phone Utility for communication with other users on your system or any other VAX/VMS system connected to it. See Chapter 9 for details.

PRINT

PRINT file-spec[,...]

Creates a printer or terminal queue for printing the specified files. The default queue is SYS$PRINT; a different queue name can be specified in the command.

The **file-spec[,...]** is the name or names of files to be printed. For multiple files, separate the file specifications with commas or plus signs. In the instance of multiple files, **PRINT** concatenates files into a single job, giving the job the name of the first file. Wildcard characters are allowed in the directory specification, filename, file type, and version number fields.

Command Qualifiers

/AFTER=time
/NOAFTER

Instruct the system whether to print a job after a specified time of day. Time can be specified either as an absolute time or a combination of absolute and delta times. If the specified time has already passed, the system will queue the job for immediate printing. Absolute time is actual time, as in 1 P.M., 2:30 A.M., or 14:50 in 24-hour clock notation as well as TODAY, TOMORROW, and YESTERDAY. Delta time is change time, or a particular period of time counted from the present time, as in 90 minutes from this moment.

The format for delta time is [ddd-][hh:mm:ss.cc]. The fields are

- ddd   Number of days, shown as an integer in the range of 0-9999.
- hh   Number of hours, shown as an integer in the range from 0-23.
- mm   Number of minutes, shown as an integer in the range of 0-59.
- ss   Number of seconds, shown as an integer in the range of 0-59.
- cc   Number of hundredths of seconds, shown as an integer in the range of 0-99.

Delta times build from the left and can be truncated from the right. Here are some examples of specifications:

5 =	5 days from now.
3	3 hours from now.
:27	27 minutes from now.
4-:32	4 days and 32 minutes from now.
7:23	7 hours and 23 minutes from now.

/BACKUP
/NOBACKUP

Selects files for printing on the basis of their most recent backup. This qualifier is used in conjunction with the **/BEFORE** or **/SINCE** qualifier. The **/BACKUP** qualifier is incompatible with **/CREATED**, **/EXPIRED**, or **/MODIFIED**. The default is **/CREATED**.

/BEFORE=[time]
/NOBEFORE

Selects files for printing that are dated before the time specified. In addition to time values, the keywords **TODAY**, **TOMORROW**, and **YESTERDAY** can be used. If no time is specified, the system will assume **TODAY**.

/BURST[=keyword]
/NOBURST

BURST instructs the system to print a *burst* page before the specified file. A burst page includes the name of the user submitting the job, the job entry number and other information, and it serves to identify the ownership of the printing job. A burst page is printed over the perforation of the page and precedes a flag page (see **FLAG**), making it easy for the operator to see where print jobs or files begin.

/BURST can be optionally placed between PRINT and file-spec, in which case the keywords **ALL** or **ONE** can be added. **ALL** instructs the system to precede each file in a multiple-file job with a burst and flag page; **ONE** instructs the system to use a burst page only for the first copy of the first file in the job (see **/COPIES=n**).

/NOBURST is used to override any relevant defaults assigned to the printer queue.

/CHARACTERISTICS = (characteristic[,...])

Instructs the system to use one or more special characteristics available on specific printers, such as ink color.

The command **SHOW QUEUE/CHARACTERISTICS** will display any characteristics defined for the system. The command **SHOW QUEUE/FULL** will display characteristics available on a particular queue.

If a Print job is specified with a characteristic not available on the queue, the job will not execute and will remain in a pending queue. The system manager will have to stop the queue to retrieve the job and change its characteristics or those of the queue.

/CONFIRM
/NOCONFIRM (default)

Instruct the system whether to query the user for confirmation of each print operation. See Figure 10-1 on page 161 for appropriate responses.

A DICTIONARY OF SELECTED DCL COMMANDS AND STATEMENTS □ 203

/COPIES = n

Instructs the system to print **n** copies of a job. If the qualifier is not used, the default is 1 copy.

If **/COPIES = n** comes immediately after the **PRINT** command, each file in the list is printed the specified number of times. If the **/COPIES = n** qualifier comes following one of the file specifications, only that file is affected.

/CREATED (default)
/NOCREATED

Selects files for printing on the basis of their creation dates. This qualifier is used in conjunction with the **/BEFORE** or **/SINCE** qualifier. The **/CREATED** qualifier is incompatible with **/BACKUP, /EXPIRED,** or **/MODIFIED.**

/DELETE
/NODELETE (default)

Instruct the system to delete a file or files after printing. If the **/DELETE** qualifier comes immediately after the **PRINT** command, each file in the list is deleted. If the **/DELETE** qualifier comes following one of the file specifications, only that file is affected.

Obviously, this qualifier should be used with care.

/EXCLUDE = (file-spec[,...])
/NOEXCLUDE

Excludes any specified files from a wildcard **PRINT** command.

/EXPIRED
/NOEXPIRED

Select files for printing on the basis of their expiration dates. This qualifier is used in conjunction with the **/BEFORE** or **/SINCE** qualifier. The **/EXPIRED** qualifier is incompatible with **/BACKUP, /CREATED,** or **/MODIFIED.** The default is **/CREATED.**

/FEED (default)
/NOFEED

/FEED instructs the system to automatically insert form feeds near the end of a page. The number of lines per form can be set with the **/FORM** qualifier.

/FLAG[= keyword]
/NOFLAG

/FLAG instructs the system to print a *flag* page before the specified file. A flag page includes the name of the user submitting the job, the job entry number, and other information; it serves to identify the ownership of the printing job. (See also **/BURST**.)

The keywords **ALL** or **ONE** can be added to a **/FLAG** qualifier placed between the **PRINT** command and the file specifications. **ALL** instructs the system to precede each file in a multiple-file job with a flag page; **ONE** instructs the system to use a flag page only for the first copy of the first file in the job.

/NOFLAG is used to override any relevant defaults assigned to the printer queue.

/FORM = type

Instructs the system to use a particular type of form to print a job. Forms are specified with a numeric value or alphanumeric name, as determined by the system operator or other qualified user.

The **SHOW QUEUE/FORM** command will display any form types and characteristics defined for the system. The command **SHOW QUEUE/FULL** will display forms and characteristics available on a particular queue.

If a Print job is specified with a form type not available on the queue, the job will not execute and will remain in a pending queue. The system manager will have to stop the queue to retrieve the job and change its form types or those of the queue.

/HEADER
/NOHEADER (default)

Instruct the printer whether to print a heading at the top of each output page.

/HOLD
/NOHOLD (default)

Instruct the system whether to print a file immediately or hold it until it is released.

To release a job, use the command **SET QUEUE/RELEASE/ENTRY**.

/IDENTIFY (default)
/NOIDENTIFY

Instruct the system whether to display a message on the current output device listing the job number of the print job and the name of the queue in which it has been entered.

/JOB_COUNT=n

Instructs the system to print the entire job **n** times. Allowable values for **n** are 1 to 255.

/MODIFIED
/NOMODIFIED

Selects files for printing on the basis of the date of their last modification. This qualifier is used in conjunction with the **/BEFORE** or **/SINCE** qualifier. It is incompatible with **/BACKUP**, **/CREATED**, or **/EXPIRED**. The default is **/CREATED**.

/NAME=job-name

Specifies a name string to identify a job. The name string can be from 1 to 39 characters in length. The job name will be shown in the SHOW QUEUE display and is printed on the flag page for the job.

If no job name is specified, the system selects as the name string the filename of the first file in a job.

/NOTE=string

Specifies a message, of up to 255 characters, to appear on the flag page for the job.

/NOTIFY
/NONOTIFY (default)

Instruct the system whether to broadcast a message to the terminal notifying the user when a print job has been completed or aborted.

/OPERATOR = string

Instructs the system to send a message, of up to 255 characters, to the operator. When the job begins execution, the printer queue pauses and the message is sent to the operator. This qualifier can be used in a system where an operator is available to change paper or ink, or perform other special operations upon a request from a user on the system.

/PAGES = ([lowlim,]uplim)

Instructs the system to print only the specified pages in the job.

The **lowlim** specifier is the first page in the group of pages the user wants printed. If no lowlim is given, the printing will begin on the first page of the file. The **uplim** specifier is the last page of the file the user wants printed. The symbol " " can be used to specify printing to the end of a file.

Here are some examples:

PRINT/PAGES = 12 prints the first 12 pages of a file.

PRINT/PAGES = (6,12) prints pages 6 through 12.

PRINT/PAGES = (6,"") prints from page 6 to end of file.

/PRIORITY = n

Specifies a priority for the print job. Values range from 0 to 255, with 0 the lowest priority and 255 the highest.

Users without special privileges cannot raise their print priority value above the limit set by the system operator.

/QUEUE = queue-name[:]

Instructs the system to place the print job in the specified queue. The default print queue is SYS$PRINT.

/REMOTE

Instructs the system to print specified files on a remote node. The files to be printed must exist on the remote node, and the file specification must include the name of the remote node.

Unlike local print jobs, multiple files queued by a single **PRINT/REMOTE** command are considered separate jobs.

The following qualifiers are the only ones compatible with **/REMOTE**: **/BACKUP**, **/BEFORE**, **/BY_OWNER**, **/CONFIRM**, **/CREATED**, **/EXCLUDE**, **/EXPIRED**, **/MODIFIED**, and **/SINCE**.

/RESTART (default)
/NORESTART

Instruct the system whether a print job can restart after a crash or a **STOP/QUEUE/REQUEUE** command.

/SINCE[=time]
/NOSINCE

Select files for printing that are dated after the time specified. In addition to absolute or combined absolute and delta time values, the keywords **TODAY**, **TOMORROW**, and **YESTERDAY** can be used. If no time is specified, the system will assume **TODAY**.

/SPACE
/NOSPACE (default)

Instruct the system whether to double-space the file on output. The default is **/NOSPACE**, for single-spaced output.

/TRAILER[=keyword]
/NOTRAILER

Instruct the system whether to print a trailer page at the end of the file. The trailer page includes the job entry number and information about the user submitting the job and the files being printed.

The keywords **ALL** or **ONE** can be added to a **/TRAILER** qualifier placed between the **PRINT** command and the file specifications. **ALL** instructs the system to follow each file in a multiple-file job with a trailer page; **ONE** instructs the system to use a trailer page only for the last copy of the last file in the job.

/**NOTRAILER** is used to override any defaults assigned to the printer queue.

PURGE

PURGE[file-spec[,...]]

Deletes all versions of files except the highest-numbered version.

The **file-spec[,...]** identifies one or more files to be purged. If more than one file is listed, separate them with commas or plus signs. If no file specification is included in the command, all files in the current directory are subject to a PURGE.

Command Qualifiers

/BACKUP

Selects files for purging on the basis of their most recent backup. This qualifier is used in conjunction with the **/BEFORE** or **/SINCE** qualifier. It is incompatible with **/CREATED**, **/EXPIRED**, or **/MODIFIED**. The default is **/CREATED**.

/BEFORE = [time]

Selects files for purging that are dated before the time specified. In addition to absolute or combined absolute and delta time values, the keywords **TODAY**, **TOMORROW**, and **YESTERDAY** can be used. If no time is specified, the system will assume **TODAY**.

/CONFIRM
/NOCONFIRM (default)

Instructs the system whether to query the user for confirmation of each purge operation. See Figure 10-1 on page 161 for appropriate responses.

Here is an example of use of the PURGE/CONFIRM command:

$PURGE/CONFIRM <Return>

$DISK1:[SANDLER]1988SALESCAL.W20;6, delete? [N]:**y**
%PURGE-I-FILPURG,
  $DISK1:[SANDLER]1988EDITCAL.W20;6 deleted (6 blocks)

$DISK1:[SANDLER]1988SALESCAL_VERSION2.W20;2,
                                        delete? [N]:**y**
%PURGE-I-FILPURG,
  $DISK1:[SANDLER]1988EDITCAL_VERSION2.W20;2
  deleted (6 blocks)

%PURGE-I-TOTAL, 2 files deleted (12 blocks)

/CREATED (default)

Selects files for purging on the basis of their creation dates. This qualifier is used in conjunction with the **/BEFORE** or **/SINCE** qualifier. It is incompatible with **/BACKUP**, **/EXPIRED**, or **/MODIFIED**.

/ERASE
/NOERASE (default)

When a file is deleted with a **DELETE** or **PURGE** command, the area in which the file had been stored is simply made available to the system for other storage purposes. For security purposes, the **/ERASE** command qualifier will overwrite the storage location with a pattern to make the data inaccessible.

/EXCLUDE = (file-spec[,...])

Excludes any specified files from a wildcard **PURGE** command.

/EXPIRED

Selects files for purging on the basis of their expiration dates. This qualifier is used in conjunction with the **/BEFORE** or **/SINCE** qualifier. It is incompatible with **/BACKUP**, **/CREATED**, or **/MODIFIED**. The default is **/CREATED**.

/KEEP = n

Instructs the system to keep **n** versions of each file in the directory, retaining the highest version number and **n-1** lower version numbers. Without the **/KEEP** qualifier, all but the highest-numbered versions are deleted.

/LOG
/NOLOG (default)

Instructs the system whether to display on screen the file specifications of files as they are purged.

/MODIFIED

Selects files for purging on the basis of the date of their last modification. This qualifier is used in conjunction with the **/BEFORE** or **/SINCE** qualifier. It is incompatible with **/BACKUP**, **/CREATED**, or **/EXPIRED**. The default is **/CREATED**.

/SINCE[= time]

Selects files for purging that are dated after the time specified. In addition to absolute or combined absolute and delta time values, the keywords **TODAY**, **TOMORROW**, and **YESTERDAY** can be used. If no time is specified, the system will assume **TODAY**.

READ

READ logical-name[:] symbol-name

Reads a single record from the specified input file, and then assigns the contents of that record to the specified symbol name. This command is used in command files.

RECALL

RECALL [command-specifier]

Displays on screen previously entered commands that can be reprocessed, or edited and reprocessed.

Up to 20 commands, with a total of 1025 characters, are retained in a RECALL buffer. As many as 255 characters can be recalled at one time. Displayed commands are not processed until the Return key is pressed; the displayed command can be edited using the command line editor.

The **command-specifier** is the number or leading substring of the command to be recalled. Command numbers are in the range from 1 to 20, with the most recently entered command numbered 1 and the oldest 20.

The leading substring consists of the first few characters of a command string—enter as many characters as necessary to provide a unique identification. If there are **REPLY**, **RENAME**, and **READ** commands in the buffer, for instance, you must enter at least three characters to provide a unique leading substring. If the substring is not unique, **RECALL** will provide the most recently entered match.

A **RECALL** command itself is not stored in the buffer.

Command Qualifier

/ALL

Instructs the system to display all commands stored in the RECALL buffer, along with their command numbers.

RENAME

RENAME input-file-spec[,...] output-file-spec

Renames a file or files, changing directory, filename, file type or file version as specified in the command.

The **input-file-spec[,...]** is the name or names of files to be changed. Wildcard characters can be used in the directory, filename, file type, or version number fields. With wildcards, all files whose specifications match the criteria are renamed. The **output-file-spec** is the new file specification for the input file.

If the output file specification includes a version number, the **RENAME** command will use that number. If the input file specification or the output file specification contains an asterisk wildcard in the version number field, **RENAME** uses the version number of each input field for the corresponding output file. If no file exists for the specified output file, **RENAME** creates the file and gives it a version number of 1. If a file exists with the same filename and file type specified for the output file, **RENAME** gives the output file a version number one greater than the highest existing version, unless the **/NONEW_VERSION** command qualifier is included.

Command Qualifiers

/BACKUP

Selects files for renaming on the basis of their most recent backup. This qualifier is used in conjunction with the **/BEFORE** or **/SINCE** qualifier. It is incompatible with **/CREATED**, **/EXPIRED**, or **/MODIFIED**. The default is **/CREATED**.

/BEFORE = [time]

Selects files for renaming that are dated before the time specified. In addition to absolute or combined absolute and delta time values, the keywords **TODAY**, **TOMORROW**, and **YESTERDAY** can be used. If no time is specified, the system will assume **TODAY**.

/CONFIRM
/NOCONFIRM (default)

Instructs the system whether to query the user for confirmation of each RENAME operation. See Figure 10-1 on page 161 for appropriate responses.

/CREATED (default)

Selects files for renaming on the basis of their creation dates. This qualifier is used in conjunction with the **/BEFORE** or **/SINCE** qualifier. The **/CREATED** qualifier is incompatible with **/BACKUP**, **/EXPIRED**, or **/MODIFIED**.

/EXCLUDE = (file-spec[,...])

Excludes any specified files from a wildcard **RENAME** command.

/EXPIRED

Selects files for renaming on the basis of their expiration dates. This qualifier is used in conjunction with the **/BEFORE** or **/SINCE** qualifier. It is incompatible with **/BACKUP**, **/CREATED**, or **/MODIFIED**. The default is **/CREATED**.

/LOG
/NOLOG (default)

Instructs the system whether to display on screen the file specifications of files as they are renamed.

/MODIFIED

Selects files for renaming on the basis of the date of their last modification. This qualifier is used in conjunction with the **/BEFORE** or **/SINCE** qualifier. It is incompatible with **/BACKUP**, **/CREATED**, or **/EXPIRED**. The default is **/CREATED**.

/NEW_VERSION (default)
/NONEW_VERSION

Instructs the system whether to automatically assign a new version number to the output file of a **RENAME** operation if a file with the same filename and file type already exists. If **/NONEW_VERSION** is used and there is a file with the same filename and file type as the specified output filename, the system will display an error message.

/SINCE[=time]

Selects files for renaming that are dated after the time specified. In addition to absolute or combined absolute and delta time values, the keywords **TODAY**, **TOMORROW**, and **YESTERDAY** can be used. If no time is specified, the system will assume **TODAY**.

REQUEST

REQUEST "message-text"

Sends a message to the system operator's terminal. A reply can be requested. The system operator uses the restricted command **REPLY** to send responses to users with requests.

The **"message-text"** is the message to be displayed at the specified operator terminal or terminals. The note can be as long as 128 characters; if there is more than one word in the note, the text must be enclosed with quote marks.

Command Qualifiers

/REPLY

Requests a response from the system operator.

If you include **/REPLY** in the command, a message such as the following will be displayed on your terminal:

%OPCOM-S-OPRNOTIF, operator notified, waiting...hh:mm:ss

A response from the operator will be displayed on your terminal as follows:

%OPCOM-S-OPREPLY, message text

If you request a reply, no other commands can be entered until the operator sends a response. To exit from this condition, type the Ctrl-C key combination. The system will respond with

REQUEST - Enter message or cancel with ^Z
REQUEST - Message?

You can enter a new message at the prompt or use the Ctrl-Z combination exit back to the DCL prompt.

/TO[= (operator[,...])]

Selects one or more operators to receive the message. The default sends a message to all terminals identified as operator terminals. Several operators can be included in the **/TO** qualifier, separated by commas and enclosed within parentheses.

The following operator names are acceptable:

CARDS: operators handling card reader requests.

CENTRAL: central system operators.

CLUSTER: operators handling cluster-related queries.

DEVICES: operators handling disk and tape requests.

DISKS: operators handling disk volume requests.

NETWORK: operators handling network queries.

OPER1–OPER12: system-identified operators 1 through 12.

PRINTER: operators handling printer requests.

SECURITY: operators handling security requests.

TAPES: operators handling tape volume requests.

RETURN

RETURN [status-code]

Within a command procedure, **RETURN** terminates a **GOSUB** subroutine procedure. Control is returned to the command following the **GOSUB** command that called the subroutine.

The **status-code** is a numeric value for the global symbol $STATUS. If the user specifies a status code, DCL will interpret the code as a condition code; if a code is not specified, the current value of $STATUS is saved.

RUN

RUN file-spec

Instructs the system to place an image into execution in the process, and creates a subprocess or a detached process to execute the specified image.

For further details, see the VAX/VMS DCL Dictionary and VAX/VMS DCL Concepts Manual.

RUNOFF

RUNOFF file-spec[,...]

Invokes the Digital Standard Runoff (DSR) text formatter program to format ASCII files. For complete details on this program, consult the VAX Digital Standard Runoff (DSR) Reference Manual.

RUNOFF allows the user to specify the amount of text on a page; the position of text on a page; and character styles, including boldface, underlines, and overwriting.

The **file-spec[,...]** consists of one or more ASCII files with text and DSR commands to be formatted by the Runoff program. If no file type is included, the program will assume a file type of .RNO. Filenames must be separated by commas. DSR will produce an output file with the same filename as the input file. Wildcard characters are not allowed in the file specification.

Command Qualifiers

/BACKSPACE

Instructs DSR to perform character-by-character rather than line-by-line overprinting. Line-by-line is the default.

/BOLD[=n]
/NOBOLD

Instruct DSR whether to boldface characters flagged for such treatment in the text. The numeric specifier with the **/BOLD** qualifier is used to indicate how many times the flagged text is overprinted; **/BOLD** without a number is the same as **/BOLD=1**, calling for the flagged text to be overprinted once. If **/NOBOLD** or **/BOLD=0** is specified, flagged text is not overprinted.

/CHANGE_BARS[="character"]
/NOCHANGE_BARS

Instruct DSR whether to include change bars in the formatted file, indicating text that has been altered.
   The default character is the vertical bar (|).
Substitute characters can be included in the **/CHANGE_BARS** qualifier as a character within quote marks or as an octal, decimal, or hexadecimal value.
   The **/NOCHANGE_BARS** qualifier suppresses any specifications for change bars in the text.

/DEBUG[=(option[,...])]

Instructs DSR to include commands in the output file for editing or debugging purposes. Allowable option keywords are **CONDITIONALS**, **CONTENTS**, **FILES**, **INDEX**, and **SAVE_RESTORE**, as well as **ALL** to include all five options. For further information, consult the VAX Digital Standard Runoff (DSR) Reference Manual.

/DEVICE = (option[,...])

Instruct DSR whether to produce an LNI output file intended for printing on a Digital LN01, LN01E, or LN03 laser printer, or on another device that can emulate one of those printers. Consult the VAX Digital Standard Runoff (DSR) Reference Manual for further details about LNI files.

Options available for use with **/DEVICE** are LN01, LN01E, and LN03. Emphasis and orientation options are **ITALIC**, **UNDERLINE**, **PORTRAIT**, and **LANDSCAPE**.

/DOWN[= n]
/NODOWN (default)

Instruct DSR whether to insert the specified number of blank lines at the top of each printed page, before any headers. The **/DOWN** qualifier without an **n** value results in the insertion of five blank lines.

Note that the number of blank lines specified in the qualifier does not affect the number of text lines printed on a page, which is set with a **.PAGE SIZE** command within DSR.

Using **/NODOWN** or **/DOWN = 0** results in no blank lines except for those associated with the print device or the header format.

/FORM_SIZE = n

Used as an element of the control of the maximum number of lines that can be output on a page. The maximum number must include header lines, footnotes, and page numbers. Consult the VAX Digital Standard Runoff (DSR) Reference Manual for further details.

/INTERMEDIATE[= file-spec]
/NOINTERMEDIATE (default)

Instruct DSR whether to produce an intermediate output file available for use as input to the DSR table of contents or indexing utilities. The qualifier results in an output file with the same name as the input file, plus a file type of .BRN. The output file can be given a different file name by specifying it after the **/INTERMEDIATE** qualifier.

For more information on the table of contents or indexing utilities, consult the VAX Digital Standard Runoff (DSR) Reference Manual.

/LOG
/NOLOG (default)

Instruct DSR whether to display information—at the completion of processing—on the version number of the DSR program in use, the number of diagnostic messages reported, the number of output pages produced, and the output file specification.

If errors are encountered in processing, DSR sends a message to the terminal even if the **/NOLOG** qualifier is in effect.

/MESSAGES = (option[,...])

Instructs DSR on the preferred destination for DSR error messages. Allowable options are

    OUTPUT: to send messages to the output MEM file.
    USER: to send messages to the terminal.

If both options are specified, they should be separated by commas and enclosed in parentheses.

The default is **/MESSAGES = (OUTPUT,USER)** which sends messages to both the output MEM file and the user's terminal.

/OUTPUT[= file-spec]
/NOOUTPUT

Instruct DSR where to send the output. If neither qualifier is used, or if **/OUTPUT** is used without a file specification, the output filename is the same as the input filename.

/NOOUTPUT instructs the system not to create an output file; in combination with the **/INTERMEDIATE** qualifier,

/**NOOUTPUT** will create only the intermediate .BRN file and not a formatted output file.

/PAGES = string

Instructs DSR to output only the pages specified in the string. The default instruction for DSR is to output all of the pages in a file.

The range of page numbers is given by a starting and ending page, separated by a colon, as in

/PAGES = 12:20

To specify more than one range of page numbers—up to a maximum of five ranges—separate each range with a comma and enclose the entire string in quote marks, as in

/PAGES = "12:20,24:32,44:56"

If you specify only a starting page, output will begin at that page and continue to the end of the file.

To print just a single page, use that page number as the starting and ending specification:

/PAGES = 12:12

To output an entire appendix, use only the letter for that appendix, as in

/PAGES = "A"

To output an entire index, use the word **INDEX**, as in

/PAGES = "INDEX"

To output only specific appendix or index pages, use the title of the section as a prefix to the number, as in

/PAGES = "A-12:20,INDEX-15:INDEX-30"

/PAUSE
/NOPAUSE (default)

Instruct DSR whether to pause after printing each page of output. The **/PAUSE** qualifier can be used to halt a printer to allow insertion of single pieces of paper. When output is halted, the bell at the terminal will ring; pressing the spacebar at the terminal will cause processing to resume.

The **/PAUSE** qualifier should not be used in a batch process, since the user is not monitoring the progress of the job.

/RIGHT=[n]
/NORIGHT (default, except for LN01 printer)

Instruct the printer whether to shift the text on each page **n** spaces to the right. If **/RIGHT** is specified without a number, text will be shifted five spaces. If a value of 0 or the **/NORIGHT** qualifier is used, no shift is made.

/SEQUENCE
/NOSEQUENCE (default)

Instruct DSR whether to generate input file sequence numbers in the output file.

/SIMULATE
/NOSIMULATE (default)

Instruct DSR whether to use line feeds or form feeds to advance to the top of each page. **/SIMULATE** allows printers and other output devices that do not have formfeed capability to emulate devices that do. The system will issue enough line feed characters at the end of a page to make the text skip to the top of the next page.

The **/SIMULATE** qualifier also includes an automatic pause before the first page of output; hit the space bar to begin processing.

RUNOFF/CONTENTS

RUNOFF/CONTENTS file-spec[,...]
RUNOFF/CONTENTS file-spec[+...]

Invokes the Digital Standard Runoff table of contents utility. DSR will create a file, with the file type of .RNT.

The input file for this command is an intermediate binary file produced by the **RUNOFF/INTERMEDIATE** command. For details on the use of the DSR table of contents utility, see the VAX Digital Standard Runoff (DSR) Reference Manual.

If multiple filenames are included in the command and are separated by commas, DSR will create a separate .RNT file for each input file. If multiple filenames are included in the command and are separated by plus signs, the utility will create a single .RNT file with a table of contents for all the input files.

Command qualifiers for **RUNOFF/CONTENTS** allow specification of characteristics, including boldface or underlining, header levels, running page numbers or chapter-linked page numbers, and section number formats.

Command Qualifiers

/BOLD
/NOBOLD

Instruct DSR whether to boldface characters flagged for such treatment in chapter headings and header titles. If **/NOBOLD** is specified, flagged text is not overprinted.

/DEEPEST_HEADER=n

Instructs DSR how many levels of headers are to be output in the table of contents. Any number of header levels can be specified by **n**. The default is 6.

/INDENT
/NOINDENT (default)

Instruct DSR how many spaces the header levels after Level 1 are to be indented in the table of contents. If this qualifier is omitted, or if **/NOINDENT** is specified, all header levels below Level 1 are indented 2 spaces. If **/INDENT** is included in the command, each level of header after Level 1 is indented 2 spaces beyond the starting point of the preceding level.

/LOG
/NOLOG (default)

Instruct DSR whether to display the name of each input file as it is processed, the name of each input file after it is processed, and the name of the output file that is created.

If errors are encountered in processing, DSR sends a message to the terminal even if the **/NOLOG** qualifier is in effect.

/OUTPUT[= file-spec]
/NOOUTPUT

Instruct DSR where to send the output. If neither qualifier is used, or if **/OUTPUT** is used without a file specification, the output filename is the same as the input filename.

/NOOUTPUT instructs the system not to create an output file.

/PAGE_NUMBERS = (option[,...])

Instructs DSR whether to include running page numbers or chapter-linked page numbers, and how many levels of headers have page references in tables of contents. Allowable options for this qualifier are

> **LEVEL = n:** directs that header levels up to and including header level n have page numbers listed in the table of contents. The default is 6.
> **NORUNNING:** selects chapter-linked page numbers, the default.
> **RUNNING:** selects running page numbers.

/REQUIRE = file-spec
/NOREQUIRE (default)

Instruct DSR whether to change or delete the default heading of "CONTENTS" on the first page of a table of contents.

To change the heading, create or edit a file with the new heading, then use the filename of that file as the file-spec for the /REQUIRE qualifier. To eliminate a heading, use as a file-spec a null, or empty, file.

/SECTION_NUMBERS (default)
/NOSECTION_NUMBERS

Instruct DSR whether to display section numbers in the table of contents. **/NOSECTION_NUMBERS** eliminates display of section numbers for all header levels.

/UNDERLINE
/NOUNDERLINE (default)

Instruct DSR whether to underline characters flagged for such treatment in chapter and header titles. If **/NOUNDERLINE** is specified, flagged text is not underlined.

RUNOFF/INDEX

RUNOFF/INDEX file-spec[,...]
RUNOFF/INDEX file-spec[+...]

Invokes the Digital Standard Runoff index utility. DSR will create a file with the file type .RNX.

The input file for this command is an intermediate binary file produced by the **RUNOFF/INTERMEDIATE** command.

For details on the use of the DSR index, see the VAX Digital Standard Runoff (DSR) Reference Manual.

If multiple filenames are included in the command and are separated by commas, DSR will create a separate .RNX file for each input file. If multiple filenames are included in the command and are separated by plus signs, the utility will create a single .RNX file with an index for all the input files.

Command qualifiers for **RUNOFF/INDEX** allow specification of characteristics including running page numbers or chapter-linked page numbers, the number of lines of index entries on each page, and special text and heading on the first page of the index.

Command Qualifiers

/LINES_PER_PAGE=n

Specifies to DSR the number of lines of index entries to be printed on each page. Not included in the value of **n** are the lines required for headings and footings. The default value of **n** is 55 lines.

You must calculate a new value for **n** if the default environment is changed because of the use of subtitles in the document using the RNX file, if the page length for the printed document will be other than 58 lines per page, or if any **.LAYOUT** parameter other than 0 is used. .LAYOUT is a command or parameter of DSR. It is defined in DSR Reference Manual, but is beyond the scope of this book.

For more details on calculating **n**, see the VAX Digital Standard Runoff DSR Reference Manual.

/LOG
/NOLOG (default)

Instruct DSR whether to display the name of each input file as it is processed, the name of each input file after it is processed, and the name of the output file that is created.

If errors are encountered in processing, DSR sends a message to the terminal even if the **/NOLOG** qualifier is in effect.

/OUTPUT[= file-spec]
/NOOUTPUT

Instruct DSR where to send the output. If neither qualifier is used, or if **/OUTPUT** is used without a file specification, the output filename is the same as the input filename.

/NOOUTPUT instructs the system not to create an output file.

/PAGE_NUMBERS = (option[,...])

Instructs DSR whether to include running page numbers or chapter-linked page numbers in the index. Allowable options for this qualifier are

  NORUNNING: selects chapter-linked page numbers, the default.
  RUNNING: selects running page numbers.

/REQUIRE = file-spec
/NOREQUIRE (default)

Instruct DSR whether to change or delete the default heading of "INDEX" on the first page of an index.

To change the heading, create or edit a file with the new heading, then use the filename of that file as the file-spec for the **/REQUIRE** qualifier. To eliminate a heading, use as a file-spec a null file.

For further details and a sample file, see the VAX Digital Standard Runoff (DSR) Reference Manual.

/RESERVE = n
/NORESERVE (default)

You can reserve space at the top of the first page of an index, to be used for either text or white space, in conjunction with the **/REQUIRE = file spec** qualifier. The value of **n** is the number of lines of text or white space to be inserted.

SEARCH

SEARCH file-spec[,...] search-string[,...]

Searches through one or more files for the string or strings specified in the command, and lists all lines that contain the strings.

The **file-spec[,...]** is the name or names of files to be searched. At least one filename must be specified; if two or more are included, they must be separated by commas. Wildcard characters are allowed in the file specification. The **search-string[,...]** is the string or strings to be searched for.

If the string includes any lowercase letters or nonalphanumeric characters or spaces, it should be enclosed in quote marks.

Command Qualifiers

/EXACT
/NOEXACT (default)

By default, **SEARCH** does not distinguish between uppercase and lowercase letters. Use of the **/EXACT** qualifier requires an exact match in the search.

/EXCLUDE = (file-spec[,...])

Used with a wildcard specification, **/EXCLUDE** specifies filenames not to be searched. Directory names and device names cannot be included in an **/EXCLUDE** qualifier.

/FORMAT = option

Specifies reformatting of output records created by the **SEARCH** command. Available options are

> **TEXT**: substitutes ANSI mnemonics for control characters encountered in the text, except for terminal-formatting characters including carriage feed, linefeed, and formfeed. **TEXT** is the default.
> **PASSALL**: performs no translation of control characters.
> **DUMP**: adds terminal-formatting characters to the list of characters translated to ANSI mnemonics by **TEXT**.
> **NONULLS**: identical to **DUMP**, but also removes any null characters from the input file.

/HEADING (default)
/NOHEADING

Instruct **SEARCH** whether to print filenames and window separators in the output. With the default format, **SEARCH** prints filenames only when more than one file is specified or a wildcard specification is used. The window separator, a string of 30 asterisks, is printed between groups of lines that come from different files. If the **/WINDOW** qualifier is used, the window separator uses only 15 asterisks (see **/WINDOW** below).

/LOG
/NOLOG (default)

Instruct **SEARCH** whether to produce a list of the filenames and number of records and matches for each file searched and display them on the current output device.

/MATCH = option

Instructs SEARCH how to deal with multiple search strings. Available options are

> **OR**: A match occurs if any of the search strings are found.

AND: A match occurs only if all of the search strings are found in the record.

NOR: A match occurs only if the record does not include any of the search strings.

NAND: A match occurs only if the record does not include all of the search strings.

If only a single search string is specified, the **OR** and **AND** options and the **NOR** and **NAND** options yield identical results.

/NUMBERS
/NONUMBERS (default)

Instruct **SEARCH** whether to display the source line number on the left margin of each line.

/OUTPUT[=file-spec]
/NOOUTPUT

Unless one of these qualifiers is specified, output from a **SEARCH** command is sent to the current default output device. Under **/OUTPUT**, the results of the search are sent to a file with the specified filename.

/STATISTICS
/NOSTATISTICS (default)

Instruct **SEARCH** whether to display statistics about its work. Statistics displayed are number of files searched, number of records searched, number of characters searched, number of records matched, number of lines printed, buffered I/O count, direct I/O count, number of page faults, elapsed CPU time, and elapsed time.

/WINDOW[=(n1,n2)]
/NOWINDOW (default)

Specify how many lines, if any, are listed along with the line containing the matched string.

The specifier **n1** refers to the number of lines above the matched string; the specifier **n2** refers to the number of lines below the matched string. Either number can be set at 0.

If **/WINDOW** is given with just one number, **n–1** lines are listed along with the matched string. Half of the lines are output above the matched string and half below; if **n–1** yields an odd number, the extra line goes below the matched string.

If **/WINDOW = 0** is given, **SEARCH** will display the names of each file containing a match, but no records.

If **/WINDOW** is omitted, or if the **/NOWINDOW** qualifier is in effect, only the line with the match is displayed.

SET

SET option

Defines or changes file and device characteristics for the duration of the current terminal session or batch job.

Descriptions of **SET** commands available to the user follow. Additional **SET** commands accessible to the system operator and other privileged users are described in the VAX/VMS DCL Dictionary.

SET ACL

SET ACL object-name

Modifies the Access Control List (ACL) of an object.

The **object-name** is the object that will have its ACL modified. Wildcard characters are not permitted in object names. For further details, consult the VAX/VMS DCL Dictionary.

SET BROADCAST

SET BROADCAST = (class-name[,...])

Allows the user to screen out certain types of incoming messages to the terminal.

The **class-name(s)** are the types of messages to be enabled or disabled at the terminal. If two or more classes are included in the command, they must be separated by commas and enclosed within parentheses.

For example,

SET BROADCAST = (NOMINAL, NOPHONE)

Screens out Mail and Phone, and

SET BROADCAST = (MAIL, PHONE)

resumes acceptance of Mail and Phone.

You can issue the **SHOW BROADCAST** command to see a list of any message classes being screened out. The following classes can be specified:

ALL: All types of messages are accepted.
[NO]DCL: Ctrl-T and **SPAWN/NOTIFY** messages.
[NO]GENERAL: all ordinary **REPLY** messages or messages from **$BRDCST**.
[NO]MAIL: notification of incoming mail.
[NONE]: all message types disabled.
[NO]OPCOM: messages from OPCOM.
[NO]PHONE: messages from the Phone utility.
[NO]QUEUE: messages from the Queue Manager.
[NO]SHUTDOWN: messages from **REPLY/SHUTDOWN**.
[NO]URGENT: messages from **REPLY/URGENT**.
[NO]USER1–[NO]USER16: messages from the specified groups of users.

SET CONTROL

SET [NO]CONTROL[= (T,Y)]

Specifies the terminal's reaction to the Ctrl-T (statistical display) and/or the Ctrl-Y (escape from current operation) commands.

If both Ctrl-T and Ctrl-Y are specified in the command, separate them by a comma and enclose both within a set of parentheses.

Ctrl-Y can be used in most interactive terminal sessions to interrupt the current command, command procedure, or program image. If **SET NOCONTROL = Y** is specified, an INTERRUPT message is displayed on screen, but the operation is not disrupted. **SET NOCONTROL = Y** also turns off the Ctrl-C cancel function for most programs.

Ctrl-T temporarily interrupts the current command, procedure, or image to display statistical information about the current process, including the node and user names, the current time, current process, CPU usage, number of page faults, level of I/O activity, and memory usage. If **SET NOCONTROL=T** is specified, the terminal will not respond to a Ctrl-T command. (Ctrl-T works only when **SET TERMINAL/BROADCAST** has been specified at the system or local level.)

SET DEFAULT

SET DEFAULT device-name:

SET DEFAULT [Directory-Name]

Used to change the default directory name and/or default device for the current process.

The **device-name[:]** is the name of a device and/or directory name to be used as the default device or directory in subsequent file specifications. If a physical device name is specified, it must end with a colon; if a directory name is specified, it must be enclosed in square brackets.

Here are some examples of use:

$SET DEFAULT [SANDLER]   <Return>

changes default directory to SANDLER;

$SET DEFAULT DISK1:   <Return>

changes default device to DISK1;

$SET DEFAULT DISK1:[SANDLER]   <Return>

changes directory and device.

SET DEVICE/ACL

SET DEVICE/ACL[=(ace[,...])] device-name

Permits modification of the Access Control List (ACL) of a device. For full details on ACLs and Access Control Entries (ACEs), consult the VAX/VMS DCL Concepts Manual and the VAX/VMS DCL Dictionary.

The **device-name** is the name of the device to have its ACL modified. Wildcard characters are not permitted. The (ace[,...]) is the name or names of ACEs to be modified. Separate multiple ACEs with commas and enclose the list in parentheses. If no ACE is included in the command, the entire access control list is modified.

SET DIRECTORY

SET DIRECTORY directory-spec[,...]

Allows modification of the characteristics of one or more directories.

The **directory-spec[,...]** is the name or names of directories to be modified. A complete directory specification, enclosed in square brackets, must be entered. If two or more directories are specified, they should be separated with commas. Wildcard characters are permitted in specifications.

Command Qualifiers

/ACL

Associates an Access Control List with the specified directory or directories.

/BACKUP

Selects directories on the basis of their most recent backup. This qualifier is used in conjunction with the **/BEFORE** or **/SINCE** qualifier. It is incompatible with **/CREATED, /EXPIRED,** or **/MODIFIED**. The default is **/CREATED**.

/BEFORE=[time]

Selects directories that are dated before the time specified. In addition to time values, the keywords **TODAY**, **TOMORROW**, and **YESTERDAY** can be used. If no time is specified, the system will assume **TODAY**.

/CONFIRM
/NOCONFIRM (default)

Instruct the system whether to query the user for confirmation of each directory operation. Appropriate responses are shown in Figure 10-1 on page 161.

/CREATED (default)

Selects directories on the basis of their creation dates. This qualifier is used in conjunction with the **/BEFORE** or **/SINCE** qualifier. The **/CREATED** qualifier is incompatible with **/BACKUP**, **/EXPIRED**, or **/MODIFIED**.

/EXCLUDE = (directory-spec[,...])

Exclude any specified directories from a wildcard command.

/EXPIRED

Selects directories on the basis of their expiration dates. This qualifier is used in conjunction with the **/BEFORE** or **/SINCE** qualifier. It is incompatible with **/BACKUP**, **/CREATED**, or **/MODIFIED**. The default is **/CREATED**.

/LOG
/NOLOG (default)

Instruct the system whether to display the directory specification of each directory as it is modified.

/MODIFIED

Selects directories on the basis of the date of their last modification. This qualifier is used in conjunction with the **/BEFORE** or **/SINCE** qualifier. It is incompatible with **/BACKUP**, **/CREATED**, or **/EXPIRED**. The default is **/CREATED**.

/SINCE[= time]

Selects directories that are dated after the time specified. In addition to absolute or combined absolute and delta time values, the keywords **TODAY**, **TOMORROW**, and **YESTERDAY** can be used. If no time is specified, the system will assume **TODAY**.

/VERSION_LIMIT[=n]

Specifies the total number of versions of individual files that the specified directory will retain. If no value for **n** is given, the system assumes a value of 0, which allows the full Files-11 capacity of 32,767 versions.

If the version limit is changed for a directory, the new limit will apply only to files created after the change has been made.

SET DIRECTORY/ACL

SET DIRECTORY/ACL[=(ace[,...])] directory-spec[,...]

Allows modification of the Access Control List of one or more directories. For full details on ACLs and Access Control Entries (ACEs), consult the VAX/VMS DCL Concepts Manual and the VAX/VMS DCL Dictionary.

The **directory-spec[,...]** is the name or names of directories to have their ACL modified. Device name is optional, and wildcard characters are permitted. If two or more directories are specified, they must be separated by commas. If the **/EDIT** command qualifier is used, only one directory specification can be made and it cannot include wildcard characters. The **(ace[,...])** is the name or names of Access Control Entries to be modified. If no ACE is specified, the entire ACL is open for modification.

SET FILE

SET FILE file-spec[,...]

Allows modification of the characteristics of one or more files.

The **file-spec** is the name of the file or files to be modified. If two or more files are specified, they must be separated by commas.

Command Qualifiers

/ACL

Associates an Access Control List with the specified file or files.

/BEFORE = [time]

Selects files that are dated before the time specified. In addition to time values, the keywords **TODAY**, **TOMORROW**, and **YESTERDAY** can be used. If no time is specified, the system will assume **TODAY**.

/CONFIRM
/NOCONFIRM (default)

Instruct the system whether to query the user for confirmation of each **SET FILE** operation. Appropriate responses are shown in Figure 10-1 on page 161.

/CREATED (default)

Selects files on the basis of their creation dates. This qualifier is used in conjunction with the /BEFORE or /SINCE qualifier.

/DATA_CHECK[= (READ,WRITE)]
/DATA_CHECK[= (NOREAD,NOWRITE)]

Instruct the system whether to perform a READ or WRITE data check, or both, during file transfers. If neither is specified, the default calls for a WRITE data check to be performed on the file.

/ENTER = new-file-spec

Allows assignment of a second, or alias, name for a file. Both names, though, refer to the same file.
    To remove an alias name but not the file to which it refers, use the **SET FILE/REMOVE** qualifier.

/ERASE_ON_DELETE

Instructs the system to physically erase files when a **DELETE** or **PURGE** command is used, rather than merely mark the disk space as available for later use by the system. **ERASE_ON_**

DELETE is used as part of the maintenance of security for sensitive files or information.

/EXCLUDE[= (file-spec...)]

Excludes any specified files from a wildcard command.

/EXPIRATION_DATE = date
/NOEXPIRATION_DATE

Instruct the system whether to assign an expiration date to specified files. If 0 is specified, today's date is used.

/LOG
/NOLOG (default)

Instruct the system whether to display the file specification of each file as it is modified.

/NODIRECTORY

Removes the directory attributes of a file, allowing deletion of a damaged directory file even if it contains other files. When a damaged or corrupted directory file is deleted, all files contained within it are lost.

The **ANALYZE/DISK_STRUCTURE/REPAIR** command can be used to retrieve lost files. See the VAX/VMS DCL Concepts Manual for details.

/PROTECTION[= (code)]

Allows modifications to or resetting of the protection level for files. If no protection code is included in the command qualifier, the access level of the specified files is set to the current default level.

/REMOVE

Allows removal of one of the names of the file with more than one name, without deleting the file. The file can still be accessed by any other name still in effect.

If a file with only one name has its name removed, the **ANALYZE/DISK_STRUCTURE** utility must be used. See **SET FILE/ENTER** and the VAX/VMS DCL Concepts Manual for more details.

/SINCE[=time]

Selects files that are dated after the time specified. In addition to absolute or combined absolute and delta time values, the keywords **TODAY**, **TOMORROW**, and **YESTERDAY** can be used. If no time is specified, the system will assume **TODAY**.

/UNLOCK

Instructs the system to unlock a file that has been improperly closed.

/VERSION_LIMIT[=n]

Specifies the total number of versions an individual file can have. If no value for **n** is given, the system assumes a value of 0, which allows the full Files-11 capacity of 32,767 versions.

SET FILE/ACL

SET FILE/ACL[= (ace[,...])] file-spec[,...]

Allows modification of the Access Control List of one or more files. For full details on ACLs and Access Control Entries (ACEs), consult the VAX/VMS DCL Concepts Manual and the VAX/VMS DCL Dictionary.

The **file-spec[,...]** is the name or the names of files to have their ACL modified. Wildcard characters are permitted. If two or more files are specified, they must be separated by commas. If the **/EDIT** command qualifier is used, only one file specification can be made and it cannot include wildcard characters. The **(ace[,...])** is the name or names of Access Control Entries to be modified. If no ACE is specified, the entire ACL is open for modification.

SET HOST

SET HOST nodename

Connects the terminal, through the current host processor, to another processor, called the remote processor. Both processors must be running the DECnet network, and you must have an account on the remote system in order to log in after the remote connection has been made. The **SHOW NETWORK** command can be used to list the names of nodes accessible to your node.

The **LOGOUT** command is used to exit from a connection to a host; if you have **SET HOST** to a remote host, the **LOGOUT** will return you to the local host and a second **LOGOUT** will be required to exit the system entirely.

It is possible to connect to multiple hosts, establishing a series of connections from local to remote hosts. As an example, from HOST1 you could **SET HOST host2** to connect through HOST1 to HOST2. After signing on to HOST2, you could **SET HOST host3** to another remote host, in this case establishing a path from one remote host through another to the local host. The first **LOGOUT** would sign off from HOST3; the second from HOST2, and the third from the local HOST1. You can make a quick exit from remote connections through use of the Ctrl-Y key combinations, struck several times. The system will query to ask if you want to return to the original node. A **Y** or **YES** will return to the local node.

Command Qualifier

/LOG[=file-spec]
/NOLOG (default)

Instruct the system whether to maintain a log file of the entire session. If **/LOG** is used without a file specification, the log file is given the name SETHOST.LOG.

SET HOST/DTE

SET HOST/DTE terminal-name

Connects the system to a remote system through an outgoing terminal line directly or with a modem.

You must have proper privileges to assign a channel to the specified terminal port, or the device protection of the terminal port must be set at a level low enough for you to make changes. Check with the system manager for instructions on your system and information on any special requirements of the local or remote system.

The **terminal-name** is the name of the outgoing terminal line.

Once connected to the remote system, you must log in to that system, and can then use DCL commands. To exit from the remote system, type the Ctrl-Backslash (\) combination.

Command Qualifiers

/DIAL = (NUMBER:number[,MODEM_TYPE:modem-type])

Instructs an attached modem to dial a telephone number. The **NUMBER:number** element is required; the **MODEM_TYPE** element is optional and can be used to specify a modem protocol of DF03 or DF112, or another type of modem identified to the system by the system operator. The default is DF03.

Here is an example of the command qualifier:

$SET HOST/DTE TTA6:/DIAL = (NUMBER:2256278,MODEM_ TYPE:DF03)

/LOG[= file-spec]
/NOLOG

Instruct the system whether to maintain a log of the entire session. If the **/LOG** qualifier is used without a file specification, the default name for the log is SETHOST. LOG.

The log will include any noise transmitted along with the file; therefore the use of the **/LOG** qualifier is not recommended as a means of file transfer.

SET KEY

SET KEY

Changes the current state for key redefinitions. See **DEFINE/KEY** for instructions on defining keys.

Command Qualifiers

/LOG (default)

/NOLOG

Instruct the system whether to display a message showing that the key state has been set.

/STATE = statename
/NOSTATE

Identify the state to be set. If the **/STATE** qualifier is not used or if **/NOSTATE** is used, the current state is not changed. Here is an example of use:

SET KEY/STATE = advance_edit

SET MESSAGE

SET MESSAGE [file-spec]

Instructs the system on the display format for messages. Messages can also be overridden or supplemented. Consult the VAX/VMS DCL Concepts Manual and the VAX/VMS DCL Dictionary.

The **file-spec** is the name of an optional file of messages. In order to compile a list of messages, it is necessary to use the Message Utility. Consult the VAX/VMS Message Utility Reference Manual for details.

SET PASSWORD

SET PASSWORD

Instructs the system to change the login password. The system manager can control the right to change passwords as well as the length of passwords and can assign expiration dates to passwords.

Passwords can include alphanumeric characters from A to Z, 0 through 9, the dollar sign, and underscore. (Lowercase characters are converted to uppercase by the system.)

There is also a random password generator facility in VMS which can be used to create a nonsense password.

When the **SET PASSWORD** command is used, the system will first ask for the present password. This is done to prevent a user who may have come across a signed-on but unsupervised terminal from changing the password. Next the system asks for a new password and then asks that it be entered a second time for verification. For security reasons, the old and new passwords are not displayed on the screen as they are entered. Here is the form:

$SET PASSWORD <Return>

Old password:

New password:

Verification:

In order to maintain the security of the system and your own files, you should change your password regularly. Common recommendations for security of passwords include

1. Change passwords monthly.
2. Create passwords of six or more characters.
3. Select passwords that are not obvious to strangers and friends (avoid your nickname and the names of your children, for example).
4. Don't write down your password on your desk calendar or in the front of your telephone directory.

Command Qualifiers

/GENERATE[= value]

Requests the system to generate a password. Five random passwords will be displayed on screen and you can select one of them; pressing Return will bring five new passwords to the screen. The optional **value** in the qualifier limits the length of the generated password. The system will create a password between value n and $n + 2$ characters in length. The passwords are designed to include pronounceable syllables, and the list includes an aid to pronunciation.

Here is an example of the /GENERATE qualifier in use.

$SET PASSWORD/GENERATE

Old password:

zoafzy   zoaf-zy
kiegry   kie-gry
ultezbun   ul-tez-bun
limgea   lim-gea
dajdyxuf   daj-dyx-uf

Choose a password from this list, or press RETURN to get a new list.
New password:

Verification:

/SECONDARY

Permits the change of a secondary password if one is in use, or creates one. Once a secondary password is in use, two password prompts will be displayed at login. To remove a secondary password, run the **SET PASSWORD/SECONDARY** command and hit the Return key instead of typing in a new password.

One interesting use of a secondary password is to require that two different persons, each knowing one of the passwords, sign on together for certain accounts.

SET PROCESS

SET PROCESS [process-name]

Instructs the system to change execution characteristics of the specified or current process for the current terminal session or job.

The **process-name** is the name of the process to have its characteristics changed.

Consult the VAX/VMS DCL Concepts Manual and the VAX/VMS DCL Dictionary for further details.

SET PROMPT

SET PROMPT[= string]

Allows the user to change the DCL prompt.

The **string** is the name of the string to replace the default $ prompt of DCL. Any valid ASCII character can be used in the string, which can be as short as one character. If you use spaces or lowercase letters in the string, they must be enclosed in quote marks; otherwise spaces are removed and lowercase letters are converted to uppercase automatically.

Here is an example of use of the command:

$SET PROMPT = "Yes, boss?:"   <Return>

From this point on, instead of a bare dollar sign, the DCL prompt will be:

Yes, boss?:

New prompts are retained for as long as the current session is maintained. In order to make the new prompt permanent, the **SET PROMPT** command and string should be included as a line in the LOGIN.COM file.

SET PROTECTION

SET PROTECTION[=(code)]file-spec[,...]

Instructs the system to apply a particular level of protection to a file or group of files. Read the VAX/VMS DCL Concepts Manual for full details.

The **code** is the protection to be applied. Details are in the VAX/VMS DCL Concepts Manual. The **file-spec[,...]** is the name or names of files for which protection is to be changed. Wildcard characters can be used in the directory, filename, file type, and version fields. If you omit the version number, protection will be changed only for the highest existing version of a file.

Command Qualifiers

/CONFIRM
/NOCONFIRM (default)

Instruct the system whether to query the user for confirmation of each **SET PROTECTION** operation. See Figure 10-1 on page 161 for appropriate responses.

/LOG
/NOLOG (default)

Instruct the system whether to display the file specification of each file after protection has been reset.

SET PROTECTION/DEFAULT

SET PROTECTION[= (code)]/DEFAULT

Instructs the system to set the default level of protection for all files to be created during a terminal session or batch job.

The **code** is the level of protection to be applied, except when a different level is specified by a **SET PROTECTION** or **CREATE** command. If no protection code is specified, the current default level of protection remains in effect.

For details on codes for protection, see the VAX/VMS DCL Concepts Manual.

SET RESTART_VALUE

SET RESTART_VALUE = string

In a command procedure, **SET RESTART_VALUE** establishes a test value for restarting portions of batch jobs. The command does not work as an interactive command.

The **string** is the test value for the batch job, and can contain as many as 255 characters.

SET RIGHTS_LIST

SET RIGHTS_LIST id-name[,...]

Permits the modification of the process or system rights list. The **/DISABLE** or **/ENABLE** command qualifier must be used with the command. For full details, see the VAX/VMS DCL Concepts Manual.

The **id-name[,...]** represents the identifier or identifiers to be added or removed. The **id-name** is a string of 1 to 31 alphanumeric characters, underscores, and dollar signs, containing at least one nonnumeric character.

Command Qualifiers

/ATTRIBUTES = (keyword[,...])

Available attribute keywords are

DYNAMIC—specifies whether unprivileged holders of the identifiers can add or remove them from the process rights list.
NODYNAMIC (default)
NORESOURCE (default)
RESOURCE—specifies whether holders of the identifiers can charge resources to them.

/DISABLE

Removes the specified identifiers from the process or system rights list. Incompatible with the **/ENABLE** qualifier.

/ENABLE

Adds the specified identifiers to the process or system rights list. Incompatible with the **/DISABLE** qualifier.

/IDENTIFICATION = pid

Specifies the process identification value (**pid**) of the process with the rights list to be modified. This qualifier cannot be used with the **/PROCESS** or **/SYSTEM** qualifier. If neither **/IDENTIFICATION** nor **/PROCESS** is specified, the system will assume the current process.

/PROCESS[= process-name]

Specifies the process name of the process with the rights list to be modified. This qualifier cannot be used with the **/IDENTIFICATION** or **/SYSTEM** qualifier. If neither **/IDENTIFICATION** nor **/PROCESS** is specified, the system will assume the current process.

/SYSTEM

Instructs the system to perform the addition or removal of an identifier on the system rights list. **/SYSTEM** cannot be used with **/PROCESS** or **/IDENTIFICATION**.

SET SYMBOL

SET SYMBOL

In a command procedure, **SET SYMBOL** controls access to local and global symbols. The command allows the user to mask global and local symbols from an outer procedure level at inner procedure levels. For full details, see the VAX/VMS DCL Concepts Manual.

Command Qualifier

/SCOPE = (keyword,...)

Allows symbols to be treated as undefined. Available keywords are

> **LOCAL**—removes any symbol translation limits set under the current procedure level.
> **NOLOCAL**—makes any local symbols defined in an outer procedure level to be considered as undefined by the current procedure and any inner procedure level.
> **GLOBAL**—restores access to all global symbols.
> **NOGLOBAL**—makes all global symbols inaccessible to the current procedure level and all inner procedure levels unless a specific instruction is issued.

SET TERMINAL

SET TERMINAL [device-name[:]]

Modifies specific characteristics of the terminal. For full details, see the VAX/VMS DCL Concepts Manual, the VAX/VMS I/O User's Reference Manual, and the manual for the specific terminal or terminals in use.

The **device-name[:]** is the name of the terminal to be affected by the **SET TERMINAL** command. If no device is specified, the modification will be made to the current SYS$COMMAND device, if such device is a terminal. If it is not a terminal, the system will issue an error message.

Command Qualifiers

/ADVANCED_VIDEO
/NOADVANCED_VIDEO

Specify whether the terminal in use has advanced video attributes, including the ability to display 132 columns of data. If terminal width is set at 132 columns and the **/ADVANCED_VIDEO** qualifier is issued, the terminal page limit is set at 24 lines. If **NOADVANCED_VIDEO** is used on a terminal set at 132 columns, the terminal page limit is set at 12 lines.

/ALTYPEAHD
/NOALTYPEAHD

In conjunction with the **/PERMANENT** qualifier, control the size of the type-ahead buffer for the terminal.

/ANSI_CRT
/NOANSI_CRT

Instruct the terminal whether to use ANSI CRT programming standards.

/APPLICATION_KEYPAD

Instructs the system to set the keypad to APPLICATION_KEYPAD so that the DEFINE/KEY facility can be used. The default is /NUMERIC_KEYPAD.

/AUTOBAUD
/NOAUTOBAUD

Used in conjunction with the **/PERMANENT** qualifier, **/AUTOBAUD** enables automatic baud rate detection on a terminal line at login, with a default speed of 9600 baud.

/BLOCK_MODE
/NOBLOCK_MODE

Instruct the system whether the terminal can perform block mode transmission, local editing, and field protection.

/BROADCAST (default)
/NOBROADCAST

Instruct the system whether the terminal is to receive broadcast messages such as MAIL notices and REPLY messages. The **/NOBROADCAST** qualifier blocks all messages and is used when the terminal is being used as a noninteractive device or when the user does not want output interrupted by messages.

See the **SET BROADCAST** command to enable or disable specific classes of messages.

/CRFILL[=formula]

Required for use with some non-Digital terminals and other devices, this qualifier instructs the system to generate fill characters after the pressing of the Return key on the terminal. The default value is **/CRFILL**=0. The recommended formula is a number from 0 to 9 with sufficient null characters to ensure that the Return instruction executes completely before the next real character is sent. If the terminal manufacturer does not provide the appropriate formula, the user will have to experiment to find the proper number of null characters.

/DEC_CRT[=(value1,value2)]
/NODEC_CRT[=(value1,value2)]

Tell the system whether the terminal conforms to DEC VT100 family standards, including escape sequences. A value of 1, the default, instructs that DEC_CRT terminal characteristics be used; a value of 2 instructs that DEC_CRT2 characteristics be used, supporting minimum VT200 standards.

For more information see the VAX/VMS I/O User's Reference Manual and specific manuals for the terminals to be used.

/DEVICE_TYPE=terminal-type

Tells the system the terminal type in use, automatically selecting the default characteristics for that terminal.

Available terminal types include

VT300	PRO_SERIES	LQP02
VT200	LA210	UNKNOWN
VT100	LA120	FT1–FT8
VT101	LA100	
VT102	LA38	
VT105	LA36	
VT125	LA34	
VT131	LA12	
VT132	LN03	
VT173	LN01K	
VT52		
VT55		
VT05		

FT1–FT8 are user-definable foreign terminals. You can find a description of characteristics for most Digital terminals in Table DCL-15 of the VAX/VMS DCL Concepts Manual.

/DIALUP
/NODIALUP (default)

Tell the system whether the terminal is a dialup terminal.

/DISCONNECT
/NODISCONNECT (default)

Instruct the system whether to discontinue a process if the line detects a hangup. **/DISCONNECT** can be used only in conjunction with the **/PERMANENT** qualifier. For more details, see **CONNECT** and **DISCONNECT** commands.

/DISMISS
/NODISMISS (default)

Instruct the terminal how to handle parity errors. (Parity errors are generated as part of the error-checking features of many communications protocols.) If **/DISMISS** is specified, the terminal driver ignores data with errors; with **/NODISMISS** in effect, the terminal driver terminates the current I/O with an error status.

/ECHO (default)
/NOECHO

Instruct the terminal whether to echo to the screen input lines it receives. With **/NOECHO** in effect, the terminal will display only the data a system or program writes to it.

/EDIT_MODE
/NOEDIT_MODE

Instruct the system whether the terminal can perform ANSI advanced editing functions.

/EIGHT_BIT
/NOEIGHT_BIT

Instruct the system whether the terminal uses 8-bit ASCII character code.

/FRAME=n

An element of the communication protocol, **/FRAME** specifies to the system the number of data bits the terminal driver expects for each character. The value of **n** can range from 5 to 8.

/FORM
/NOFORM

Instruct the terminal driver whether to translate a formfeed character into one or more line feeds or whether to pass through the formfeed without acting on it.

/FULLDUP
/NOFULLDUP (default)

Instruct the terminal whether to operate as a full-duplex or half-duplex device. These qualifiers are complementary to **/HALFDUP**, since **/FULLDUP** is the same as **/NOHALFDUP**.

/HALFDUP (default)
/NOHALFDUP

Instruct the terminal whether to operate as a full-duplex or half-duplex device. **/HALFDUP** is the same as **/NOFULLDUP**.

/HANGUP
/NOHANGUP (default)

Instruct the terminal whether the modem is to be hung up when the user logs out.

/HARDCOPY
/NOHARDCOPY

Instruct the system whether the terminal is a hard-copy or video terminal, also affecting how the terminal interprets certain input keys, including delete or rubout keys. The qualifier is complementary to **/SCOPE**, since **/HARDCOPY** is the same as **/NOSCOPE**.

/HOSTSYNC
/NOHOSTSYNC

Instruct the system whether to synchronize the flow of input from the terminal with handshaking protocols. With **/HOSTSYNC** in effect, the system sends a Ctrl-S or Ctrl-Q to respectively enable or disable acceptance of input.

/INSERT

Instructs the terminal to operate in the **/INSERT** mode for editing. The default mode is **/OVERSTRIKE**, in which characters are overtyped in editing.

/LOWERCASE
/NOLOWERCASE

See **UPPERCASE.**

/NUMERIC_KEYPAD (default)

Instructs the terminal to use the **/NUMERIC_KEYPAD** mode so that keys on the numeric keypad generate numbers and punctuation characters.

/OVERSTRIKE (default)

Instructs the terminal to use the **/OVERSTRIKE** mode. Compare to **/INSERT**.

/PAGE[= n]

Instructs the system on the page length of the terminal. On hard-copy terminals, the value of **n** equals the number of print lines between perforations on the paper; when the terminal receives a formfeed character, it advances the paper to the next perforation. A value of 0 treats each formfeed as a linefeed.

/PARITY[= option]
/NOPARITY[= option]

Instruct the system on the parity setting for the terminal. Available options are **EVEN** and **ODD**. If **/PARITY** is used without an option, the system will assume **/PARITY = EVEN**.

/PASTHRU
/NOPASTHRU (default)

Instruct the system whether to interpret special characters or to pass all data to an application program without acting on characters.

/PRINTER_PORT
/NOPRINTER_PORT

Tell the system that the terminal has a printer port available.

/REGIS
/NOREGIS

Instruct the system whether the terminal can use ReGIS graphics commands.

/SCOPE
/NOSCOPE

Instruct the system whether the terminal is a video terminal, also affecting how the device reacts to certain keys. These qualifiers are complementary to **/HARDCOPY**, since **/SCOPE** is the same as **/NOHARDCOPY**.

/SECURE_SERVER
/NOSECURE_SERVER (default)

Instruct the system whether the Break key on the terminal logs out the current process. With **/SECURE_SERVER** in effect, the Break key will initiate the login sequence when there is no current process underway.

/SIXEL_GRAPHICS
/NOSIXEL_GRAPHICS

Instruct the system whether the terminal can use the REGIS-defined SIXEL graphics protocol.

/SOFT_CHARACTERS
/NOSOFT_CHARACTERS

Instruct the system whether the terminal can work with a user-defined character set.

/SPEED = **rate**

Sets the speed at which the terminal receives and sends data. If one rate is given, input and output baud rates are set at the same speed; to give rates for each, list two speeds separated by a comma. Consult the hardware manual for your terminal for allowable baud rates.

/TAB
/NOTAB

Instruct the terminal how to handle tab characters. If you use **/NOTAB**, all tab characters are expanded to spaces, and tab stops are assumed to be at eight-character intervals. The **/TAB** qualifier prevents the system from converting tabs to spaces, but has the terminal process the tab characters.

/UNKNOWN

Instructs the system that the terminal in use is not a recognized type. The system will use the default terminal characteristics for unknown terminals.

/UPPERCASE
/NOUPPERCASE

Instruct the terminal whether to translate all lowercase letters to uppercase. The qualifier is complementary to **/LOWERCASE**, since **/UPPERCASE** is the same as **/NOLOWERCASE**.

/WIDTH = n

Instructs the terminal as to the number of characters on each input or output line, in the range from 1 to 511. If the **/WRAP** qualifier is in effect, the terminal will produce a carriage return and line feed when any line reaches the column position specified by the width value.

/WRAP (default)
/NOWRAP

Instruct the terminal whether to produce a carriage return and line feed at the end of a line, as determined by the terminal width.

SET WORKING_SET

SET WORKING_SET

Instructs the system to redefine the default size of the working set, or to establish a new upper limit for the working set size that can be changed by an image executed by a process. See the VAX/VMS DCL Concepts Manual for more details.

SHOW ACCOUNTING

SHOW ACCOUNTING

Displays elements of the system for which ACCOUNTING is enabled. See the discussion of ACCOUNTING in the VAX/VMS DCL Concepts Manual and the VAX/VMS DCL Dictionary for details.

SHOW ACL

SHOW ACL

Displays the Access Control List of an object.
The command assumes the object is a file. If it is not, the following command qualifier can be used:

/OBJECT_TYPE = type

The following keywords can be used to identify the type of object:

> **FILE** (default—a Files-11 disk file)
> **DEVICE**
> **SYSTEM_GLOBAL_SECTION**
> **GROUP_GLOBAL_SECTION**
> **LOGICAL_NAME_TABLE**

SHOW BROADCAST

SHOW BROADCAST

Displays the message classes disabled by the **SET BROADCAST** command (if any).

Command Qualifier

/OUTPUT[= file-spec]
/NOOUTPUT

Instruct the system where to send the output of the command. If neither qualifier is used or if **/OUTPUT** is used without a file specification, the output is sent to the current process default output stream or device.

Here is an example of the command and a sample response from the system:

$SHOW BROADCAST <Return>

Broadcasts are currently disabled for:

PHONE

MAIL

USER1

$

SHOW DEFAULT

SHOW DEFAULT

Displays current default device and directory names. Current equivalence strings, if any, are also displayed.
   The information listed tells the user what defaults the system will use whenever a file specification does not provide full information in all fields.
   Here is a sample response from the system:

$SHOW DEFAULT <Return>

$DISK1:[SANDLER]

15-AUG-1987 17:29:20

SHOW DEVICES

SHOW DEVICES [device-name[:]]

Displays the status of the specified device. The **device-name[:]** is the name of the device about which information is sought.
   To obtain information about a specific device or a generic class of devices, specify the device name. If you truncate the name of the device, the command will supply information on all

devices beginning with the characters included in the command. If the controller designation is not included, the command will list all devices on all controllers with the specified unit number; and if the unit number is not included, the command lists all devices on the specified controller. If you include neither a device name parameter nor any other qualifier, the command will yield a list of characteristics of all devices on the system, except for mailbox-related devices.

Here is an example of use of the **SHOW DEVICES** command:

$SHOW DEVICES   <Return>

Device Name	Device Status	Error Count	Volume Label	Free Blocks	Trans Count	Mnt Cnt
BLUEFISH$DUA0:	Online	0				
BLUEFISH$DUA1:	Offline	0				
BLUEFISH$DUA2:	Online	0				
BLUEFISH$DUB3:	Mounted	0	MICROVMS	103077	93	1
BLUEFISH$MSA0:	Online	9				
BLUEFISH$MUA0:	Online	0				
TXA7:	Unavailable	113				

Command Qualifiers

/ALLOCATED

Displays all devices that are currently allocated to processes. Can be used with generic device names or partial device names.

/BRIEF (default)

Yields a brief display of information about specified devices.

/FULL

Yields a complete display of information about specified devices. Here is an example of use of the command:

$SHOW DEVICES/FULL <Return>

Disk BLUEFISH$DUA0:, device type RD53, is online, file-oriented device, shareable, available to cluster, error logging is enabled.

Error count	0	Operations completed	0
Owner process	" "	Owner UIC	[0,0]
Owner process ID	00000000	Dev Prot S:RWED,O:RWED,G:RWED,W:RWED	
Reference count	0	Default buffer size	512

/MOUNTED

Yields a list of all devices currently with volumes mounted.

/OUTPUT[=file-spec]
/NOOUTPUT

Instruct the system where to send the output of the command. If no file specification is given, and in the absence of either command qualifier, output is sent to the current default output stream or device.

/NOOUTPUT suppresses all output.

/WINDOWS

Displays the number of windows and the total size of all windows for files open on a volume.

SHOW ERROR

SHOW ERROR

Displays the error count for any device with a count greater than 0.

Command Qualifiers

/FULL

Displays the error count for all devices, including devices with a count of 0.

/OUTPUT[= file-spec]
/OUTPUT = SYS$OUTPUT (default)

Instruct the system where to send the output of the command. If no file specification is given, or in the absence of the command qualifier, output is sent to the current default output stream or device.

SHOW KEY

SHOW KEY [keyname]

Displays any key redefinitions put into effect by the **DEFINE/KEY** command.

The **keyname** is the name of a specific key the user seeks information about. You can find the list of redefinable keys and their names under the **DEFINE/KEY** command.

Command Qualifiers

/ALL

Instructs the system to display all key definitions of the current state.

/BRIEF (default)
/NOBRIEF

Instruct the system whether to display only the key definition and state. **/BRIEF** is equivalent to **/NOFULL**.

/DIRECTORY

Instructs the system to display the names of all states for which keys have been redefined. The **/DIRECTORY** qualifier is not compatible with any of the other qualifiers for the **SHOW KEY** command.

/FULL
/NOFULL (default)

Instruct the system whether to display all qualifiers associated with definitions. The **/FULL** and **/NOBRIEF** qualifiers are equivalent.

/STATE = (state-name[,...])
/NOSTATE

Request display of key redefinitions in the specified state. If you omit the **/STATE** qualifier or use the **/NOSTATE** qualifier, key definitions in the current state are displayed.

SHOW LOGICAL

SHOW LOGICAL [logical-name[:],[...]]

Displays all logical names in one or more logical name tables, or displays the current equivalence string or strings assigned to a specified logical name or names.

    The **logical-name[:],[...]** is the name of one or more logical names about which information is to be displayed. Logical names can be from 1 to 255 characters; a logical name table can be up to 31 characters in length. If no logical name is included as a parameter of the command, **SHOW LOGICAL** will display all logical names in the specified logical name tables.

    For more details, consult the VAX/VMS DCL Concepts Manual.

SHOW MEMORY

SHOW MEMORY

Displays information about memory resources of the system, including physical memory, process entry slots and balance slots, nonpaged and paged dynamic memory, and space in paging and swap files.

    The **SHOW MEMORY** command displays statistics on the following: physical memory usage, bad page list, number of pages allocated to VMS, slot usage, fixed-size pool areas in packets, dynamic memory usage in bytes, paging file usage in pages, lookaside list, and dynamic memory. For more details on memory terms and uses, see the VAX/VMS DCL Concepts Manual and the VAX/VMS DCL Dictionary.

Command Qualifiers

/ALL (default)

Instructs the system to display all available information, as if the **/FILES**, **/PHYSICAL_PAGES**, **/POOL**, and **/SLOTS** qualifiers had been used.

Here is an example of use of the **SHOW MEMORY/ALL** command:

$SHOW MEMORY/ALL   <Return>

System Memory Resources on 15-AUG-1987 17:30:03.45

Physical Memory Usage (pages):	Total	Free	In Use	Modified
Main Memory (16.00Mb)	32768	27703	4918	147

Slot Usage (slots):	Total	Free	Resident	Swapped
Process Entry Slots	50	35	15	0
Balance Set Slots	50	37	13	0

Fixed-Size Pool Areas (packets):	Total	Free	In Use	Size
Small Packet (SRP) List	2000	1791	209	96
I/O Request Packet (IRP) List	366	234	132	208
Large Packet (LRP) List	49	26	23	656

Dynamic Memory Usage (bytes):	Total	Free	In Use	Largest
Nonpaged Dynamic Memory	399872	115120	284752	79184
Paged Dynamic Memory	189952	110448	79504	103072

Paging File Usage (pages):	Free	In Use	Total
DISK$MICROVMS:[SYS0.SYSEXE]SWAPFILE.SYS	16160	3840	20000
DISK$MICROVMS:[SYS0.SYSEXE]PAGEFILE.SYS	18847	1153	20000
	17763	2229	19992

Of the physical pages in use, 3471 pages are permanently allocated to VMS.

15-AUG-1987 17:30:16

/FILES

Instructs the system to display information about usage of each paging and swap file currently installed.

/FULL

Used in conjunction with the **/POOL** or **/FILES** qualifier to display additional information about the usage of each pool area or paging and swap file.

/OUTPUT[=file-spec]
/NOOUTPUT

Instruct the system where to send the output of the command. If neither qualifier is used or if no file specification is used with **/OUTPUT**, the output is sent to the current process default output stream or device. The **/NOOUTPUT** qualifier suppresses any output.

/PHYSICAL_PAGES

Displays information about the amount of physical memory and the number of free and modified pages in the system.

/POOL

Displays information on usage of each dynamic memory (pool) area.

/SLOTS

Displays information about availability of vector and balance slots.

SHOW NETWORK

SHOW NETWORK

Displays information about the local node as a member of the network, if one exists.

The command will display the current network as follows:

Node: the name of each available node in the network, with its node address and node name.

Links: the number of logical links between the local node and any available remote node.

Cost: the total line cost, as defined by the system manager, of a path to a remote node.

Hops: the number of intermittent nodes and the target node.

Next hop to node: the outgoing physical line to the remote node, with node address and nodename of the next hop to the target node.

Here is an example of the use of the **SHOW NETWORK** command and a sample response from a small network:

$SHOW NETWORK <Return>

VAX/VMS Network status for local node 1.1 BLUEFISH on 18-AUG-1987 09:26:10.68

Node	Links	Cost	Hops	Next Hop to Node
1.1 BLUEFISH	2	0	0	(Local) — > 1.1 BLUEFISH

18-AUG-1987 09:26:13

Command Qualifier

/OUTPUT[=file-spec]
/NOOUTPUT

Instruct the system where to send the output of the command. If neither qualifier is used or if no file specification is used with the /OUTPUT command, the output is sent to the current process default output stream or device. The **/NOOUTPUT** qualifier suppresses any output.

SHOW PRINTER

SHOW PRINTER device-name[:]

Displays characteristics currently defined for a system printer. Printer characteristics are put into effect by the **SET PRINTER** command, which is available only to those with operator privileges.

SHOW PROCESS

SHOW PROCESS [process-name]

Displays information about a process or subprocess in the current process tree.

Command Qualifiers

/ACCOUNTING

Displays accounting statistics for the current session.

/ALL

Displays all information available, including default information of the **SHOW PROCESS** command as well as the additional information produced by the **/ACCOUNTING**, **/PRIVILEGES**, and **/QUOTAS** qualifiers. For current processes, the information generated by the **/MEMORY** and **/SUBPROCESSES** qualifiers will also be displayed.

Figure 10-2 shows an example of part of the display from a **SHOW PROCESS/ALL** command:

$SHOW PROCESS/ALL   <Return>

17-AUG-1987 09:33:46.42   VTA 130:   User: SANDLER
Pid: 00000562   Proc. name: SANDLER   UIC: [EDIT,SANDLER]
Priority: 4   Default file spec: $DISK1:[SANDLER]

Devices allocated: VTA130:

Process Quotas:
  Account name: EDIT
  CPU limit: Infinite   Direct I/O limit: 18
  Buffered I/O byte count quota: 35904   Buffered I/O limit: 18
  Timer queue entry quota: 50   Open file quota: 59
  Paging file quota: 18960   Subprocess quota: 6
  Default page fault cluster: 64   AST limit: 78
  Enqueue quota: 200   Shared file limit: 0
  Max detached processes: 0   Max active jobs: 0

Accounting information:
  Buffered I/O count: 279   Peak working set size: 645
  Direct I/O count: 181   Peak virtual size: 1553
  Page faults: 1756   Mounted volumes: 0
  Images activated: 9
  Elapsed CPU time: 0 00:00:13.77
  Connect time: 0 00:02:53.94

Process privileges:
  TMPMBX   may create temporary mailbox
  NETMBX   may create network device
  GRPPRV   group access via system protection

Process rights identifiers:
 INTERACTIVE
 DIALUP
 FREELANCE
 SYS$NODE_BLUEFISH

Process Dynamic Memory Area
  Current Size (bytes)   153600   Current Total Size (pages)   300
  Free Space (bytes)   149360   Space in Use (bytes)   4240
  Size of Largest Block   149248   Size of Smallest Block   8
  Number of Free Blocks   4   Free Blocks LEQU 32 Bytes   1

Processes in this tree:

SANDLER (*)

17-AUG-1987 09:34:03

/CONTINUOUS

Yields a continuously updated display of information about the current process.

While the continuous display is running, you can display a map of pages in the virtual address space of the process by pressing the V key. For further details, see the VAX/VMS DCL Dictionary.

/CONTINUOUS cannot be used with the **/OUTPUT** qualifier.

A DICTIONARY OF SELECTED DCL COMMANDS AND STATEMENTS □ 265

/IDENTIFICATION = pid

Specifies the process identification of the process under examination. Incompatible with a process name parameter in the command.

/MEMORY

Yields a display of the current process's use of dynamic memory area.

/OUTPUT[= file-spec]
/NOOUTPUT

Instruct the system where to send the output of the command. If neither qualifier is used or if **/OUTPUT** is used without a file specification, the output is sent to the current process default output stream or device.
   /OUTPUT cannot be used with the **/CONTINUOUS** qualifier.

/PRIVILEGES

Displays user privileges and identifiers of the process.

/QUOTAS

Displays current quotas or limits for each resource.

/SUBPROCESSES

Displays any subprocesses owned by the current process.

SHOW PROTECTION

SHOW PROTECTION

Displays default file protection to be applied to any new files created during the current terminal session or batch job.
   Here is an example of use of this command:

$SHOW PROTECTION   <Return>

SYSTEM = RWED, OWNER = RWED, GROUP = RE,
                                    WORLD = NO ACCESS

17-AUG-1987 09:34:19

SHOW QUEUE

SHOW QUEUE [queue-name]   <Return>
Yields a display of information about queues and jobs currently in queues.
    The **queue-name** is a specified queue. If the **queue-name** is not included in the command, the system will display information about all queues initialized for the system. If there are any jobs on any of the queues, information about those jobs will also be displayed. Wildcard characters can be used in the parameter.
    Here is an example of use of the **SHOW QUEUE** command:

$SHOW QUEUE   <Return>

Batch queue SYS$BATCH, on BLUEFISH::

Terminal queue SYS$HARRIS, on BLUEFISH::$PRINTER3, mounted form DEFAULT

Terminal queue SYS$LASER, on BLUEFISH::LTA100:, mounted form WPSPLUS (stock = DEFAULT)

Printer queue SYS$LINE, on BLUEFISH::$PRINTER1, mounted form WPSPLUS (stock = DEFAULT)

Terminal queue SYS$PRINT, on BLUEFISH::LTA101:, mounted form REMOTE (stock = DEFAULT)

17-AUG-1987 09:34:33

Command Qualifiers

/ALL

Produces a display of all job entries in specified queues. The default condition of the **SHOW QUEUE** command is a display of only those jobs owned by the current process.

Here is an example of the **SHOW QUEUE/ALL** command and a partial response from the system:

$SHOW QUEUE/ALL   <Return>

Jobname	Username	Entry	Status
no privilege		1859	Holding until 18-AUG-1987 07:00

Terminal queue SYS$HARRIS, on BLUEFISH::$PRINTER3, mounted form DEFAULT

Terminal queue SYS$LASER, on BLUEFISH::LTA100:, mounted form WPSPLUS (stock=DEFAULT)

Printer queue SYS$LINE, on BLUEFISH::$PRINTER1, mounted form WPSPLUS (stock=DEFAULT)

Terminal queue SYS$PRINT, on BLUEFISH::LTA101:, mounted form REMOTE (stock=DEFAULT)

   17-AUG-1987 09:35:08

/BATCH

Lists any batch queues and any jobs in those queues owned by the current process.

/BRIEF (default)

Yields a brief listing of information about job entries in queues, including queue name, username, job number, and for applicable queues, current form and stock mounted. See **/FULL**.

/DEVICE

Produces a list of all printer, terminal, and server queues, as well as any jobs in the queues that are owned by the current process.

/FILES

Instructs the system to produce a brief listing of information about job entries in the queue with a list of files associated with each job.

/FULL

Produces a full list of information about all queues and any jobs in the queue owned by the current process. Information on queues includes queue name and type and any settings for the queue. Information on jobs includes full file specification, date and time of submission, and any specified settings for the job.

Here is an example of use of the **SHOW QUEUE/FULL** command:

$SHOW QUEUE/FULL <Return>

Batch queue SYS$BATCH, on BLUEFISH::
  /BASE_PRIORITY=4 /JOB_LIMIT=3
  /OWNER=[SYSTEM] /PROTECTION=(S:E,0:D,G:R,W:W)

Terminal queue SYS$HARRIS, on BLUEFISH::$PRINTER3, mounted form DEFAULT
  /BASE_PRIORITY=4
  /DEFAULT=(FEED,FORM=DEFAULT) Lowercase /OWNER=[SYSTEM]
  /PROTECTION=(S:E,0:D,G:R,W:W)

Terminal queue SYS$LASER, on BLUEFISH::LTA100:, mounted form WPSPLUS (stock=DEFAULT)
  /BASE_PRIORITY=4
  /DEFAULT=(FEED,FORM=REMOTE (stock=DEFAULT)) Lowercase
  /OWNER=[SYSTEM] /PROCESSOR=LATSYM/PROTECTION= (S:E,0:D,G:R,W:W)
  /RETAIN=ERROR

Printer queue SYS$LINE, on BLUEFISH::$PRINTER1, mounted form WPSPLUS (stock=DEFAULT)
  /BASE_PRIORITY=4 /DEFAULT=(FEED,FORM=DEFAULT) /OWNER=[SYSTEM]
  /PROTECTION=(S:E,0:D,G:R,W:W)

Terminal queue SYS$PRINT, on BLUEFISH::LTA101:, mounted form REMOTE (stock=DEFAULT)
  /BASE_PRIORITY=4

A DICTIONARY OF SELECTED DCL COMMANDS AND STATEMENTS □ 269

/DEFAULT = (FEED,FORM = REMOTE (stock = DEFAULT)) Lowercase
/OWNER = [SYSTEM] /PROCESSOR = LATSYM /PROTECTION = (S:E,O:D,G:R,W:W)
/RETAIN = ERROR

17-AUG-1987 09:35:29

/OUTPUT[= file-spec]
/NOOUTPUT

Instructs the system where to send the output of the command. If neither qualifier is used or if **/OUTPUT** is used without a file specification, the output is sent to the current process default output stream or device.

SHOW QUEUE/CHARACTERISTICS

SHOW QUEUE/CHARACTERISTICS [characteristic-name]

Instructs the system to display characteristic names and numbers on queues.

The **characteristic-name** is the specified characteristic. If no characteristic is included in the command, **SHOW QUEUE/CHARACTERISTICS** will display information for all characteristics on the system.

Here is an example of use of the **SHOW QUEUE/CHARACTERISTICS** command:

$SHOW QUEUE/CHARACTERISTICS   <Return>

Characteristic name	Number
WPCORP$DOCUMENT	127

17-AUG-1987 09:35:51

Command Qualifier

/OUTPUT[= file-spec]
/NOOUTPUT

Instruct the system where to send the output of the command. If neither qualifier is used or if **/OUTPUT** is used without a file specification, the output is sent to the current process default output stream or device.

SHOW QUEUE/FORM

SHOW QUEUE/FORM [form-name]

Instructs the system to display form names and numbers on queues.

The **form-name** is a specified form name. If no **form-name** is included in the command, **SHOW QUEUE/FORM** will display information for all forms on the system.

Here is an example of use of the **SHOW QUEUE/FORM** command:

$SHOW QUEUE/FORM   <Return>

Form name	Number	Description
DEFAULT	0	System-defined default
LAS10 (stock=DEFAULT)	21	LAS10
LAS12M (stock=DEFAULT)	24	LAS12M
LASLAND (stock=DEFAULT)	27	LASLAND
LASSMALL (stock=DEFAULT)	25	LASSMALL
PR10 (stock=DEFAULT)	1	PR10
PRBIG (stock=DEFAULT)	8	PRBIG
PRBIGM (stock=DEFAULT)	9	PRBIGM
PRLQ (stock=DEFAULT)	5	PRLQ
PRLQM (stock=DEFAULT)	6	PRLQM
REMOTE (stock=DEFAULT)	50	REMOTE
REMOTE1 (stock=DEFAULT)	132	REMOTE1
WPSPLUS (stock=DEFAULT)	1101	WPSPLUS

17-AUG-1987 09:36:19

Command Qualifiers

/BRIEF (default)

Displays the name, stock, number, and description of the form.

/FULL

Displays more complete information, including form names, numbers, descriptions, and any **DEFINE/FORM** settings.

/OUTPUT[=file-spec]
/NOOUTPUT

Instruct the system where to send the output of the command. If neither qualifier is used or if **/OUTPUT** is used without a file specification, the output is sent to the current process default output stream or device.

SHOW QUOTA

SHOW QUOTA

Instructs the system to display the current disk quota for a specific user on a specific disk. The display also shows a calculation of the amount of space available and the amount of allowable overdraft.

SHOW STATUS

SHOW STATUS

Instructs the system to show the status of the current process.
 Information includes current time and date, elapsed CPU time used by the current process, the number of page faults, the open file count, buffered I/O count, direct I/O count, current working set size, and the current amount of physical memory occupied by the current process.
 The information yielded by **SHOW STATUS** is similar to that produced by the Ctrl-T key combination on systems with that function enabled.
 Here is an example of the use of the **SHOW STATUS** command:

$SHOW STATUS   <Return>

Status on 17-AUG-1987 09:36:48.33   Elapsed CPU : 0 00:00:22.47
Buff. I/O: 552   Cur. ws. :   406   Open files :   1
Dir. I/O :   218   Phys. Mem. : 198   Page Faults :   3023

17-AUG-1987 09:36:50

SHOW SYMBOL

SHOW SYMBOL [symbol-name]

Instructs the system to show the current value of a local or global symbol.

The command searches the local symbol table of the current command level first, and then moves on to the local symbol tables of the preceding command levels, then to the global symbol table of the specified symbol.

Command Qualifiers

/ALL

Instructs the system to display the current values of all symbols in the specified symbol table. The system assumes the use of the local symbol table unless **/GLOBAL** is specified.

/GLOBAL

Instructs the system to search only the global symbol table.

/LOCAL

Instructs the system to search only the local symbol table.

/LOG (default)
/NOLOG

Instruct the system whether to generate a message if a symbol value is truncated because it is longer than 255 characters.

SHOW SYSTEM

SHOW SYSTEM

Instructs the system to display a list of all processes, with information about the status of each process.

Here is an example of use of the **SHOW SYSTEM** command:

$SHOW SYSTEM   <Return>

VAX/VMS V4.5 on node BLUEFISH 17-AUG-1987 09:36:58.38 Uptime 7 14:07:05

Pid	Process Name	State	Pri	I/O	CPU	Page flts	Ph.Mem
00000040	NULL	COM	0	0	6 17:36:52.43	0	0
00000041	SWAPPER	HIB	16	0	0 00:02:50.41	0	0
00000044	JOB_CONTROL	HIB	9	25831	0 00:03:26.14	222860	97
00000046	OPCOM	LEF	7	1043	0 00:00:11.69	8844	64
00000047	SYMBIONT_0001	HIB	6	4332	0 00:06:49.76	18882	45
00000048	NETACP	HIB	10	3694	0 00:00:45.24	24539	78
00000049	EVL	HIB	6	193	0 00:01:01.46	149234	46 N
0000004A	REMACP	HIB	8	15	0 00:00:00.20	80	56
0000004B	SYMBIONT_0002	HIB	6	42048	0 00:05:28.32	89127	55
0000004C	SYMBIONT_0003	HIB	6	6666	0 00:00:56.54	12362	47
0000004D	DK_DUB3	HIB	3	283901	0 04:15:01.88	906622	70
0000044F	TESSA	LEF	4	685	0 00:00:13.07	2107	209
00000090	WILLIE	LEF	9	30240	0 00:04:56.14	56098	143
00000518	_LTA288:	LEF	5	503	0 00:00:08.76	999	898
00000562	SANDLER	CUR	4	774	0 00:00:22.94	3063	365
000001E4	JANICE	HIB	8	5281	0 00:00:47.73	7175	63

The *Pid* is the process identification code, a 32-bit binary value that identifies a process. *Process Name* is a 1–15 character string. State is the activity level of the process (including COM for computing, HIB for hibernation, LEF for local event flag, and WAIT for wait). *Pri* is the current priority level of the process: the higher the number, the higher the priority. *I/O* is total process I/O count—the number of I/O operations involved in the execution of the process, including direct I/O and buffered I/O. *CPU* is charged CPU time, the amount of time that a process has used. *Page flts* is the number of page faults, the exceptions caused by references to pages not in the process's working set. *Ph.Mem* is physical memory occupied. The final column of the display can show a process indicator, with B for Batch, S for Subprocess, and N for a network process.

If the process is swapped out, the message "-swapped out-" will be displayed in some of the columns. Swapping is the shaving of memory resources between general processes, acccomplished by writing a working set to secondary storage (swapping out) and reading another working set into physical memory (swapping-in).

Command Qualifiers

/BATCH

Instructs the system to display system information only on batch jobs.

/FULL

Instructs the system to display the User Identification Code in addition to the default information.

/NETWORK

Instructs the system to display system information only on network processes.

/OUTPUT[=file-spec]
/NOOUTPUT

Instruct the system where to send the output of the command. If neither qualifier is used or if **/OUTPUT** is used without a file specification, the output is sent to the current process default output stream or device.

/PROCESS (default)

Instructs the system to display information on all system processes.

/SUBPROCESSES

Instructs the system to display information only on subprocesses.

SHOW TERMINAL

SHOW TERMINAL [device-name[:]]

Instructs the system to display the current characteristics of a terminal, as put into effect by the **SET TERMINAL** command. If a device name is not specified in the command, the characteristics of the current SYS$COMMAND device are shown.

A DICTIONARY OF SELECTED DCL COMMANDS AND STATEMENTS □ 275

Here is an example of use of the command:

$SHOW TERMINAL <Return>

Terminal: _VTA130:   Device_Type: VT200_Series   Owner: SANDLER
Physical terminal: _TXA7:

| Input: | 1200 | LFfill: | 0 | Width: | 80 | Parity: | None |
| Output: | 1200 | CRfill: | 0 | Page: | 24 | | |

Terminal Characteristics:
  Interactive   Echo   Type_ahead   No Escape
  Hostsync   TTsync   Lowercase   Tab
  Wrap   Scope   Remote   Eightbit
  Broadcast   No Readsync   No Form   Fulldup
  Modem   No Local_echo   Autobaud   Hangup
  No Brdcstmbx   No DMA   Altypeahd   Set_speed
  Line Editing   Overstrike editing   No Fallback   Dialup
  No Secure server   Disconnect   No Pasthru   No Syspassword
  No SIXEL Graphics   No Soft Characters   Printer port   Numeric Keypad
  ANSI_CRT   No Regis   No Block_mode   Advanced_video
  Edit_mode   DEC_CRT   DEC_CRT2
17-AUG-1987 09:37:36

Command Qualifier

/OUTPUT[= file-spec]
/NOOUTPUT

Instruct the system where to send the output of the command. If neither qualifier is used or if no file specification is used with the **/OUTPUT** command, the output is sent to the current process default output stream or device. The **/NOOUTPUT** qualifier suppresses any output.

SHOW TIME

SHOW [DAY]TIME

Instructs the system to display the current date and time. The **SHOW DAYTIME** command yields the same response as **SHOW TIME**.

Here are sample commands and responses:

$SHOW DAYTIME <Return>

18-AUG-1987 09:25:46

$SHOW TIME <Return>

18-AUG-1987 09:25:50

SHOW TRANSLATION

SHOW TRANSLATION logical-name

Instructs the system to search logical name tables for the specified logical name. The first equivalence name of the first match is displayed.

SHOW TRANSLATION is similar to **SHOW LOGICAL**, except that **SHOW TRANSLATION** executes from within DCL, while **SHOW LOGICAL** executes an image. **SHOW TRANSLATION** does not cause the current image to exit and does not deassign user mode logical names.

Command Qualifier

/TABLE = name

Specifies to the system the name of a table to be searched. If no table name is specified, the system will search all logical tables defined by the system under the logical name LNM$DCL_LOGICAL.

SHOW USERS

SHOW USERS [username]

Instructs the system to display the username, terminal name, and process identification code of all interactive users on the system, or a specified interactive user.

The **username** is the name of a specific user. If a string is used in the command, the system will display information on all users whose usernames begin with the string. If no username is specified in the command, **SHOW USERS** will display a list of all interactive users.

Here is an example of use of the command:

$SHOW USERS   <Return>

VAX/VMS Interactive Users
17-AUG-1987 09:37:46.17
Total number of interactive users = 11

Username	Process Name	PID	Terminal	
BASHFUL	BASHFUL	00000617	LTA287:	
DOC	DOC	0000056D	LTA274:	
DOPEY	DOPEY	000003EC	LTA273:	
GRUMPY	GRUMPY	00000316	LTA286:	
JANICE	JANICE	0000046B	LTA272:	
KEEFE	KEEFE	00000355	LTA285:	
OPERATOR	OPERATOR	0000044F	LTA283:	
SANDLER	SANDLER	00000562	VTA130:	TXA7:
SLEEPY	SLEEPY	00000090	LTA14:	
TESSA	_LTA288:	00000518	LTA288:	
WILLIE	WILLIE	00000663	LTA295:	

17-AUG-1987 09:37:55

If the command had been entered as

$SHOW USERS DO   <Return>

the result would have been

VAX/VMS Interactive Users
17-AUG-1987 09:37:46.17
Total number of interactive users = 11

Username	Process Name	PID	Terminal
DOC	DOC	0000056D	LTA274:
DOPEY	DOPEY	000003EC	LTA273:

17-AUG-1987 09:37:55

Command Qualifier

/OUTPUT[= file-spec]
/NOOUTPUT

Instruct the system where to send the output of the command. If neither qualifier is used or if no file specification is used with the **/OUTPUT** qualifier, the output is sent to the current process default output stream or device. The **/NOOUTPUT** qualifier suppresses any output.

SHOW WORKING_Set

SHOW WORKING_SET

Instructs the system to display the working set limit, quota, and extent for the current process. Here is an example of use of the **SHOW WORKING_SET** command:

$SHOW WORKING_SET   \<Return\>

Working Set   /Limit = 256   /Quota = 512   /Extent = 2048
Adjustment enabled   Authorized Quota = 512   Authorized Extent = 2048
18-AUG-1987 09:26:04

Command Qualifier

/OUTPUT[= file-spec]
/NOOUTPUT

Instruct the system where to send the output of the command. If neither qualifier is used or if no file specification is used with **/OUTPUT**, the output is sent to the current process default output stream or device. The **/NOOUTPUT** qualifier suppresses any output.

SORT

SORT input-file-spec[,...] output-file-spec

Invokes the VAX Sort Utility to reorder the records in a file. For details, see the VAX/VMS Sort/Merge Utility Reference Manual.

SPAWN

SPAWN [command-string]

Instructs the system to create a subprocess of the current process. The TMPMBX or PRMMBX user privileges must be enabled by the system operator; **SPAWN** and its associated **ATTACH** commands cannot be used if the terminal has an associated mailbox.

The subprocess created by the **SPAWN** command copies the context from the parent process, including all process logical names and logical name tables except those marked by the **CONFINE** qualifier or those created in executive or kernel mode; the default disk and directory; key definitions; current keypad state; current prompt string; all symbols except $RESTART, $SEVERITY, and $STATUS; current **SET MESSAGE** settings; current process privileges; and control and verification states.

The current command tables of the process are not copied.

For more details on the **SPAWN** command, see the VAX/VMS DCL Dictionary and the VAX/VMS DCL Concepts Manual.

Command Qualifiers

/CLI = cli
/NOCLI

Specify to the system whether an alternate command language interpreter (CLI) will be used by the subprocess. If no CLI name is specified, the subprocess will use the same interpreter as the parent process.

/INPUT = file-spec

Specifies to the system the name of an input file with DCL commands to be executed by the spawned subprocess. If a command string is included in the **SPAWN** command, the string is processed before the input file.

/KEYPAD (default)
/NOKEYPAD

Instruct the system whether keypad symbols and the current keypad state are copied from the parent process to the subprocess. The default calls for such copying; to block them, use the **/NOKEYPAD** qualifier.

/LOG (default)
/NOLOG

Instruct the system whether to display the name of the assigned subprocess name with messages about transfer of control between the processes.

/LOGICAL_NAMES (default)
/NOLOGICAL_NAMES

Instruct the system whether to pass logical names and logical name tables to the subprocess.

/NOTIFY
/NONOTIFY (default)

Instruct the system whether to broadcast a message to the terminal notifying that a subprocess has been completed or aborted. **/NOTIFY** should be used with the **/NOWAIT** qualifier, and cannot be used when the **SPAWN** is executed from within a non-interactive process.

/OUTPUT=file-spec

Instructs the system to write the output of the **SPAWN** command to the specified file.

/PROCESS=subprocess-name

Specifies to the system a name for the subprocess to be created. If this qualifier is not used, a unique process name is created by the system with the same base name as the parent process and a unique number.

/PROMPT[= string]

Specifies a different prompt string for the subprocess. By default, the subprocess uses the same prompt string as the parent process. The string can be as short as one character. Any valid ASCII character can be used in the string; in order to use spaces, lowercase letters, or nonalphanumeric characters in the string, you must enclose it within quote marks.

/SYMBOLS (default)
/NOSYMBOLS

Instruct the system whether to pass DCL global and local symbols to the subprocess, with the exception of the $RESTART, $SEVERITY, and $STATUS symbols.

/TABLE = command-table

Specifies an alternate command table to be used by the subprocess.

/WAIT (default)
/NOWAIT

Instruct the system whether to wait until the current subprocess is completed before new commands can be issued in the parent process. The **/NOWAIT** qualifier allows you to issue new commands while the specified subprocess is running.

If you issue the /NOWAIT command as part of an interactive session, the use of the **/OUTPUT** qualifier is recommended in order to direct output from the subprocess to a file rather than the terminal—otherwise the terminal will be used by more than one process at the same time.

STOP

STOP [process-name]

Terminates executions of a command, command procedure, image, subprocess, or detached process.

The **process-name** is the name of the process within your group to be stopped. To stop a process outside of your group, you must use the **/IDENTIFICATION = pid** qualifier.

If you use neither a **process-name** nor the **/IDENTIFICATION** qualifier with the **STOP** command, the image executing in the current process is stopped.

STOP results in an abnormal termination of the current image, and exit-handling routines of the image (if any) are not invoked. The **EXIT** command will give control to the exit-handling routines.

See the VAX/VMS DCL Dictionary for more details on the effect of **STOP** on processes interrupted by Ctrl-Y or other means.

Command Qualifier

/IDENTIFICATION = pid

Specifies to the system the process identification code of the process to be stopped. Leading zeros can be left off.

STOP/QUEUE/ABORT

STOP/QUEUE/ABORT queue-name[:]

Instructs the system to stop an executing job on the specified output queue. The current job is deleted from the queue, and the queue continues processing any other jobs waiting.

When a print job is aborted, the system will attempt an orderly halt, including completion of printing of the job in progress.

Execute privileges for the specified queue or operator privileges are required to use this command.

STOP/QUEUE/ENTRY

STOP/QUEUE/ENTRY = entry-number queue-name[:]

Instructs the system to stop an executing job on the specified batch queue. The queue continues processing any other jobs waiting.

Execute access to the specified queue or operator privileges are required to use this command.

STOP/QUEUE/NEXT

STOP/QUEUE/NEXT queue-name[:]

Instructs the system to stop a queue after any current job's complete execution.
   Execute access to the specified queue or operator privileges are required to use this command.

STOP/QUEUE/REQUEUE

STOP/QUEUE/REQUEUE[=queue-name]
STOP/QUEUE/REQUEUE queue-name[:]
STOP/QUEUE/ENTRY=entry-number/REQUEUE
STOP/QUEUE/ENTRY[=queue-name]queue-name[:]

Instructs the system to stop an executing job on the specified queue and then requeue the job for later execution. The queue does not stop and will process other jobs waiting.
   Execute or delete access to the specified queue or operator privileges are required to use this command.

STOP/QUEUE/RESET

STOP/QUEUE/RESET queue-name[:]

Immediately stops a queue and returns control to the system.
   Execute access to the specified queue or operator privileges are required to use this command.

SUBMIT

SUBMIT file-spec[,...]

As part of a command procedure, **SUBMIT** enters one or more command procedures into a batch job queue.

SYNCHRONIZE

SYNCHRONIZE [jobname]

Instructs the system to place the process issuing the command into a wait state until a specified job completes execution.

The **jobname** is the name of the job that was defined when the job was submitted. If the specified job is not in the system, an error message is sent.

Command Qualifiers

/ENTRY = entry-number

Tells the system the assigned entry number of a job. If **/ENTRY** and a **jobname** are included in the same command, the system will ignore the **jobname** and use the **entry-number**.

/QUEUE = queue-name[:]

Tells the system the name of the queue where the job was entered or is executing. If this qualifier is not used, the default batch job queue is assumed.

TYPE

TYPE file-spec[,...]

Displays the contents of a file or a group of files.

The **file-spec[,...]** is the name of a file or files to be displayed. If no file type is included, the system assumes a file type of .LIS. If two or more files are included, they should be separated by commas or plus signs. Files are displayed in the order in which they were specified. Wildcard characters can be used in the directory name, filename, file type, and file version number fields.

The display is sent to the default output device.

The display of a file or files initiated with the TYPE command can be controlled with the following special characters:

1. Ctrl-C stops the **TYPE** command for the current file. If just one file has been specified, Ctrl-C will cancel the display of just that file; if more than one file was requested, Ctrl-C will move on to the next file specified in the command.

A DICTIONARY OF SELECTED DCL COMMANDS AND STATEMENTS □ 285

2. Ctrl-S temporarily suspends output; Ctrl-Q resumes the output display at the point of interruption.
3. Ctrl-O suppresses display but does not suspend the command processing. Entering Ctrl-O again while the **TYPE** command is still processing will resume display at the point where the **TYPE** command is processing if there was just a single file specified; if there was more than one file specified in the command, Ctrl-O will resume display when the next file in the list is reached.
4. Ctrl-Y interrupts the execution of the file. The **CONTINUE** command can be entered to resume the command if no subsequent image-calling commands have been issued. The display will resume at the point of interruption.

Command Qualifiers

/BACKUP

Selects files for a **TYPE** command on the basis of their most recent backup. This qualifier is used in conjunction with the **/BEFORE** or **/SINCE** qualifier. It is incompatible with the **/CREATED**, **/EXPIRED**, and **/MODIFIED** command qualifiers. **/CREATED** is the default.

/BEFORE[= time]
/SINCE[= time]

Select only those files dated before or since the time specified in the command qualifier. The time can be a date, in the form of 06-JUL, or it can be one of the keywords **TODAY**, **TOMORROW**, or **YESTERDAY**. If no time is specified in the command, DCL assumes **TODAY**.

/CONFIRM
/NOCONFIRM (default)

Tell the system whether to query the user before each **TYPE** operation is performed. See Figure 10-1 on page 161 for proper responses.

/CREATED (default)

Instructs the system to select files based on their dates of creation. This command qualifier is used in conjunction with the **/BEFORE** or **/SINCE** qualifier. It is not compatible with the **/BACKUP**, **/EXPIRED**, and **/MODIFIED** command qualifiers.

/EXCLUDE = (file-spec[,...])

Instructs the system to exclude the specified file or files from a wildcard command.

/EXPIRED

Instructs the system to select files based on their expiration dates. This command qualifier is used in conjunction with the **/BEFORE** or **/SINCE** qualifier. It is not compatible with the **/BACKUP**, **/CREATED**, and **/MODIFIED** command qualifiers. **/CREATED** is the default specification.

/MODIFIED

Instructs the system to select files based on their date of last modification. This command qualifier is used in conjunction with the **/BEFORE** or **/SINCE** qualifier. It is not compatible with the **/BACKUP**, **/CREATED**, and **/EXPIRED** command qualifiers. **/CREATED** is the default specification.

/OUTPUT[= file-spec]
/NOOUTPUT

Instruct the system where to send the output of the command. If no file specification is used with **/OUTPUT** or if neither qualifier is used, the output is sent to the current default output stream or device. If **/NOOUTPUT** is specified, output is suppressed.

/PAGE
/NOPAGE (default)

Instruct the system whether to display output from the **TYPE** command one screen at a time. **/PAGE** is incompatible with **/OUTPUT**.

/SINCE[=time]

See /BEFORE.

UNLOCK

UNLOCK file-spec[,...]

Reopens for access a file that has been improperly closed.
   The **file-spec[,...]** is the name or names of files to be unlocked. If more than one file is included in the command, the filenames must be separated by commas or plus signs. Wildcard characters are permitted in file specifications.

Command Qualifiers

/CONFIRM
/NOCONFIRM (default)

Tell the system whether to query the user before each **UNLOCK** operation is performed. See Figure 10-1 on page 161 for proper responses.

/LOG
/NOLOG (default)

Instruct the system whether to display the file specification of each file as it is unlocked.

WAIT

WAIT delta-time

Instructs the system to put the current process into a wait state until the specified period of time has passed.
   See the VAX/VMS DCL Dictionary and the VAX/VMS DCL Concepts Manual for more details on use of the **WAIT** command in an interactive statement or as part of a command procedure, as well as an explanation of the proper use of delta time values.

WRITE

WRITE logical-name expression[,...]

Writes specified data as one record in the output file indicated by the logical-name included in the command.

The **logical-name** is the logical name assigned to the file that will receive the record. The **OPEN** command assigns a logical name to a file and places that name in the process logical name table. The process permanent files with the logical names SYS$INPUT, SYS$OUTPUT, SYS$ERROR, and SYS$COMMAND can also be used. The **expression[,...]** represents the data to be written to the output file.

The **WRITE** command can place records in sequential, relative, and indexed sequential access files that have been opened for writing. The file must have been opened with either the **/WRITE** or **/APPEND** qualifier of the **OPEN** command, except for the process permanent files with the logical names of SYS$INPUT, SYS$OUTPUT, SYS$ERROR, and SYS$COMMAND, which do not have to be explicitly opened.

Data can be specified with character string expressions. See the VAX/VMS DCL Concepts Manual and the VAX/VMS DCL Dictionary for more details.

The maximum record size is less than 1,024 bytes, unless the **/SYMBOL** qualifier is used.

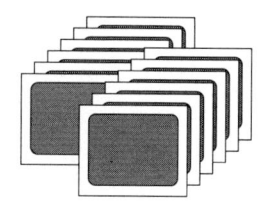

11 Error Messages

If you are very, very careful in all that you do, and very, very lucky, you will never make an error on the computer and all will be well with the world. For the rest of us mortals, though, VAX/VMS will regularly greet us with *error messages* pointing out problems and miscues. There are several thousand such error messages, with multiple versions of many of them, waiting just below the surface of an ordinary computer session.

In this chapter, you'll find a selection of the error messages an ordinary user is most likely to encounter in a VAX/VMS session. The nature of the error will be explained, and some possible corrective actions will be given. More detailed explanations of all errors in this chapter, as well as more technical errors aimed at system managers and programmers, can be found in Digital's VAX/VMS System Messages and Recovery Procedures Reference Manual.

TYPES OF ERROR MESSAGES

You may receive several types of messages during any computer session. *Success* and *informational messages* inform you that the system has performed a request. *Warning messages* indicate that the system may have performed some, but not all, of the request, and that the command or the program output should be verified. *Error messages* inform you that the output or program result is incorrect, but the system may attempt to continue execution. *Fatal error messages* declare that the system cannot continue execution of the request.

Error messages begin with a percent sign or a hyphen, and occur in the following form:

%FACILITY-L-IDENT, text

The meanings of the individual elements are as follows;

%—Indicates an error message.
FACILITY—The name of the operating system facility or the program issuing the message.
L—Level of severity of the problem, with the following categories:

    S Success

    I Informational

    W Warning

    E Error

    F Fatal error

IDENT—A code for the error.
TEXT—A description of the error and suggestions for fixes.

If two or more error messages are strung together, they are connected with a hyphen. By displaying the status of several elements of the command, such *linked* messages can provide you great assistance in determining the cause of an error.

Here is an example of a DCL error message:

% DCL-W-MAXPARM, too many parameters = reenter command with fewer parameters

Two classes of facilities will generate messages without IDENTS: System Bootstrap Utility (BOOT or SYSBOOT) and System Initialization (SYSINIT). Both of these classes are within the province of the system manager. Three other classes of facilities will yield error messages without IDENTS or FACILITY names: the EDT editor, the DSR Digital Standard Runoff program, and the Diskquota utility.

RECOVERING FROM AN ERROR

The fact is, alas, that nearly all errors are those of the human user or the human system operator. These could be mistakes in entering data, incorrect or inappropriate commands, or *bugs* in the human-designed machine operating system software itself. Another class of error is the result of mechanical or electrical failure. For example, the computer will issue an error message if the user attempts to use a piece of equipment that is broken, turned off, or disconnected from the system in some way.

In any case, the prospect of receiving one of these error messages should hold no terror for a computer user. A properly designed operating system such as VAX/VMS helps the user to diagnose the nature of the error and in many cases suggests a solution to the problem.

Command Entry Errors

Error messages that come back immediately from the command interpreter during an interactive session are the result of an error in entering a command. They usually include a portion of the rejected command line, indicating to the user where the mistake occurred.

An error that occurs during the execution of a command may be the result of an invalid value for a parameter or qualifier. Use the DCL command **HELP** to look up the proper form on screen, or read the VAX/VMS DCL Dictionary for the proper values.

Errors in file specifications or device names can be caused by a number of actions, including

- a mistake in entering the filename itself.
- a device name not terminated with a colon.
- a directory name not enclosed in brackets.
- a filename with more than 39 characters.
- an error in specifying the version number.
- an error in identifying the node name.
- a connection to the specified target node not able to be made.

Unavailable Resources

If a file or a device is not available for use, an error message will be generated; the solution is to make the device available or issue a different command calling on a different, available device.

Another reason for which a resource may be unavailable is the user's lacking the proper privilege for the resource; the solution is to use another resource or obtain a proper privilege for the desired resource.

The program or operating system may be set up to immediately return to the user if a resource is not available, or it may continue execution and retry the service later.

Programming and Hardware or Software Errors

If the program image terminates because of an error in the program or the system hardware or software, the error message will display some information about the error. Make a record of the message and notify the system operator of the error.

VMS ERROR MESSAGE DIRECTORY

Following is a listing of some of the more common error messages that refer to the DCL Command Language Interpreter, the EDT text editing program, and the VMS System itself. A full listing of error codes can be found in the Guide to VAX/VMS and the VAX/VMS System Manager's Reference Manual.

Consult the following list of facility codes for explanations of abbreviations and for referral to the proper Digital reference manual for more details.

List of Facility Codes

Abbreviation	Facility	Manual
ACCOUNTING	Accounting Utility	VAX/VMS Accounting Reference Manual
AUTHORIZE	Authorize Utility	VAX/VMS Authorize Utility Reference Manual

List of Facility Codes

Abbreviation	Facility	Manual
BACKUP	Backup Utility	VAX/VMS Backup Utility Reference Manual
BAD	Bad Block Locator Utility	VAX/VMS Bad Block Locator Utility Reference Manual
BOOT	System Bootstrap Facility	VAX/VMS System Manager's Reference Manual; Guide to VAX/VMS
CDU	Command Definition Utility	VAX/VMS Command Definition Utility Reference Manual
CLI	Command Language Interpreter (DCL)	Guide to Using DCL and Command Procedures on VAX/VMS
CONVERT	Convert Utility	VAX/VMS Convert and Convert/Reclaim Utility Reference Manual
CREF	Cross-Reference Utility	Guide to Programming on VAX/VMS
DCL	Digital Command Language	VAX/VMS DCL Dictionary
DEBUG	VAX Debugger	VAX/VMS Debugger Reference Manual
DIFF	**DIFFERENCES** Command	VAX/VMS DCL Dictionary
DISKQUOTA	Diskquota Utility	VAX/VMS Disk Quota Utility Reference Manual
DISM	**DISMOUNT** Command	VAX/VMS DCL Dictionary
DUMP	File Dump Utility	VAX/VMS DCL Dictionary
EDT	EDT Editor	VAX EDT Reference Manual
EVL	Event Logger	VAX/VMS Networking Manual

ERROR MESSAGES

List of Facility Codes

Abbreviation	Facility	Manual
EXCHANGE	Exchange Utility	VAX/VMS Exchange Utility Reference Manual
FDL	Create or Edit/FDL Utility	VAX/VMS File Definition Language Reference Manual
INIT	**INITIALIZE VOLUME** Command	VAX/VMS DCL Dictionary
INSTALL	Install Utility	VAX/VMS Install Utility Reference Manual
JBC	Job Controller	VAX/VMS System Services Reference Manual
LATCP	Local Area Transport Control Program	VAX/VMS LAT Control Program Reference Manual
LBR	Librarian	VAX/VMS Librarian Reference Manual
LIB	RTL General Procedures	VAX/VMS Run-Time Library Routines Reference Manual
LIBRAR	**LIBRARY** Command	VAX/VMS Librarian Reference Manual
LINK	VAX Linker	VAX/VMS Linker Reference Manual
LOGIN	Login Processor	VAX/VMS DCL Dictionary; VAX/VMS System Manager's Reference Manual
MACRO	VAX Macro Assembler	VAX Macro and Instruction Set Reference Volume
MAIL	Personal Mail Utility	VAX/VMS Mail Utility Reference Manual
MESSAGE	Message Utility	VAX/VMS Message Utility Reference Manual
MONITOR	Monitor Utility	VAX/VMS Monitor Utility Reference Manual

List of Facility Codes

Abbreviation	Facility	Manual
MOUNT	**MOUNT** Command	VAX/VMS DCL Dictionary
MTH	RTL Math Procedures	VAX/VMS Run-Time Library Routines Reference Manual
NCP	Network Control Program	VAX/VMS Networking Manual
NET	DECnet Test Program Protocol	VAX/VMS Networking Manual
OPCOM	Operator Communication	VAX/VMS System Manager's Reference Manual
OTS	Language Independent RTL Support Procedures	VAX/VMS Run-Time Library Routines Reference Manual
PATCH	VAX Image File Patch	VAX/VMS Patch Utility Reference Manual
PSI	VAX Packetnet System Interface	VAX/VMS Networking Manual
PSM	Print Symbiont	VAX/VMS Utility Routine Reference Manual
REM	Set Host Facility	VAX/VMS DCL Dictionary
RENAME	**RENAME** Command	VAX/VMS DCL Dictionary
RMS	VAX RMS Services	VAX Record Management Services Reference Manual
RUNOFF	Digital Standard Runoff Utility	VAX Digital Standard Runoff (DSR) Reference Manual
SDA	System Dump Analyzer	VAX/VMS System Dump Analyzer Reference Manual
SEARCH	**SEARCH** Command	VAX/VMS DCL Dictionary
SHR	Set Facility Shared Messages	VAX/VMS DCL Dictionary

List of Facility Codes

Abbreviation	Facility	Manual
SMB	Symbiont Services	VAX/VMS Utility Routines Reference Manual
SMG	RTL Screen Management Procedures	VAX/VMS Run-Time Library Routines Reference Manual
SORT	VAX/Sort/Merge Utility	VAX/VMS Sort/Merge Utility Reference Manual
STR	RTL String Procedures	VAX/VMS Run-Time Library Routines Reference Manual
SUBMIT	**SUBMIT** Command	VAX/VMS DCL Dictionary
SUMSLP	SUMSLP Batch Editing Utility	VAX/VMS SUMSLP Utility Reference Manual
SYSBOOT	System Bootstrap Facility	VAX/VMS System Manager's Reference Manual; Guide to VAX/VMS Software Installation
SYSGEN	System Generation Utility	VAX/VMS System Generation Utility Reference Manual; VAX/VMS System Manager's Reference Manual
SYSINIT	System Initialization	VAX/VMS System Manager's Reference Manual
SYSTEM	VAX/VMS System Services	VAX/VMS System Services Reference Manual
UETP	User Environment Test Package	Guide to VAX/VMS Software Installation
VAXTPU	VAX Text Processing Utility	VAX Text Processing Utility Reference Manual
VERIFY	Verify Utility	VAX/VMS Verify Utility Reference Manual

Selected VMS Error and Information Messages

'.' required

> Facility: EDT
>
> Details: The command is missing a period, or whatever other character is specified in the error message within the quote marks.
>
> Corrective action: Reenter the command, including the requested special character if appropriate.

'AS' required

> Facility: EDT
>
> Details: The word **AS** was missing from the **DEFINE KEY** command.
>
> Corrective action: Reenter the command with the proper syntax.

ABEND, 'string' aborted

> Facility: Several
>
> Details: A program phase has aborted prematurely.
>
> Corrective action: None.

ABFNAM, ambiguous lexical function name - supply more characters

> Facility: CLI
>
> Details: Too few characters were used in a truncated version of a lexical function name, resulting in a name that was not unique.
>
> Corrective action: Reenter the command with additional letters of the function name included.

ABKEYW, ambiguous qualifier or keyword - supply more characters

> Facility: CLI
>
> Details: Too few characters were used in a truncated version of a keyword or qualifier, resulting in a name that was not unique.

Corrective action: The rejected portion of the command is displayed within backslashes (\\ ). Reenter the command with additional letters included.

ABKW, ambiguous keyword on line

Facility: FDL

Details: An ambiguous abbreviation for an attribute keyword was used.

Corrective action: Enter a more specific abbreviation.

ABORT, abort

Facility: SYSTEM

Details: An attempted operation was aborted by the $CANCEL system service.

Corrective action: Notify system operator.

ABORT, abort

Facility: SYSGEN

Details: Part of a set of linked error messages.

Corrective action: Perform action indicated in the accompanying messages.

Aborted by Ctrl-C

Facility: EDT

Details: The user entered the Ctrl-C key combination after entering a command in keypad change-mode. All text disappears from the screen.

Corrective action: Press Return if text is not returned to the screen.

ABPRIKW, ambiguous primary keyword on line n

Facility: FDL

Details: An ambiguous abbreviation for an attribute keyword was used.

Corrective action: Provide a more specific abbreviation.

ABSENT, entity or value absent from command string

> Facility: CLI
>
> Details: An entity value has not been specified in the command line.
>
> Corrective action: None.

ABSYMD, abbreviated symbol definition conflict - rename symbol

> Facility: CLI
>
> Details: A newly defined abbreviated symbol is ambiguous with an existing symbol; the new symbol is not entered.
>
> Corrective action: Display the current symbols for information and reenter the new symbol with an unambiguous symbol name.

ABVERB, ambiguous command verb - supply more characters

> Facility: CLI
>
> Details: Too few characters were used in a truncated version of a command name to make the command name unique.
>
> Corrective action: Reenter the command with additional characters.

ACCONFLICT, file access conflict

> Facility: SYSTEM
>
> Details: The attempt to access the specified file failed because the type of access requested conflicted with the current file access.
>
> Corrective action: 1) Establish who has the file open and wait for the file to be closed; 2) check for a programming error.

ACNTEXC, you are at maximum allowed processes for your account name

> Facility: LOGIN
>
> Details: The user has made an attempt to log in when the maximum number of processes in the user's account have already logged in.

Corrective action: Log off another process or wait until the system is less busy.

ACSIGN, access control string ignored

Facility: REM
Details: The access control string specified in a **SET HOST** command was ignored by the remote terminal facility.
Corrective action: None.

ADDFIL, error adding 'file-name' to job

Facility: PRINT and SUBMIT
Details: The system was unable to add the specified file to a batch or print job. An accompanying message provides additional information.
Corrective action: Correct the error and reenter the command.

Advance past bottom of buffer

Facility: EDT
Details: The user has tried to move the cursor past the end of the buffer, indicated on screen with the [EOB] marker.
Corrective action: Move the cursor above the [EOB] marker.

ALLOC, 'device' allocated

Facility: CLI
Details: The specified device is already allocated.
Corrective action: None.

AMBIG, ambiguous field name or class name 'class-name'

Facility: SHOW
Details: The field or class name entered is not unique.
Corrective action: Reenter the field or class name with additional characters. Use the **HELP FIELDS** or **HELP CLASSES** to obtain a list of available fields or classes.

AMBIGNAME, Variable 'name' cannot be a procedure at line 'integer'

> Facility: VAXTPU
>
> Details: The user is attempting to use an identifier as a procedure, when that identifier has previously been used as a variable.
>
> Corrective action: Use a different name for the procedure.

APPENDEDB, input-file-spec appended to output-file-spec (nnn blocks)

> Facility: Several.
>
> Details: An informational message confirming that an input file has been appended to the specified output file. The number of blocks or number of records is also displayed.
>
> Corrective action: None.

ARGREQ, missing argument - supply all required arguments

> Facility: CLI
>
> Details: All required arguments were not included when a lexical function was invoked.
>
> Corrective action: Supply required arguments.

ATTACHED, terminal now attached to process 'process name'

> Facility: CLI
>
> Details: An informational message from the DCL command **ATTACH** when it attaches to a process.
>
> Corrective action: None.

Attempt to CUT or APPEND to current buffer

> Facility: EDT
>
> Details: In a CUT or APPEND operation, the user named the current text buffer as the destination text buffer. The default destination is the PASTE text buffer.
>
> Corrective action: Copy the text to an intermediate buffer.

302 □ ERROR MESSAGES

Attempt to PASTE the current buffer

>Facility: EDT
>
>Details: The EDT command PASTE attempted to paste text into the same text buffer where the text to be pasted resides.
>
>Corrective action: Copy the text to an intermediate buffer.

Attempt to reenter EDT

>Facility: EDT
>
>Details: Within callable EDT, the user attempted to recall EDT without having exited.
>
>Corrective action: Exit from EDT first.

Backup past top of buffer, 0

>Facility: EDT
>
>Details: The user attempted to move the cursor beyond the first line of the buffer.
>
>Corrective action: Press any key to move the cursor below the top of the buffer.

BADBUFWRITE, Error occurred writing buffer 'buffer name'

>Facility: VAXTPU
>
>Details: An I/O error occurred during the writing of the contents of a buffer to a file. An accompanying message should specify the reason for the error.
>
>Corrective action: Correct the specified error and reenter.

BADCHAR, Unrecognized character in input on line 'integer'

>Facility: VAXTPU
>
>Details: A control character or other unrecognized character was found.
>
>Corrective action: Remove the unrecognized character and recompile.

BADCOPIES, 'nnn' is an invalid number of copies

>Facility: Several.

>Details: The specified number of copies is not within the allowable range.

>Corrective action: Correct the number of copies and reenter the command.

BADDELIM, invalid delimiter following 'command'

>Facility: Several.

>Details: An invalid character was included in a command. The message displays the rejected portion of the command.

>Corrective action: Check the command for spelling or syntax errors and reenter the command.

BADEXCL, directory or device not allowed in /EXCLUDE = exclude-item

>Facility: SEARCH

>Details: The specified excluded item is a network node name, device name, or directory name.

>Corrective action: Correct the command to specify only a filename, file type, or version number.

BADFILEVER, bad file version number

>Facility: SYSTEM

>Details: The file version number in a file specification is not acceptable. The specification may not have a version number greater than 32,767 or one that contains nonnumeric characters.

>Corrective action: Correct the version number and reenter.

BADHOUR, you are not authorized to login at this time

>Facility: LOGIN

>Details: The user's authorization file is set up so that the user is not allowed to log in at this time.

Corrective action: Wait until the allowed time or have the system operator change the authorization file.

BADJOBID, 'name' is a bad job identifier

Facility: Several.

Details: The job identifier indicated in the **/ENTRY** qualifier is missing or not valid.

Corrective action: Correct the job identifier. Consult the **SHOW QUEUE** command.

BADJOBNAME, 'name' is an invalid job name

Facility: Several.

Details: The jobname indicated in the **/NAME** qualifier is missing or not valid.

Corrective action: Correct the job identifier. Consult the **SHOW QUEUE** command.

BADLOGIC, internal logic error detected [at PC location]

Facility: Several.
Details: An internal software error has been detected.
Corrective action: Contact the system manager.

BADLOGICPC, internal logic error detected at PC = location

Facility: Several.

Details: An internal software error has been detected, and the value of the PC at the time of the error is indicated.

Corrective action: Contact the system manager.

BADMATCH, invalid option for /MATCH = match-option

Facility: SEARCH

Details: The option specified for **/MATCH** is not valid. An accompanying message should provide more details.

Corrective action: Reenter the command with a valid match option.

BADTIME, 'time-spec' is an invalid time specification

> Facility: Several.
>
> Details: An invalid time specification was entered.
>
> Corrective action: Reenter with a proper time specification. See the VAX/VMS DCL Dictionary for allowable forms.

BADVALUE, value is an invalid keyword value

> Facility: Several.
>
> Details: An unacceptable value was used for the indicated command qualifier.
>
> Corrective action: Check the command string for an error in spelling or syntax and reenter.

BUFOVF, command buffer overflow - shorten expression or command line

> Facility: CLI
>
> Details: A command string, with any continuation lines, is longer than the buffer available to the command interpreter to store commands.
>
> Corrective action: Shorten and reenter the command, or break the command into more than one command.

CTRL-C ignored

> Facility: EDT
>
> Details: The user attempted to use Ctrl-C to interrupt an operation that EDT does not allow to be aborted in this manner.
>
> Corrective action: Informational.

CAPTIVE, this command cannot be executed; Your account is CAPTIVE

> Facility: MAIL
>
> Details: The user attempted to issue a **SPAWN** command, but the user's account is CAPTIVE.
>
> Corrective action: Contact system manager.

CLIFAIL, error activating command interpreter 'interpreter'

> Facility: LOGIN
>
> Details: An error was detected in the attempt to invoke the command interpreter for the user's process. An accompanying message will provide additional information.
>
> Corrective action: Correct the error indicated in the message.

CMDINPUT, error reading command input

> Facility: LOGIN
>
> Details: An error was detected while the system was attempting to read the input file. A common cause is a read timeout while waiting for the username or password. An accompanying message will provide further information.
>
> Corrective action: Correct the problem indicated in the message and try again.

COMMA, requested value is terminated by a comma

> Facility: CLI
>
> Details: The value that was entered was terminated with a comma, implying that additional values are on the list.
>
> Corrective action: None.

Command buffer exhausted

> Facility: EDT
>
> Details: The change mode command string exceeds the allowed 255 characters.
>
> Corrective action: Reenter the command as several shorter strings.

Command file could not be closed
Command file could not be opened

> Facility: EDT
>
> Details: The startup command file could not be closed, or the command file specified in the command line could not be opened. An accompanying message should give more details on the error.

Corrective action: Correct the problem indicated in the message.

CONFLICT, illegal combination of command elements - check documentation

Facility: CLI

Details: Two or more qualifiers, keywords, or parameters that are not allowed to be combined were used in the same command line.

Corrective action: Correct the command.

CONFQUAL, conflicting qualifiers

Facility: Several.

Details: Two or more conflicting qualifiers were used.

Corrective action: Consult the VMS **HELP** command or the VAX/VMS DCL Dictionary for guidance and reenter the commands.

COPIEDB, input-file-spec copied to output-file-spec (nnn blocks)

Facility: Several.

Details: An informational message showing the names of files copied and the number of blocks or records copied.

Corrective action: None.

CREATED, 'file-spec' created

Facility: Several.

Details: An informational message when a new file or directory is created.

Corrective action: None.

CREPRIJOB, error creating print job on queue 'queue-name'

Facility: MAIL

Details: An error was detected when the user attempted to create a print job to queue a message for printing. An accompanying message should indicate the reason for the failure.

Corrective action: Correct the specified problem.

DEFKEY, 'state' key 'key name' has been defined

Facility: CLI
Details: The specified key was previously defined.
Corrective action: None.

DEFOVF, too many command procedure parameters - limited to eight

Facility: CLI
Details: More than eight parameters were invoked in a single command procedure.
Corrective action: Reenter the command with no more than eight parameters.

DELETED, 'file-name' deleted

Facility: Several.
Details: An informational message that displays the file specification of a successfully deleted file.
Corrective action: None.

DELKEY, 'state' key 'key name' has been deleted

Facility: CLI
Details: The specified key was previously deleted.
Corrective action: None.

DELVER, explicit version number or wild card required

Facility: Several.
Details: The DCL command **DELETE** requires a version number for each specified file.
Corrective action: Reenter the command with an explicit version number for files to be deleted, or use a wildcard character in the version field.

DEVALLOC, device already allocated to another user

Facility: SYSTEM

Details: The attempt to allocate a device has failed because the device is already allocated by another user. Only one user at a time can access an allocated device.

Corrective action: 1) Wait until the current owner has deallocated the device; 2) specify a different device and reenter the command; or 3) specify a generic device name in the allocate request.

DEVICEFULL, device full - allocation failure

Facility: SYSTEM

Details: Space cannot be allocated for a file because the device is full, or a request for contiguous space cannot be honored because the specified number of contiguous blocks is not available.

Corrective action: Verify the status of the device. Purge or delete unneeded private files; if the device is a system device, notify the system operator.

DEVNOTALLOC, device not allocated

Facility: SYSTEM

Details: The specified device in a deallocate request is not allocated.

Corrective action: Verify the device name or logical name and reenter the command.

DIRALLOC, directory allocation failure

Facility: SYSTEM

Details: The file system did not allocate space to increase the size of a directory file. Directory files must be contiguous, and this error may be caused by the disk being too full or the disk's free space being too fragmented to provide sufficient contiguous space.

Corrective action: Consult the system manager to reorganize the disk's free space or restructure the application to use smaller directory files.

DIRNOTEMPTY, directory file is not empty

    Facility: SYSTEM

    Details: The directory the user attempted to delete contained files and could not be deleted.

    Corrective action: Verify that you indeed want to delete the directory. Delete all files before the directory is deleted. If the directory is corrupted, the DCL command **SET FILE/NODIRECTORY** can remove its status as a directory, allowing it to be deleted.

DRVERR, fatal drive error

    Facility: SYSTEM

    Details: An input or output operation has failed because of an error in a disk or magnetic tape drive.

    Corrective action: Consult the system operator.

Editor aborted

    Facility: EDT

    Details: The EDT editor encountered difficulties and aborted the session.

    Corrective action: Use the journal file of EDT to recover edited work.

ENDABORT, 'name' compilation aborted

    Facility: Several

    Details: Errors prevented the compilation of the specified name from being completed.

    Corrective action: Correct the errors and recompile.

ENDED, 'name' ended
ENDEDD, 'name' ended at 'system date and time'
ENDEDT, 'name' ended at 'system time'

    Facility: Several

    Details: An informational message that a program phase has been ended.

    Corrective action: None.

Entity must be WORD, SENTENCE, PAGE, or PARAGRAPH

> Facility: EDT
>
> Details: The EDT command of **SET ENTITY** was entered without one of the four allowed entity options: **WORD**, **SENTENCE**, **PAGE**, or **PARAGRAPH**.
>
> Corrective action: Reenter the command with a proper entity.

Error in command

> Facility: EDT
> Details: An invalid command was entered.
> Corrective action: Correct the command.

Error in command option

> Facility: EDT
> Details: An EDT command included an invalid qualifier.
> Corrective action: Correct the command.

Error in range specification

> Facility: EDT
> Details: The specified EDT command requires a complete range specification.
> Corrective action: Correct the command.

Error opening terminal for input
Error opening terminal for output

> Facility: EDT
> Details: EDT could not access the specified terminal for input or output, as indicated.
> Corrective action: Correct the problem.

Error reading from input file

> Facility: EDT

Details: EDT could not read the input file. The problem could lie in the main input file, the journal file if it is being used, or the startup command file if it is being used.

Corrective action: Correct the problem.

Error writing to output file

Facility: EDT

Details: EDT could not produce an output file. The problem could lie in the MAIN buffer copy, the journal file, or in a file requested as part of a **WRITE** command.

Corrective action: Determine the reason for the failure and correct problem.

EXCPUTIM, CPU time limit expired

Facility: SYSTEM

Details: The user's allotted CPU time limit has been reached.

Corrective action: Request the system manager grant more CPU time to the user or remove restrictions.

EXISTS, 'file-spec' already exists

Facility: Several.

Details: An informational message that the directory included in the **CREATE/DIR** command already exists.

Corrective action: None.

EXPRCLM, exceeded subprocess quota

Facility: SYSTEM

Details: An image was not allowed to continue executing or a command would not execute because the process exceeded its subprocess limit.

Corrective action: Consult system manager to see if the subprocess quota should be increased.

EXPSYN, invalid expression syntax - check operators and operands

Facility: CLI

Details: An arithmetic expression in a DCL command was not correct in syntax. The invalid expression could be the result of missing operators between values or symbol names, of unmatched parentheses, or of undefined symbol names interpreted as character strings.

Corrective action: Determine the cause of the failure and correct the command.

EXQUOTA, exceeded quota

Facility: SYSTEM

Details: An image could not continue execution or a command could not execute because the process exceeded a resource quota or limit.

Corrective action: Consult the DCL command **SHOW PROCESS/QUOTAS** to see current quotas and determine which one was exceeded. Delete any unneeded subprocesses. Consult the system manager to determine if the process quotas should be increased.

File attributes error

Facility: EDT
Details: EDT cannot edit the file because of its attributes.
Corrective action: None.

File specification required

Facility: EDT

Details: The filename or file specification was not included in an **INCLUDE, PRINT**, or **WRITE** command.

Corrective action: Reenter the command with the proper file specification.

FILEMPTY, file 'filename' has no folders

Facility: MAIL
Details: Within Mail, a **DIR/FOLDER** command has been

issued, but the current mail file has no folders and no messages could be found.

Corrective action: None.

FILEPURGED, oldest file version purged

Facility: SYSTEM

Details: The newest file version exceeded the maximum number of versions of that file allowed, and therefore the oldest file version has been deleted.

Corrective action: None.

FILNOTDEL, error deleting 'file-spec'

Facility: Several

Details: The specified file could not be deleted. An informational message usually accompanies details of the problem.

Corrective action: Fix the problem identified in the message and reenter.

FILNOTPUR, error deleting 'file-spec'

Facility: Several

Details: An error was encountered during the attempt to delete the specified file. An accompanying message explains the reason for the error.

Corrective action: Correct the problem identified in the message and reenter.

FILPURGED, 'file-spec' deleted

Facility: Several

Details: An informational message with the file specification of a file being deleted.

Corrective action: None.

HANGUP, data set hang-up

Facility: SYSTEM

Details: The associated terminal data set has been hung up.

Corrective action: None.

HIGHVER, higher version of 'output file' already exists

Facility: Several

Details: In specifying a version number of an output file, the user gave an explicit version number lower than that of an existing version.

Corrective action: None.

IDXFILEFULL, index file is full

Facility: SYSTEM

Details: The maximum size for the index file has been reached and no more files can be written on the volume.

Corrective action: If the volume is private, delete any unwanted files. If the volume is a system one, notify the system manager.

ILLSELF, illegal self reference

Facility: SYSTEM

Details: An illegal attempt has been made to suspend all action on your own job.

Corrective action: None. The job is not suspended.

Include file could not be closed

Facility: EDT

Details: The specified file could not be closed by EDT while using the **INCLUDE** command. A problem exists at the system level that prevents the closure of the file.

Corrective action: Determine the system problem, correct it, and reenter command.

Include file could not be opened

Facility: EDT

Details: The specified file could not be opened by EDT while using the **INCLUDE** command. A problem exists at the system level that prevents the opening of the file.

Corrective action: Determine the system problem, correct it, and reenter command.

Include file does not exist

Facility: EDT

Details: A file specification with an **INCLUDE** command does not exist, or exists in a directory other than the one specified or implied by the command.

Corrective action: Enter a correct file specification.

Include file record too large, truncated to 255 characters

Facility: EDT

Details: EDT can handle no more than 255 characters on a line. The file the user intends to include is longer than that, and EDT will truncate the line.

Corrective action: None.

Input file could not be closed

Facility: EDT

Details: The file named in the **EDIT/EDT** command line or in the line mode **INCLUDE** command line could not be closed by EDT. A problem exists at the system level that prevents the closure of the file.

Corrective action: Determine the system problem, correct it, and reenter command.

Input file could not be opened

Facility: EDT
Details: The specified file could not be opened by EDT.
Corrective action: Check the command syntax and directory listings. Correct command and reenter it.

Input file does not exist

> Facility: EDT
>
> Details: A file specification does not exist, or exists in a directory other than the one specified or implied by the command. When a new file is created using the EDT editor, this message is displayed as an indication that a new file is being created.
>
> Corrective action: No action is necessary if you intend to create a new file. Otherwise, enter a correct file specification.

Input file does not have standard text file format

> Facility: EDT
>
> Details: The file does not have standard file attributes such as carriage returns at the ends of lines.
>
> Corrective action: An informational warning. EDT will allow the user to continue editing the file, but difficulties could be encountered in editing nonstandard elements.

Input record too large, truncated to 255 characters

> Facility: EDT
>
> Details: EDT can handle no more than 255 characters in a record. The record the user intends to include is longer than that, and EDT will truncate it. This message can also occur because of an attempt to edit a file that does not contain ASCII text.
>
> Corrective action: None.

INSFMEM, insufficient dynamic memory

> Facility: SYSTEM or SYSGEN
>
> Details: A command or image has exhausted all available dynamic memory in the system pool, and the request cannot be completed.
>
> Corrective action: Consult the system manager to determine if there has been a programming error or if additional memory needs to be allocated.

INSFPRM, missing command parameters - supply all required parameters

Facility: CLI

Details: One or more required parameters are missing from a command and the command cannot be executed.

Corrective action: Complete the command procedure.

Insufficient memory

Facility: EDT

Details: EDT has insufficient memory available to complete the last command. This message can occur in situations where the user defines a new text buffer or uses the EDT command of **DEFINE KEY**.

Corrective action: Exit from EDT and restart the editing session. To avoid the problem, define fewer keys and text buffers or decrease the size of the text buffers.

Invalid buffer name

Facility: EDT

Details: Unacceptable syntax used for the buffer name in an EDT command.

Corrective action: Correct the syntax and reenter.

Invalid entity

Facility: EDT

Details: The entity portion of the EDT change mode command is improper.

Corrective action: Reenter the command with a valid entity.

Invalid option for that command

Facility: EDT

Details: The **/OPTION** qualifier was used with an EDT command that does not work with that qualifier.

Corrective action: Reenter the command without the **/OPTION** qualifier.

Invalid parameter for SET or SHOW

Facility: EDT

Details: Parameters entered as part of a **SET** or **SHOW** command will not work with EDT.

Corrective action: Reenter the command with a valid parameter.

Invalid string

Facility: EDT

Details: EDT could not handle the string entered, for example, a search string longer than 64 characters.

Corrective action: Reenter the command with a valid string.

Invalid subcommand

Facility: EDT

Details: An improper name for an EDT change mode subcommand has been used.

Corrective action: Reenter the subcommand with a valid name. Use the **HELP CHANGE SUBCOMMANDS** display for assistance.

Invalid value in SET command

Facility: EDT

Details: An invalid keyword was used with the EDT command **SET**.

Corrective action: Reenter the command with a valid keyword.

INVCMD, unrecognized command 'command'

Facility: MAIL

Details: An invalid command has been entered.

Corrective action: Reenter with a valid Mail command.

INVFILSPE, invalid file specification 'file-spec'

Facility: PRINT and SUBMIT

Details: The file specification in the command is invalid. Files must be disk files and may contain a nodename only if the **/REMOTE** qualifier has been specified.

Corrective action: Correct the command and reenter.

INVLOGIN, login information invalid at remote node

Facility: SYSTEM

Details: An incorrect login attempt for a DECnet logical link connection was made, and the access control string specified was incorrect.

Corrective action: If the default access control was used, notify the system manager to update the DECnet configuration database with correct information. Correct the command and reenter.

INVUIC, invalid UIC - must be of the form [group,member]

Facility: CLI

Details: The command includes an invalid UIC or a UIC improperly entered. The group and member elements of a UIC must be contained within square brackets and must be separated by a comma.

Corrective action: Correct the command and reenter.

IVATIME, invalid absolute time - use
DD-MMM-YYYY:HH:MM:SS.CC format

Facility: CLI

Details: The specified absolute time was entered in an incorrect format.

Corrective action: Reenter the time in the form shown in the error message.

IVCHAR, invalid numeric value - check for invalid digits

> Facility: CLI
>
> Details: The command interpreter was unable to execute a command because it came to a character string in a context where it expected a numeric value.
>
> Corrective action: Check the command string for undefined or incorrectly spelled symbol names, a missing radix operator preceding a hexadecimal or octal value, an illegal value following a radix operation, or a syntax error. Correct the command and reenter.

IVDTIME, invalid delta time - use DDDD-HH:MM:SS.CC

> Facility: CLI
>
> Details: The specified delta time value was entered incorrectly.
>
> Corrective action: Reenter the delta time in the format shown in the error message.

IVFNAM, invalid lexical function name - check validity and spelling

> Facility: CLI
>
> Details: An invalid lexical function name is used in the command.
>
> Corrective action: Consult the DCL **HELP** command or the VAX/VMS DCL Dictionary for proper style for lexical function names. Correct the command and reenter.

IVKEYNAM, unrecognized key name - check validity and spelling

> Facility: CLI
>
> Details: A keyname is specified incorrectly.
>
> Corrective action: Correct the spelling of the keyname and reenter the command.

IVKEYW, unrecognized keyword - check validity and spelling

> Facility: CLI

Details: The keyword in the command is not valid for the command. The rejected element of the command is displayed in the error message between backslashes.

Corrective action: Consult the DCL **HELP** command or the VAX/VMS DCL Dictionary for valid keywords.

IVLOGNAM, invalid logical name

Facility: SYSTEM

Details: The logical name specified is invalid. Logical names can be no more than 63 characters in length. Process names, global section names, and common event flag cluster names can be no more than 15 characters in length.

Corrective action: Verify the name and reenter the command.

IVQUAL, unrecognized qualifier - check validity, spelling, and placement

Facility: CLI

Details: A qualifier was spelled incorrectly or placed improperly in a command.

Corrective action: Correct the command and reenter it.

IVSYMB, invalid symbol name - start with an alphabetic character

Facility: CLI

Details: Symbol names must begin with an alphabetic character.

Corrective action: Correct the symbol name and reenter the command.

IVTIME, invalid time

Facility: SYSTEM

Details: A specified time value is invalid. Possible problems include a delta time of greater than 10,000 days or a calculated absolute time that is less than the system date and time.

Corrective action: Correct the error and reenter.

Journal file could not be closed

> Facility: EDT
>
> Details: In an attempt to recover a file, EDT was unable to close the journal file after processing the commands in it because of a problem at the system level.
>
> Corrective action: Correct the problem indicated in the message.

Journal file could not be opened

> Facility: EDT
>
> Details: The specified journal file could not be opened. An accompanying file system message will describe the nature of the problem.
>
> Corrective action: Correct the error noted in the message and try again.

KEYCNV, synonym 'keyname' has been converted to 'keyname'

> Facility: CLI
>
> Details: An informational message advising that the keyname specified in the **DEFINE/KEY** command is a synonym for a definable keyname. The synonym name is converted to the actual keyname prior to the definition of the key.
>
> Corrective action: None.

Line exceeded 255 characters, truncated

> Facility: EDT
>
> Details: The input line is greater than 255 characters and the excess has been deleted.
>
> Corrective action: None.

LOGIN - unrecognized qualifier keyword

> Facility: LOGIN
>
> Details: The **LOGIN** command line included an invalid qualifier.
>
> Corrective action: Correct the command line and reenter.

324 □ ERROR MESSAGES

LOGIN - user authorization failure

> Facility: LOGIN
>
> Details: An incorrect username or password (or both) was entered.
>
> Corrective action: Reenter.

LOGIN - you are at maximum allowed processes for your account name

> Facility: LOGIN
>
> Details: No more processes can be logged in under this account name.
>
> Corrective action: Wait until a current process for this account is logged off and then retry.

LOGIN - you are not authorized to log in at this time

> Facility: LOGIN
>
> Details: The user is restricted from the class of login being attempted. Login classes are LOCAL, DIALUP, REMOTE, NETWORK, and BATCH.
>
> Corrective action: Log in to a different class, or consult the system manager to see if your account has been improperly restricted.

LOGIN - you are not authorized to login at this time
LOGIN - you are not authorized to login today

> Facility: LOGIN
>
> Details: Your account is restricted from login at the present time.
>
> Corrective action: Wait until the authorized time or consult the system manager to have restrictions changed or removed.

LOGIN - your account has expired - contact your system manager

> Facility: LOGIN

Details: Accounts can be limited to a particular time period, after which it automatically becomes invalid.

Corrective action: Consult the system manager.

LOGIN - your password has expired - contact your system manager

Facility: LOGIN

Details: The system manager can assign a time limit to passwords, after which the password expires and cannot be used in login.

Corrective action: Consult the system manager.

MACRO or KEY required

Facility: EDT

Details: Within EDT, the **DEFINE** command is incomplete, missing either **MACRO** or **KEY** under the format **DEFINE MACRO** or **DEFINE KEY**.

Corrective action: Correct the command and reenter it.

Max input line of 2814749767 exceeded, file input terminated

Facility: EDT

Details: Congratulations! You have gone over the limit of 2,814,749,767 lines for an EDT buffer. EDT will accept no more lines.

Corrective action: None, except brevity.

Max line number exceeded - lines no longer ascending; resequence recommended

Facility: EDT

Details: EDT has reached its internal limit for line numbering.

Corrective action: Resequence the buffer if there are fewer lines than line numbers in it.

Max number of lines for this buffer exceeded

> Facility: EDT
> Details: No more lines can be added to the present buffer.
> Corrective action: Place other lines in a different buffer.

MAXPARM, too many parameters - reenter command with fewer parameters

> Facility: CLI
> Details: The command contains more than the allowable maximum number of parameters. The error could be caused by leaving blanks in a command where special characters such as commas or plus signs are expected; using symbol or logical names that include blank characters which would be substituted or translated; or failure to place quote marks around a character string that includes blanks.
> Corrective action: Correct the command and reenter.

MBFULL, mailbox is full

> Facility: SYSTEM
> Details: An attempt to write to a mailbox has failed because the target mailbox is full and resource wait mode is not enabled.
> Corrective action: The sender can wait until space is available. The owner of the mailbox can consult the system manager to see if the buffer space for the mailbox should be increased.

No definition

> Facility: EDT
> Details: A **SHOW KEY** definition has been requested for an undefined key.
> Corrective action: None.

No help available for that key

> Facility: EDT

Details: The current EDT Help file does not include information about the use of the key the user has pressed.

Corrective action: If there is another Help file available on the system with the requested information, use the **SET HELP** command to access that file.

No more than 65,535 lines can be processed in a single command

Facility: EDT

Details: EDT cannot work with a range of lines greater than 65,535.

Corrective action: Correct the command to specify a smaller range and reenter.

No output file name

Facility: EDT

Details: The EDT command **EXIT** was used without a specified filename.

Corrective action: Reenter the command with a filename or use the **QUIT** command.

No output file written

Facility: EDT

Details: EDT was unable to put the specified text into the specified output file because of the record format of the text.

Corrective action: Change the record format of the file before editing it.

No select range ACTIVE

Facility: EDT

Details: A range was not selected before the EDT commands of **APPEND** or **CUT** were used.

Corrective action: Select a range before the **APPEND** or **CUT** command is used.

NOCOMD, no command on line - reenter with alphabetic first character

>Facility: CLI
>Details: A command begins with a nonalphabetic character
>Corrective action: Verify the command and reenter.

NODEVAVL, no device available

>Facility: SYSTEM
>Details: An attempt was made to allocate an unavailable device.
>Corrective action: Wait until the device is available and retry, or use a different device.

NOFILPURG, no files purged for 'file-spec'

>Facility: Several
>Details: No files matching the file specifications were eligible for purging.
>Corrective action: None.

NOJOBID, job 'nnn' not found in 'queue-name' queue
NOJOBNAME, job 'name' not found in 'queue-name' queue

>Facility: Several
>Details: The attempt to modify or delete a job was not performed because the job could not be found. The message will identify the job by jobname or job identification number, depending upon the specification in the command.
>Corrective action: Verify that the job identification number or jobname was entered correctly and reenter if necessary. If the name or number is correct, the job is apparently no longer in the queue.

NOMOREMSG, no more messages

>Facility: MAIL
>Details: There are no more messages to be read.

Corrective action: None. To read messages again, use the **READ** command of Mail or change to a different folder and **READ** the messages there.

NOMSGS, no messages

Facility: MAIL
Details: There are no Mail messages.
Corrective action: None.

NOSUCHUSR, no such user 'username'

Facility: MAIL
Details: An attempt was made to send a message to a user who is not an authorized user of the system. If the mail attempt included more than one username, at least one of which was authorized, this message will appear for each unauthorized user, with the accompanying question: "Do you want to send it anyway (Y/N)?"
Corrective action: Reenter the command with a valid username if necessary.

NOTREADIN, you are not reading a message

Facility: MAIL
Details: The **MAIL** command you entered will work only when reading a message.
Corrective action: Read a message and then apply the appropriate command to it.

NULFIL, missing or invalid file specification - respecify

Facility: CLI
Details: The command interpreter expected a file specification, but none was entered.
Corrective action: Reenter the command with a file specification.

Parenthesis mismatch

>Facility: EDT

>Details: The number of right parentheses does not match the number of left parentheses in a change mode command string.

>Corrective action: Modify the change mode command string to correct.

Print file could not be closed
Print file could not be created

>Facility: EDT

>Details: EDT was unable to close or create the output file associated with the **PRINT** command. An accompanying message gives details of the problem.

>Corrective action: Correct the problem identified in the message.

Record too big, truncated to 255 characters

>Facility: EDT

>Details: An attempt was made to edit or include a file with lines longer than 255 characters. All characters beyond that length have been truncated.

>Corrective action: None.

RECTOBIG, 'record-size' byte record too large for MAIL buffer

>Facility: MAIL

>Details: An oversized record was encountered in a READ operation.

Search string cannot be null

>Facility: EDT

>Details: An EDT search request was made without specifying anything to search for.

>Corrective action: Reenter the command with a search string.

Select range is already active

> Facility: EDT
>
> Details: An attempt was made to select a range when a range was already in effect.
>
> Corrective action: None.

SENDABORT, no message sent

> Facility: MAIL
>
> Details: Ctrl-C was pressed while sending a mail message and the transmission was aborted.
>
> Corrective action: None.

SENDERR, error sending to user 'username'

> Facility: MAIL
>
> Details: An error occurred in the attempt to send mail to the specified user. An accompanying message should indicate the reason for the failure.
>
> Corrective action: Address the problem indicated in the message.

SKPDAT, image data records not beginning with $ ignored

> Facility: CLI
>
> Details: A command procedure that included lines not marked as DCL commands (by not beginning with $ marks) was encountered.
>
> Corrective action: Examine the command procedure for errors.

SPAWNED, process 'process name' spawned

> Facility: CLI
>
> Details: An informational message when the **SPAWN** command is used to spawn a subprocess.
>
> Corrective action: None.

STKOVF, command procedures too deeply nested - limit to 16 levels

> Facility: CLI
>
> Details: Within a command procedure, the maximum level of nesting was exceeded.
>
> Corrective action: Simplify the command procedure hierarchy and reduce the level of nesting.

String delimiter must be non-alphanumeric

> Facility: EDT
>
> Details: A letter, digit, or percent sign was used as a string delimiter; a nonalphanumeric character is expected.
>
> Corrective action: Correct the command to use a valid string delimiter.

String was not found

> Facility: EDT
>
> Details: The specified string could not be found.
>
> Corrective action: Verify that the string was entered properly and that EDT has been given proper instructions for searching.

SUPERSEDE, previous value of 'value' has been superseded

> Facility: CLI
>
> Details: An informational message that the specified logical name has been redefined.
>
> Corrective action: None.

SUSPENDED, process is suspended

> Facility: SYSTEM
>
> Details: The specified process was suspended or placed in a wait state. The operation cannot be performed while the specified process is suspended.
>
> Corrective action: Resume the process or retry the operation.

SYMLNG, symbol name is too long - shorten the name

> Facility: CLI
> Details: The user specified a symbol name that was too long.
> Corrective action: Shorten the symbol name and retry.

SYMOVF, no room for symbol definitions - delete some symbols

> Facility: CLI
> Details: The command interpreter cannot hold any more symbol definitions or labels.
> Corrective action: Use the DCL commands **SHOW SYMBOL** and **SHOW KEY** to determine how many global symbols and keypad symbols are defined, and delete unused symbols to recover space in the symbol table. Command procedure or procedures can also be shortened or simplified. The system manager can also adjust the size of the allowable CLI symbol table.

SYMTOOLNG, symbol 'symbol' is too long to copy to subprocess

> Facility: CLI
> Details: When the process was spawned, a logical name, logical value, symbol name, or symbol value was too long to be copied to the subprocess.
> Corrective action: The name or value should be reduced to several parts.

That key is not definable

> Facility: EDT
> Details: The key specified in an EDT **DEFINE KEY** command is not available for redefinition.
> Corrective action: Choose a different key to define.

TIMEOUT, device timeout

> Facility: SYSTEM
> Details: A requested input operation did not complete

because a timeout period elapsed—the device did react in the specified time.

Corrective action: Try again. If the problem recurs, consult the system manager to determine if it was a hardware, communications, or programming problem.

TOOMANYVER, too many higher file versions

Facility: SYSTEM

Details: The maximum number of file versions exists for the specified file, and all existing version numbers are greater than the specified version number.

Corrective action: Change the version limit for the file, or delete some unnecessary existing versions.

UAFGETERR, error reading user authorization file

Facility: MAIL

Details: An error was detected in the process of reading the user authorization file.

Corrective action: The VAX RMS status code that accompanies the message will help with correction of the problem. Correct and retry.

UNDFIL, file has not been opened by DCL - check logical name

Facility: CLI

Details: A **READ, WRITE,** or **CLOSE** command specified a file not currently opened, or one for which no logical name was assigned.

Corrective action: Reenter the command with the name of an opened file, or use the DCL command **OPEN** to open the file before an attempt is made to read or write to it.

UNDKEY, 'state' key 'keyname' is undefined

Facility: CLI

Details: An attempt was made to use the **SHOW KEY** or

DELETE/KEY command to show or delete the definition of a key that has not been redefined.

Corrective action: None.

UNDSYM, undefined symbol - check validity and spelling

Facility: CLI

Details: The command interpreter encountered a problem in evaluating a symbol.

Corrective action: Certify that the symbol is in fact defined and reenter the command. If the error was in a command procedure, correct the procedure to make certain the symbol is defined locally or globally, as required before the statement that caused the error.

Unexpected characters after end of command

Facility: EDT

Details: The command ended with one or more characters that are not part of the command.

Corrective action: Reenter the command, removing the invalid character or characters from the end of the command line.

Unrecognized command

Facility: EDT

Details: EDT did not recognize, or does not support, the command entered.

Corrective action: Verify the command syntax and spelling. Consult the Help facility and manuals. Reenter the command correctly.

USERDSABL, user 'username' cannot receive new mail

Facility: MAIL

Details: The user has attempted to send mail to a user who has been prohibited from receiving new mail.

Corrective action: None.

USEREXC, you are at maximum allowed processes for your user name

> Facility: LOGIN
>
> Details: The maximum number of processes logged to your username has already been logged in.
>
> Corrective action: Log off another process or wait until another user logs off.

USERSPEC, invalid user specification 'username'

> Facility: MAIL
>
> Details: An invalid username was included in a list of mail message recipients.
>
> Corrective action: Correct the names on the list and retry.

VALREQ, missing qualifier or keyword value - supply all required values

> Facility: CLI
>
> Details: A value is missing from the specified qualifier or keyword.
>
> Corrective action: Reenter the command correctly.

WANTOSEND, do you want to send anyway (Y/N, default is N)?

> Facility: MAIL
>
> Details: One or more of the specified addresses were unavailable.
>
> Corrective action: Type **Y** if the message should be sent to the available addresses; **N** or Return cancels the sending of the message.

WILDCONCAT, wildcard specification cannot be concatenated

> Facility: Several
>
> Details: In certain circumstances, files to be concatenated cannot be specified with wildcards.
>
> Corrective action: Respecify the files without using wildcards.

Work file failed to close
Work file failed to open

> Facility: EDT
>
> Details: EDT was unable to close or open its work file.
>
> Corrective action: Determine why the file could not be opened or closed and correct the problem.

Write file could not be closed
Write file could not be created

> Facility: EDT
>
> Details: Because of a problem at the system level, EDT was unable to create or to close a write file. An accompanying message should give details of the problem.
>
> Corrective action: Correct the problem indicated in the message.

WRITEERR, error writing 'file-spec'

> Facility: Several
>
> Details: An error was encountered while the system was attempting to write a file.
>
> Corrective action: Determine that you have the proper privileges to write to the file and that the file is open. Consult the system manager.

Glossary

Access control: The process of validating a connection, login, or file access request to see if the action is permitted under the instructions set by the system manager. Access control is usually implemented through the use of passwords.

Account: The heart of the system's accounting and library functions. Every user of the system, including many of the parts of the system itself, has an account assigned by the system manager. The computer keeps track of the privileges assigned to each account as well as the physical location of the files created by or sent to each account.

Active position: The location on the screen, indicated by the cursor, where the next typed character will appear.

Address: A number used by the operating system to identify the location of information in storage. Can be regarded as *virtual address* or *physical address*.

Allocate a device: The user can reserve a device for exclusive use. Such an action can be made only when the device is not allocated by another process.

Alphanumeric character: Any alphabetic letter in upper- or lowercase, any decimal digit, the dollar sign, or the underscore.

ANSI: American National Standards Institute.

ANSI characters: A set of characters established as a standard by the American National Standards Institute. Two types of ANSI sets are graphic and control characters. *See* Graphic characters and Control characters.

Application program: A set of computer instructions intended to perform a specific task, such as a spreadsheet, word processor, or database program.

ASCII: American Standard Code for Information Interchange.

ASCII characters: The American Standard Code for Information Interchange, a set of 8-bit binary numbers used to represent the alphabet and other symbols used by the computer in many communications, display, and printing applications. The characters and their equivalent hexadecimal codes are shown in Figure G.1.

Assembly language: A programming language that directly speaks to the computer. The VAX uses a language referred to as VAX MACRO.

Assign a channel: The creation of a software link between a user process and a device unit to allow communication with a device.

Attached processor: A secondary processor in certain types of VAX systems.

Auditing: A notation by the system that a particular event has taken place.

Authentication: The establishment of the identity and privileges of users signing on to a computer.

Auto Print Mode: A Printing Mode that sends the currently displayed line to a printer each time the on-screen cursor moves down a line because of a linefeed, formfeed, vertical tab code, or auto wrap situation. Auto Print is selectable from within the Print menu of the Set-Up series of menus. All printing functions, including Print Screen, can be initiated from the keyboard while in this mode. *See* Printing Modes for other conditions.

Autorepeat: A feature of a terminal that allows most keys to send their character repeatedly when the key is held down. The autorepeat feature can be turned on or off using the Keyboard Set-Up Screen of VT220 and VT300 terminals.

Auxiliary keyboard: *See* numeric keypad.

Batch processing: A system under which a computer accepts and stores for execution all of the commands of a particular process or program and then executes them as a group. Contrast to *real-time processing*.

HEX Code	ASCII Char	HEX Code	ASCII Char	HEX Code	ASCII Char	HEX Code	ASCII Char
00	NUL	20	SP	40	@	60	`
01	SOH	21	!	41	A	61	a
02	STX	22	"	42	B	62	b
03	ETX	23	#	43	C	63	c
04	EOT	24	$	44	D	64	d
05	ENQ	25	%	45	E	65	e
06	ACK	26	&	46	F	66	f
07	BEL	27	'	47	G	67	g
08	BS	28	(	48	H	68	h
09	HT	29	)	49	I	69	i
0A	LF	2A	*	4A	J	6A	j
0B	VT	2B	+	4B	K	6B	k
0C	FF	2C	,	4C	L	6C	l
0D	CR	2D	-	4D	M	6D	m
0E	SO	2E	.	4E	N	6E	n
0F	SI	2F	/	4F	O	6F	o
10	DLE	30	0	50	P	70	p
11	DC1	31	1	51	Q	71	q
12	DC2	32	2	52	R	72	r
13	DC3	33	3	53	S	73	s
14	DC4	34	4	54	T	74	t
15	NAK	35	5	55	U	75	u
16	SYN	36	6	56	V	76	v
17	ETB	37	7	57	W	77	w
18	CAN	38	8	58	X	78	x
19	EM	39	9	59	Y	79	y
1A	SUB	3A	:	5A	Z	7A	z
1B	ESC	3B	;	5B	[	7B	{
1C	FS	3C	<	5C	\	7C		
1D	GS	3D	=	5D	]	7D	}
1E	RS	3E	>	5E	^	7E	~
1F	US	3F	?	5F	_	7F	DEL

Figure G–1

Baud rate: The speed at which a terminal or modem communicates with the host system, printer, or other device. Baud rate is measured in bits per second.

Binary machine code: The internal language of the computer, stored and executed on the basis of a binary (two-character, 0 and 1) code. Programmers use languages, compilers, and the VAX Macro Assembler to generate the binary code for the computer.

Bit: The smallest unit of storable information, a bit can be set to one of two values: 0 (on) or 1 (off).

Block: The smallest addressable unit of data on a VMS-organized disk that can be transferred in a single I/O operator, defined as 512 contiguous bytes.

Boot: To bootstrap, or bring a program or machine to a desired state by its own action.

Boot name: The name of the device used to boot software.

Break key: A key that is recognized by some programs and operating system states as meaning a halt to a particular process or program or a disconnect. The Break key sends different commands in its ordinary, shifted, and Ctrl combinations.

Broadcast addressing: A means of sending a message to all nodes of a system.

Broadcast circuit: A circuit to which multiple nodes are connected, and across which a message can be sent to multiple receivers.

Byte: Eight contiguous bits, used by the computer to store numbers or characters. Bits are numbered from 0 to 7, going from right to left. Bit 7 is the *sign bit*, indicating a positive or negative integer. Bits are counted in binary, or two's complement, mathematics, and thus a 7-bit byte can be in the range from -128 to $+128$. Without the sign bit, the number can range from 0 to 255 in decimal counting.

Call: To transfer control to a specified routine.

Captive account: A VAX/VMS account with limited privileges. In some captive accounts, only certain commands of procedures are permitted.

CCITT: Comité Consultatif Internationale de Telegraphique et Telephonique (International Telegraph and Telephone Consultative Committee), a European communications standards committee.

Channel: A logical path connecting a user process to a physical device unit, as assigned by the operating system.

Character: A symbol represented by an ASCII code.

Character buffer: The temporary storage area used by EDT and some other programs to hold the last deleted character.

Character cell: The pixel area on the screen used to display a single graphic character.

Character encoding: The method used by a terminal or a computer to encode information. Most current systems use 8-bit codes; other systems are based on a smaller 7-bit set.

Character set: A Hard Character Set is a design for a group of characters built into the internal memory of a terminal. Typical Hard Character Sets include ASCII and DEC Supplemental Graphic sets. A Soft Character Set is a group of characters downloaded to the terminal from a computer or other source.

Character string: A contiguous set of bytes. The computer identifies a character string by giving it two attributes: an address and a length. The address is the location of the byte holding the first character of the string. The length is the number of characters in the string, stored in subsequent bytes of increasing address.

Cluster: 1) A set of pages brought into memory in a single paging operation. 2) A configuration of VAX processors.

Column: A vertical row of character positions on a screen. Most terminals can display 80 or 132 columns in width.

Command: An instruction requesting the computer to perform a defined action.

Command file: *See* Command procedure.

Command interpreter: The element of the operating system that receives, checks for errors, and parses the commands sent by the user of a command file.

Command procedure: The file containing commands and any necessary data that the command interpreter can act upon as if the instructions had been typed in by the user.

Compatibility Mode: A mode that permits the VAX's central processor to execute nonprivileged PDP-11 instructions, ensuring compatibility with software intended for that earlier series of DEC machines. *See also* Native Mode.

Compiler: An element of the system that translates a program written in a high-level language into binary machine code.

Compose Character key: A key used to initiate display and transmission of certain special characters not part of the ordinary computer keyboard. Characters are sent by typing the Compose Character key and then one or two pre-specified keyboard characters. On the LK201 keyboard used with VT220 and VT300 series terminals, a Compose Indicator illuminates while a Compose Character function is underway.

Compose sequence: *See* Compose Character key.

Composite Video Output Connector: A connector on a VT terminal that provides a video output signal to drive an external "slave" display.

Concealed device: An I/O device that has been given a logical name. The user will use and see the logical name in most system commands and responses, rather than the device name.

Condition: An error state that exists when an exception occurs. *See* Exception; Condition handler.

Condition handler: A procedure executed by the system when a process exception occurs. When the exception occurs, the computer will look for an appropriate condition handler and, within the context of the situation, follow the instructions given there.

Configuration database: A database of files containing information about the system and network components.

Console: The control unit used by the system operator to start and stop the system, monitor system operation, and perform diagnostics.

Console terminal: The hard-copy terminal connected to the central processor console.

Context switching: The act of interrupting the activity in progress and switching to another. The switching can be done by the system as it concludes one process and moves on to the next, or it can be performed by the user in certain circumstances.

Control characters: A set of characters, not usually displayed on the screen, that make the terminal perform a specific function. Examples include CR (carriage return) and LF (line feed).

Control combination: The combination of the Ctrl key on the keyboard and another character to cause a control action.

Control (Ctrl) key: A computer keyboard key that works as another shift level, sending *control characters* to the computer for action. The command is issued by holding down the Ctrl key on the keyboard and then typing a second character. In this book, and in most application programs, a command calling for use of a control character would be printed as Ctrl-A.

CPU: Central processing unit. The "brain" of the computer, as opposed to ancillary units such as memory and storage.

CRC: Cyclical redundancy check, one algorithm used in an error-detecting protocol for communications.

Ctrl: *See* Control key.

Cursor: A dash or block displayed on the screen of a terminal to indicate where the next alphanumeric character will appear. The cursor can be customized as part of the Set-Up choices on most VT terminals.

Cursor keys: The "arrow" keys on a terminal's keyboard used to move the cursor from point to point on the screen.

Data flow control: A method of synchronizing communication between a terminal and its host system or printer.

DCL: Digital Command Language.

DEC Multinational character set: The standard character set of the VT220 and VT300 series of terminals.

DEC Special Graphic character set: A group of characters with special symbols and line segments, as well as equivalents to many of the graphics characters of the ASCII character set. Also called the VT100 line-drawing character set.

DEC Supplemental Graphic character set: A set of 94 graphic characters including special characters such as letters with accents and diacritical marks used by European languages.

Decryption: The process of restoring encoded information to its original, unencoded form.

Dedicated: Pertaining to an element of a system that is assigned to a single purpose or user.

Default: The ordinary or expected element of a command. The operating system will substitute, in most cases, the default value in a command unless some other information is provided.

Detached process: A process that has no owner. Such processes are created by the job controller when a user logs in, when a batch job is begun, or when a logical link connect is requested.

Device: Any peripheral unit connected to the processor for sending, receiving, or transmitting data. Devices include printers, terminals, mass storage devices such as magnetic disks, and communication controllers and modems. A device can be *pseudo* in that it is not real but exists only for the purposes of the system.

Device driver: Software associated with each device in the system that works as an interface between the operating system and the device controller.

Diacritical marks: Symbols that are used in some languages to call for a change in the standard pronounciation of a letter, such as acute (´) and grave (`) accents and the tilde (˜).

Diagnostic: A program to test hardware, logic, or memory and report any faults it finds.

Digital Command Language: The command interpreter in a VAX/VMS system.

Directory: A file that catalogs the files stored in a particular physical location. Included in most directories are the filename, file type, and version number as well as a number that identifies the file's actual location and points to a list of its attributes.

Download (also called Down-line Load): The movement of data or instructions from the host to the terminal. Contrast to *upload*.

Downloadable Character Set (also called Down-line Loadable Character Set, or Soft Character Set): A set of characters downloaded to a terminal from the host system to supplement or replace the built-in, or hard, character set of the terminal.

DRCS: Dynamically redefinable character set. *See* Downloadable Character Set.

Drive: The mechanical element of a mass storage unit. A magnetic tape or disk, for example, is mounted on a drive.

Driver: The code and data that oversee the physical input and output of data to a device.

EBCDIC: Extended Binary Coded Decimal Interchange Code, a set of 6-bit characters used to represent data in some IBM systems. Includes all 51 COBOL characters. Compare to *ASCII*.

Echo: A characteristic of a communications setup that calls for characters typed by the user on the keyboard to be also displayed on the screen or printer.

Editing keypad: The supplemental keypad on many terminals designed to allow easy entry of editing commands, including cursor and page movement and insertion or deletion of characters.

EIA Host Port Connector: A port on the back of a VT terminal used to connect the device to a host computer either directly or through the use of a modem.

Emulation: The ability of one piece of hardware or software to act like another. For example, the VT320 terminal can emulate the earlier VT220 or VT100 series of terminals if required by a particular software application.

Encryption: The process of encoding information so that it is not easily understood by persons or devices without a copy of the decryption code.

Esc: The "Escape" character, used to initiate an Escape Sequence.

Escape Sequence: A special command to the system. The sequence begins with the ESC character and is transmitted without interpretation to the software or operating system for action.

Exception: An event detected by the hardware or software that effects a change in the normal execution of instructions. Examples include attempts to perform a privileged or reserved instruction and arithmetic traps such as overflow, underflow, and division by 0. When an event occurs that is *completely* outside of the current instruction, it is called an Interrupt.

Executable image: An image that can be run in a process.

Executive: The collection of procedures in the operating system to provide the basic control and monitoring functions.

Executive Mode: A highly privileged processor access mode, used for many of the operating system's service procedures.

Exit: An activity that occurs when an image execution is terminated, either normally or abnormally. The system deassigns I/O channels and other assignments made for the purpose of the image.

Exit handler: A procedure executed when an image exists.

Fault: A hardware exception condition that occurs in the middle of an instruction, leaving the computer's internal registers and memory in such a state that only eliminating the fault and restarting the instruction will give correct results.

Field: A set of contiguous bytes in a logical record.

FIFO (First-in, first-out): The order in which processing is performed. In other words, the computer will act upon the oldest command in its queue before coming to the most recently added command. *See also* LIFO.

File: Any named, stored program or data.

File header: A block in an index file describing a file with information needed by the system to find and use the file.

Filename: The identification of a file, employed by the user in retrieving and storing a file. Can be as many as 39 alphanumeric characters in length.

Filename extension: *See* File type.

Files-11: The disk structure used by the VAX/VMS operating system as well as some other Digital systems. VMS uses Files-11 Structure Level 2, but also supports Level 1 for compatibility with earlier systems.

File sharing: The capability of a relative or indexed file to allow access to more than one process.

File specification: The unique name of a file, identifying the node, device, directory name, file type, and version number.

File type: The field of a file specification to identify a particular class of files, such as compiler, assembly, data, and listings. Can be as many as 39 alphanumeric characters in length.

Firmware: Instructions to the computer that are encoded in a chip. Contrast to software, which has instructions stored at first on a disk or cartridge and later transferred to the volatile internal memory of the computer for execution.

Floating point data: A single precision floating point number four bytes in length, having a range from $\pm 2.9*10^{-37}$ to $\pm 1.7*10^{38}$ and a precision of approximately seven decimal digits. *See also* G_floating data and H_floating data.

Font: A style or design for characters that appear on a screen or are created by a printer.

Formfeed: In EDT, the movement of the cursor position to the start of a new page. On a printer, the movement of the paper to the top of the next sheet of continuous-form paper.

G_floating data: An extended range floating point number eight bytes in length, having a range of $\pm 0.56*10^{-308}$ to $\pm 0.9*10^{308}$ and a precision of approximately 15 decimal digits. *See also* Floating point data and H_floating data.

Generic device name: A device name that identifies the type of device but not a particular unit.

Global: Affecting the entire file, system, or image, depending upon the context. In a text file, a global replacement changes all instances of a particular string of characters to something else.

Global section: A shareable image section that can be made available to all processes in a system. Access is set by privilege.

Global symbol: A symbol that can be made to extend across a number of files or strings. The linker resolves—matches—references with definitions (*see* Linker).

Gold key: A special key on the terminal keyboard enabling alternate key functions. Used within WPS, EDT, and many other programs.

Graphic characters: A set of alphanumeric characters that can be displayed on the screen of a terminal.

Group: A set of users who have been given special access privileges to each others' directories and files, unless the files have been specifically protected. VMS organizes users under the following hierarchy: System/Owner/Group/World.

H_floating data: An extended range floating point number 16 bytes in length, having a range of $\pm 0.84*10^{-4932}$ to $\pm 0.59*10^{4932}$ and a precision of approximately 33 decimal digits. *See also* G_floating data and Floating point data.

Hanging: Slow response of the system because of a heavy load of users or compute-intensive jobs.

Hard Character Set: One of the sets of characters built into a terminal as a default design. Contrast to *Downloadable Character Sets*, also called *Soft Character Sets*.

Hard-copy terminal: A terminal that prints on paper rather than display on a video screen.

Hexadecimal number: A number in the base-16 numbering system, which uses the numerals 0 to 9 and letters A to F only. Hexadecimal numbers are used in many high-speed, high-capacity computers because they are easy to convert to the binary numbers actually processed by the computer.

Hibernation: A process made inactive, but known to the system. The system keeps track of the process's current status and can recall the process on the basis of a predefined wake request or a command from another process or the user. *See also* Suspension.

High-level language: A humanlike language for communicating with the computer to give commands or create a program. High-level languages do not include machine-specific commands that directly address a computer, such as those in assembly and machine languages. High-level languages are translated into machine code by an interpreter or compiler either before running or at the time of execution.

Holder: A user with a particular identifier.

Hold Screen: This key freezes the screen display and stops any other characters coming in from the host computer from being displayed. This function is useful when viewing a lengthy directory or file that would otherwise scroll off the screen before it could be read. The Hold Screen key is a *toggle*—pressing it once turns the mode on; pressing it a second time turns the mode off. On the LK201 and similar keyboards, a "Hold Screen Indicator" is illuminated when the freeze has been initiated.

Home: Usually defined as the top left corner of the screen or the active window of a screen.

Host: The computer or terminal server that a terminal communicates with.

Host node: Under DECnet, the host node is the node that provides services to another node.

Identifier: The signification of a user or group of users to the system. VMS has three types of identifiers: UIC identifiers, system-defined identifiers, and general identifiers.

Image: The procedures and data bound together by the linker. VMS has three types of images: executable, shareable, and system.

Image name: The name of the file in which an image is stored.

Image privileges: The privileges held by an image once installed.

Input stream: From the computer's point of view, the source of commands and data—the user's terminal, a batch stream, or a command procedure.

Interactive: Pertaining to a system in which the user and the operating system communicate directly, with the operating system acting upon commands and requests immediately.

Interrupt: An event, generally external to the process currently being executed, that changes the execution of instructions currently underway.

A keystroke from a keyboard, for example, could be a device interrupt to a process. Excluded from the definition of interrupts are exceptions and certain software calls and branches. *See also* Exceptions.

ISO: International Standards Organization.

Job: A record maintained by the computer to track a process and any subprocesses. Jobs can be either batch or interactive.

Journal file: Under the EDT editing program, a file that records all of the data and commands sent to the computer during one session. Can be used to reconstruct a file lost in an interrupted session.

K: Short for kilo. Used as a unit of measure of memory and storage, K is 2^{10}, or 1,024.

Keypad: The collection of numeric keys located at the right side of the keyboard and used in numeric data entry. On some keyboards, the numeric keypad includes cursor control keys used in manipulation of the cursor.

Keyword: A command name, qualifier, or option.

Label: A record that identifies a mass storage unit volume or file section.

LIFO (Last-in, first-out): The order in which commands are processed. Under this scheme, the most recently entered command is acted on first. *See also* FIFO.

Limit: The maximum size or number of resources allowed a particular job, as assigned by the system operator. *See also* Quota.

Line printer: A hard-copy output device that prints a single line at a time at very high speed.

Linker: A program that creates an executable program, referred to as an image, from one or more object modules produced by a language compiler or assembler. Programs must be linked before they can be executed.

LK201: The standard keyboard used by Digital with its VT220 and VT300 series of terminals.

Local Controller Mode: Used to direct the keystrokes of a terminal in

Local Mode to a directly connected printer. The mode is initiated from within the Set-Up series of menus by selecting Local Mode from the main menu and then Printer Controller Mode from the Printer Set-Up menu. *See* Printing Modes for other conditions.

Local Mode: The condition that exists when a terminal is set up as an off-line device in direct communication with a printer or other device. Contrast with *On-Line Mode*.

Locked password: A password that cannot be changed by the owner of the account, but only by the system operator.

Log: A record of performance.

Logging in: The process of identifying a user to the system. The user types in an account name and a password in response to prompts from the system. If the account name and password are registered in the system, the user will be given access to that account and all of its privileges.

Logging out: Signing off a VMS account after work is completed.

Logical name: A name, assigned by the user, that substitutes for part or all of a file specification.

Login file: A command file containing instructions automatically executed at login.

Longword: Four contiguous bytes (32 bits), with bits numbered from 0 to 31, right to left. The address of the longword is the address of the byte containing bit 0. When interpreted as a number, a longword is a two's complement integer (bit 31 is the sign bit in a signed integer). As a signed bit, a longword ranges from $-2,147,483,648$ to $2,147,483,647$. As an unsigned integer, the longword ranges in value from 0 to $4,294,967,295$.

Macro: A statement that commands a language processor to generate a predefined set of instructions for action by the system.

Mailbox: A software equivalent of a physical mailbox used for communication between VMS users. Users can address mail to a particular mailbox, and recipients open their mailbox to retrieve messages.

Mass storage device: An input/output device for the storage of data and other files while not in active use by the system. Such devices include magnetic disks, magnetic tapes, optical disks, and floppy disks.

Memory: Physical locations into which data or instructions can be placed. Each location has an address to allow the system to locate it.

Modem (short for modulator-demodulator): A device that translates (modulates) digital impulses from a computer into analog waves for transmission over telephone lines or other communications media. At the receiving end, the analog signal is converted back (demodulated) to a digital signal.

Module: In software, a portion of a program or a program library. In hardware, a physical element of a computer, as in logic module.

Multicast addressing: A mode of addressing in which a message is sent to a group of predefined nodes.

Multicast group address: An address given to a group of nodes on an Ethernet and used in multicast addressing to send a message to that group.

Multinational character set: A set of characters that goes beyond the ASCII 8-bit character set to include international alphanumeric characters, including characters with diacritical marks and special symbols.

Native image: An image whose instructions are executed in Native Mode.

Native Mode: The ordinary and primary mode of execution for a VAX processor. Under this definition, programmed instructions are interpreted as byte-aligned, variable-length instructions that operate on four data types: byte, word, longword, and quadword integers; floating and double floating character strings; packed decimals and variable-length bit fields. *See also* Compatibility-Mode.

NCP: Network Control Program.

Network: A scheme that connects separate computer systems for the interchange of data and other tasks.

Node: An individual computer system in a network.

Node address: The unique, numeric identification required for each node in a network.

Nodename: An optional alphanumeric identification for a node.

Nonvolatile RAM: Computer memory that is able to retain data even after power to the system is shut off. Such RAM is used in many terminals to store configuration settings selected through use of the Set-Up series of menus.

Normal Mode: The standard Printing Mode that allows all keyboard printing functions, including Print Screen, to be initiated from the keyboard. *See* Printing Modes for other conditions.

Null: The ASCII character with a binary value of 000. In programming, a null is an absence of information.

Numeric Keypad: A supplemental keypad on some terminals intended for rapid entry of numbers and punctuation marks. Can also be redefined to the special needs of a particular application program to allow quick entry of special commands.

NVR: *See* Nonvolatile RAM.

Object: A process that is the recipient of a logical link request, called upon to perform a specific network function or a user-defined image for a special purpose. In hardware, an object refers to a system resource such as a file or device.

Object module: The output of a language processor such as an assembler or compiler, in binary code, used as input to a linker

Octal number: A number in the base-8 numbering system, which uses the numerals 0 to 7 only. Octal numbering is used in certain applications because it is easy to convert to the binary numbers actually used by the computer.

On-Line Mode: The condition that exists when a terminal is set up to communicate with a host computer. Off-line modes include Local and Set-Up. *See also* Operational States.

Open account: An account that does not require a password for access.

Operational states: Conditions of operation for a terminal, including On-Line for communications with a host computer; Local for operations not intended to be transmitted to a host computer; and Set-Up for use of the terminal's built-in customization program.

Operating system: A set of programs that control the execution of computer programs, oversee system functions, and handle the interactive communications with the user.

Operator: The person responsible for maintenance of a computer system and the accounts of users.

Output file: A file that contains the results of an operation.

Owner: A member of a group to which a file, global section, or mailbox belongs. *See also* Group and World.

Packed decimal: Because decimal digits require only four bits for expression, two digits can be stored in a single byte using this method.

Packet: A unit of data to be routed from a source node to a destination node.

Packet switching: A scheme to more efficiently use a transmission channel by switching addressed packets in and out of the channel only as needed.

Page: In programming terms, a set of 512 contiguous byte locations, used as the unit of memory mapping and protection.

Page fault: An exception generated by a reference to a page that is not in the working set of the process. *See also* Paging.

Paging: To bring pages of an executing process into physical memory when referenced, a process at the heart of the definition of the VAX (Virtual Address Extended) architecture. When a process executes, all of its pages are placed in *virtual memory*. Only the pages in active use, though, need to reside in *physical memory*; the remaining pages reside on disk until they are needed in physical memory. Under VAX/VMS, a process is paged when it references more pages than it is allowed in its working set or when it first activates an image in memory. If the process refers to a page not in its working set, a *page fault* occurs, which causes the operating system to read in the referenced pages from wherever they are located.

Parsing: Breaking a command string into its various elements to interpret it for action.

Passwords: Character strings entered by the user and examined by the operating system to validate access to the system.

Peripheral devices: Any hardware, excluding the CPU and physical memory, that provides input or accepts output from the system. Peripherals include printers, terminals, and disk drives.

Physical address: To the computer, the address used by hardware to identify a specific location in physical memory or on-line secondary storage, such as a disk drive. In network terms, the physical address is the unique address of a specific system on an Ethernet circuit.

Physical memory: The main, internal memory of the computer.

PID: Process identification.

Pixel (Picture Element): The smallest unit of display on a video screen, used to create graphic characters and graphic displays.

Port: A connector on a terminal to allow communication with a host or another device.

Primary password: The first user password requested from the user. Some systems may ask for a secondary password.

Primary processor: The main processor in certain types of VAX computers. This processor handles input and output, scheduling, paging, and other system management functions. Such a system may have a secondary processor, called an *attached processor*, for other assignments.

Printer Controller Mode: In this condition, selectable from within the Print menu of the Set-Up menu series, the host computer has direct control of a locally connected printer. Characters sent by the host computer go directly to the printer and are not displayed on the screen. Ordinary printer control functions cannot be initiated from the keyboard while the terminal is in this mode. *See* Printing Modes for other conditions.

Printer Port Connector: A port on a VT terminal used to connect a printer directly to the terminal.

Printing Mode: *See* Auto Print mode; Normal Mode; Local Controller Mode; Printer Controller Mode.

Priority: The rank assigned to a process to allow the system to manage multiple requests for system resources.

Private section: An image section of a process that is not open for sharing among processes. Contrast with *global section*.

Privileged: Pertaining to elements of the operating system that are restricted to the use of the system itself or to specific groups of users.

Process: The context within which an image executes.

Process identification (PID): A unique numerical value assigned by the computer to allow location and tracking of a process. Processes are assigned both process identification and a process name.

Process name: An alphanumeric string used to identify processes executing under the same group number. *See also* Process identification.

Process priority: The operating system recognizes 32 levels of priority for scheduling purposes.

Process privileges: The privileges granted to a process by the system, a combination of user privileges and image privileges.

Program: A group of instructions intended to produce a particular result. *See also* Image.

Prompt: The system's indication to the user that it expects input.

Protection: The attributes assigned to a resource that limit the type of access for users.

Protocol: A set of rules defining a communications link.

Quadword: Four contiguous words, 64 bits in total, with bits numbered from 0 to 63, right to left. The address of the quadword is the address of the byte containing bit 0. When interpreted as a number, a quadword is a two's complement integer (bit 63 is the sign bit in a signed integer). As a signed bit, a quadword ranges from 2^{-63} to 2^{63}.

Qualifier: The element of a command that modifies the command through selection of an option. For example, in the command **DIR/FULL**, the **/FULL** qualifier asks for a detailed listing of information about files, rather than the short listing that is yielded by the unmodified command.

Queue: An ordered list of jobs to be processed. Jobs are generally performed in first-in, first-out (FIFO) order, but jobs can also be placed in different order on the basis of priority assigned them.

Quota: The amount of a system resource that a job is permitted to use in a particular period of time.

Random access: A memory or storage device on which all information is equally accessible at one time. Contrast with a serial storage device such as a reel of tape in which the retrieval time for any one bit depends upon the location of the bit last retrieved.

Real-time process: A process that responds to particular events as they occur, rather than when the computer is ready to respond to them. Examples would include laboratory and manufacturing process control. Contrast to *batch processing*.

Record: A set of related data.

Record length: The size of a record, in bytes.

Remote device: A device not directly connected to the local node, but available through a VAXcluster, an interconnection of VAX processors.

Resource: A physical element of a computer system such as a device or memory.

Resume: To reactivate a suspended process. Contrast with *wake*.

Return key: On a computer, the Return key can serve several different functions, depending upon the application program in use and the particular context in which it is employed. In a word processor, the Return key generates a carriage return and linefeed command, as would be used at the end of a paragraph. It can also be used to "Enter" a command for action.

Reverse video: The ability of some terminals to reverse video contrast from, for example, white letters on a black background to black letters on a white background.

Round robin: A type of time sharing that gives equal access to the CPU for images of equal priority. Each process at a given priority level executes in turn before any other process at the level.

Run-Time Procedure Library: The collection of procedures available to Native Mode images at run time.

Scrolling: The movement of text on a video screen from bottom to top or top to bottom as new information is displayed.

Secondary password: A password that may be asked of the user at login time, after the primary password has been accepted.

Served device: A device available to other nodes on a VAXcluster.

Set-Up menus: The selection of customization menus for terminals, accessible by the user. *See also* Operational states.

Set-Up Mode: The condition that exists when a terminal is set up to use its built-in customization program. *See also* Operational states and Set-Up menus.

Shareable image: An image that must be linked with one or more object modules in order to produce an executable image.

Sixel: A column of six pixels on the screen.

Soft Character Sets: *See* Downloadable Character Sets.

Sorting: The ordering of records in a particular sequence.

Source file: A text file with material ready for translation into an object module by an assembler or compiler.

Status line: A line of information that appears on many terminals in many applications to advise information about the operating modes of the terminal.

String: A connected series of characters.

Subdirectory: A subsidiary directory linked to a higher-level directory. For example, a system could have a directory containing a word-processing program, a subdirectory beneath that directory containing memos, and another subdirectory with letters.

Subprocess: A subsidiary process created by a process.

Subroutine: A routine that executes when called by another routine.

Suspension: A state in which a process is inactive, but remains known to the system. It will become active if another process requests the operating system to resume it. Contrast with hibernation.

Swapping: Sharing memory resources among several processes by writing an entire working set to secondary storage (swapping out) and reading another working set into memory (swapping in). Contrast with *paging*.

Symbiont: A process that transfers data to or from a mass storage device.

Symbol: A redefinition that represents a function or entity such as a command string or filename.

Syntax: The grammatical form of a command.

System image: The image read into memory when a system is first started up.

System password: The password asked of the user before login can begin.

Target node: The node that is to receive a memory image from another node.

Task: In network terms, an image running in the context of a process.

Timeout: The expiration of the time limit given a device or a user to provide a particular input.

Time sharing: A means of allocating computer time by dividing access to the processor into equal-sized slices and then sharing it among contending processes.

Toggle: A key with an on/off function. Pressing the key once turns a particular feature or mode on; pressing the key a second time turns the feature or mode off. Examples include the Hold Screen and Shift Lock keys.

Transparent: Refers to performance of functions that are not apparent to the user. For example, the user sees the result of a command, not the processes of parsing and executing the command.

Turnkey account: *See* Captive account.

20 mA Host Port Connector: A port on the back of a VT terminal used to connect the device to a nearby host computer using a 20 milliamp connection.

Two's complement: A means of representing an integer in binary code; a negative number is one greater than the bit complement of the corresponding positive number.

Type-ahead: The ability of a terminal to accept typed-in commands and data while the computer is processing a previously entered command. Input is held in a type-ahead buffer.

UIC: User identification code.

Universal symbol: A global symbol in a shareable image that can be used by any module linked to the image.

User authorization file: A system file created by the system manager to identify and grant access to the system for users. Included are username, password, default account, quotas, limits, and privileges for each user.

User identification code (UIC): A 32-bit value given to users of files and other activities.

Username: The name of the user entered into the system at login.

Utility: A program with functions related to the management of a system, account, or program.

VAX/VMS: Virtual Address Extension/Virtual Memory System.

Version number: In a file specification, represents the various revisions of a file since creation. The lowest version number is the oldest iteration of the file. In software terms, it represents the revision level of the product. In general, software version numbers are given as a decimal number such as 4.25 in which the numbers to the left of the decimal represent major changes while differences in the number to the right of the decimal stand for bug fixes or minor alterations and improvements.

Virtual address: A 32-bit integer that identifies the location of a byte in virtual address space.

Virtual address space: All possible virtual addresses that an image executing in the context of a process can seek or store information or instructions into.

Virtual memory: The storage locations in physical memory and on disk that are referred to by virtual addresses. As far as the program is concerned, all storage locations appear to be locations in physical memory.

Voltage Connect Switch: A slide switch on many VT terminal models that allows selection of 110 volts (U.S. domestic power source) or 220 volts (many foreign countries). In addition to the Voltage Connect Switch setting, most terminals require the proper fuse and power cord to be installed.

Volume: A mass storage medium such as a disk pack or magnetic tape.

VT Compatibility: A claim by a third-party manufacturer to provide a functional equivalent to one of the "official" VT terminals manufactured by Digital Equipment Corp. Compatibles typically are less expensive than Digital products or provide enhanced features, or both. Compatibility does not always mean exact duplication—terminals may look different, the on-screen character display may be nonstandard, and even some of the keyboard keycaps and key locations may be different. Buyers are advised to examined and test compatibles to be sure they meet particular needs.

VT52 Mode: A terminal setting that conforms with the official definition, by Digital Equipment Corp., of the VT52 terminal series. This mode employs Digital's proprietary text functions only.

VT100 Mode: A terminal setting that conforms with the official definition, by Digital Equipment Corp., of the VT100 terminal series. This mode employs standard ANSI functions as well as the full range of VT200 capabilities. The VT100 superseded the earlier VT52 terminal series and includes within it most of the earlier series' abilities as well.

VT200 Mode: A terminal setting that conforms with the official definition, by Digital Equipment Corp., of the VT200 terminal series. This mode employs standard ANSI functions as well as the full range of VT 200 capabilities. The VT200 superseded the earlier VT100 and VT52 terminal series and includes within it most of the earlier series's abilities as well.

Wait: A process enters a wait state and becomes inactive when it suspends itself, hibernates, or declares to the system that it needs to wait for an event or resource.

Wake: To reactivate a hibernating process.

Wildcard: A nonalphanumeric character used in a filename or directory in a file specification to indicate "all."

Word: Two contiguous bytes, 16 bits in total, with bits numbered from 0 to 15, right to left. The address of the word is the address of the byte containing bit 0. When interpreted as a number, a word is a two's complement integer (bit 15 is the sign bit in a signed integer). As a signed integer, a word ranges from $-32,768$ to $32,767$. When interpreted as an unsigned integer. the value is in the range from 0 to 65,535.

Working set: The set of pages in process space that an executing process can refer to without generating a page fault. Remaining pages of the process, if any, are in memory or in secondary storage.

World: All users—including system operators, system managers, and users—in an owner's group and any other group.

X.25: A protocol that specifies the interface for Packet Mode communication on data networks.

Index

Answerback, 49
APPEND, 67, 83–84, 160–161
Apple Computer Co., 2, 4
Application programs, 61
Artificial intelligence, 61
ASCII code, 10, 341
Assembler language, 61
ASSIGN, 91–94, 96–97, 158–159, 161–162
Assignment statement, 91–94, 158–159
ATTACH (Mail), 145, 162
Auto print mode, 17
Auto wrap, 42

Batch processing, 7
Baud rate, 10
Bell, 29, 52
Break key, 26, 52

Central processing unit, 7
Character input buffer (see Handshaking)
Character string expressions, 106–107
Command keys, 25
Comments (DCL), 63
Communications Set-Up, 46–49
Compilers, 60
Compose key, 25, 33–34, 53
Composing characters, 33–35, 53

COMPRESS (Mail), 145–146
Conference calls (Phone), 152
CONNECT, 162–163
CONTINUE, 163
Control character commands, 29–32
COPY, 66, 81–82, 163–166
CPU (see Central processing unit)
CREATE, 166–168
Ctrl key, 24
Cursor keys, 25

Data flow control, 10
Data/Talk key, 26
DCL (see Digital Command Language)
DEFINE, 96–99, 168–172
DELETE, 65, 82–83, 173–176
Delete key, 25
Device drivers, 4
Device name, 75
Digital Command Language, 3, 6, 60–73, 106–114, 158–288
DIRECTORY, 65, 177–184
Directory, 75, 86–87
Directory (Phone), 152–153
DISCONNECT, 184
.DIS FILE (Mail)
 (see Distribution file)
Display Set-Up screen, 41–44
Distribution file (Mail), 123–125
Do Key, 28
DSR, 8

365

366 □ INDEX

Echo, 48
EDIT, 184–189
EDT, 8
EIA Host Port Connector, 18
Electronic mail (*see* VMS Mail)
Emulation (*see* Terminal emulation)
Error messages, 289–338
Executive procedure, 159–160
EXIT, 189
Expressions (DCL), 106–114
Expressions, operations, 107–114

F keys (*see* Function keys)
F$ (*see* Lexical functions)
Facsimile (Phone), 154
Filename, 75–76
Files (VMS), 74–87
File specifications, 74–77
File type, 76
Folders (Mail), 119
Function keys, 26–28

General Set-Up screen, 44–46
Global characters, 77–87
Global symbols, 94–95
Glossary, 339–364
GOSUB, 189
GOTO, 189

Handshaking, 10–11
HELP, 189–191
Help, 70–73
Help key, 28
Help (Mail), 131–132
Help (Phone), 155
High-level language, 61
Hold (Phone), 155–156
Hold screen function key, 26
Host port, 48
Host port connector, 18, 22

IBM PC, 2, 4
IF, 191–192

Indicators, keyboard, 28–29
INQUIRE, 192
Integer string expressions, 107
Interactivity, 7
Interpreter, 5

Keyboard, 22
Keyboard Set-Up screen, 51–53
Keyclick, 29, 52
Keypad (Mail), 126–129

Label (DCL), 63
Lexical functions, 95, 192–195
LK201 (*see* Keyboard)
Local, 40
Local controller mode, 18
Local symbols, 94–95
Lock key, 25
Logging in (*see* Login)
Logging out (*see* Logout)
Logical names, 88, 96–105
Logical name tables, 101–104
Login, 55–60, 195–196
Logout, 69–70, 196–197

Machine language, 10, 60
MAIL, 116, 121–123, 197–198
Mail (*see* VMS Mail)
Master Set-Up directory, 39–41
MERGE, 198
MESSAGE, 198
Multiprocessing, 7

Natural language instructions, 61
Node name, 75
Normal mode, 17

ON, 198–199
On-line, 40
OPEN, 199–200
Operating system, 4, 61

INDEX □ 367

Parameter (DCL), 63
Password, 56–57, 58–59
PC, 2
PF keys (*see* Function keys)
PHONE, 150–152, 200
Phone (*see* VMS Phone)
PRINT, 68–69, 200–208
Printer controller mode, 17
Printer Set-Up menu, 49–51
Print screen function key, 26
Prompt, 63
PURGE, 66, 85, 208–210

Qualifier (DCL), 63

Radix operators, 92
READ, 210
RECALL, 210–211
Remote login, 57–58
RENAME, 68, 84, 211–213
Repaint screen (Ctrl W), 64
REQUEST, 213–215
Reset terminal, 41
RETURN, 215
Return key, 25
RUN, 215
RUNOFF, 215–225

Schedulers, 4
Screen blanker, 20
SEARCH, 225–228
Search lists (logical names), 104–105
SEND (Mail), 121–123
SET, 228–253
SET ACL, 228
SET BROADCAST, 228–229
SET CONTROL, 229–230
SET DEFAULT, 230
SET DEVICE/ACL, 230–231
SET DIRECTORY, 231–233
SET FILE, 233–236
SET HOST, 236–238
SET KEY, 238–239

SET MESSAGE, 239
SET PASSWORD, 239–241
SET PROCESS, 241
SET PROMPT, 241–242
SET PROTECTION, 242–243
SET RESTART_VALUE, 243
SET RIGHTS_LIST, 243–245
SET SYMBOL, 245
SET TERMINAL, 245–253
Setting password, 59
Set-Up, 17, 36–54
Set-Up function key, 26
SET WORKING_SET, 253
Shift key, 24
SHOW, 253–278
SHOW ACCOUNTING, 253–254
SHOW ACL, 254
SHOW BROADCAST, 254–255
SHOW DEFAULT, 255
SHOW DEVICES, 255–257
SHOW ERROR, 257–258
SHOW KEY, 258–259
SHOW LOGICAL, 99–100, 259
SHOW MEMORY, 259–261
SHOW NETWORK, 261–262
SHOW PRINTER, 262
SHOW PROCESS, 263–265
SHOW PROTECTION, 265–266
SHOW QUEUE, 266–271
SHOW QUOTA, 271
SHOW STATUS, 271
SHOW SYMBOL, 272
SHOW SYSTEM, 272–274
SHOW TERMINAL, 274–275
SHOW TIME, 275–276
SHOW TRANSLATION, 99, 276
SHOW USERS, 276–278
SHOW WORKING_SET, 278
SORT, 278
SPAWN, 143–145, 279–281
STOP, 281–283
String comparisons, 111–113
String conversions, 110–111
String operations, 109–114
Subdirectory (*see* Directory)
SUBMIT, 283
Symbols, 88–95
SYNCHRONIZE, 283–284

System executive, 4
System services, 4

Tab key, 24
Tab Set-Up menu, 53
Terminal emulation, 2
Terminal ID, 45
Terminals, 9–54
Timesharing, 7
TPU, 8
TYPE, 85, 284–287
Type-ahead buffer, 36

UNLOCK, 287

VAX, 3, 6–7
Verb (DCL), 63
Version number, 76
Video output (terminal), 18, 21
Virtual Address Extended (see VAX)

Virtual memory, 6
Virtual Memory System (see VAX)
VMS, 4, 6–7
VMS Mail, 115–148
VMS Mail commands, 132–148
VMS Phone, 149–157
VT terminals, 9–54
VT100 series, 11, 13
VT200 series, 11–21
VT300 series, 11–15, 21–22

WAIT, 287
Wildcard characters, 77-87
WPS-Plus, 8, 27
WRITE, 288

XON/XOFF, 10–11, 50

= (see Assignment statement)
@ (see Executive procedure)

Here's how to receive your free catalog and save money on your next book order from Scott, Foresman and Company.

Simply mail in the response card below to receive your *free* copy of our latest catalog featuring computer and business books. After you've looked through the catalog and you're ready to place your order, attach the coupon below to receive $1.00 off the catalog price of Scott, Foresman and Company Professional Books Group computer and business books.

✂ --

❏ YES, please send me my *free* catalog of your latest computer and business books! I am especially interested in

❏ IBM
❏ MACINTOSH
❏ AMIGA
❏ COMMODORE

❏ Programming
❏ Business Applications
❏ Networking/Telecommunications
❏ Other _____

Name (please print) _____

Company _____

Address _____

City _____ State _____ Zip _____

Mail response card to: Scott, Foresman and Company
Professional Books Group
1900 East Lake Avenue
Glenview, IL 60025

PUBLISHER'S COUPON	NO EXPIRATION
DATE	

SAVE $1.00

Limit one per order. Good only on Scott, Foresman and Company Professional Books Group publications. Consumer pays any sales tax. Coupon may not be assigned, transferred, or reproduced. Coupon will be redeemed by Scott, Foresman and Company Professional Books Group, 1900 East Lake Avenue, Glenview, IL 60025.

Customer's Signature _____